Mastering Responsive Web Design

Push your HTML and CSS skills to the limit and build professional grade, responsive websites

Ricardo Zea

BIRMINGHAM - MUMBAI

Mastering Responsive Web Design

First published: August 2015

Production reference: 2110915

Published by Packt Publishing Ltd.
Livery Place
35 Livery Street
Birmingham B3 2PB, UK.

ISBN 978-1-78355-023-4

www.packtpub.com

Credits

Author

Ricardo Zea

Reviewers

Jean-Marc Buytaert

Tristan Denyer

Alan Plotko

J. Pedro Ribeiro

Marija Zaric

Commissioning Editor

Usha Iyer

Acquisition Editor

Meeta Rajani

Content Development Editor

Neeshma Ramakrishnan

Technical Editor

Manali Gonsalves

Copy Editors

Roshni Banerjee

Project Coordinator

Shweta H. Birwatkar

Proofreader

Safis Editing

Indexer

Priya Sane

Production Coordinator

Shantanu N. Zagade

Cover Work

Shantanu N. Zagade

Cover Image

Ricardo Zea

About the Author

Ricardo Zea, originally from Medellín, Colombia, is a passionate and seasoned full-stack designer now located in Dayton, OH (USA). He is always looking for ways to level up his skills and of those around him. Constantly wondering how things are made on the Web, how they work, and why they work the way they do have made Ricardo a very technical designer, allowing him to explain to others the intricacies of design and the technicalities of the Web in ways that are very easy to understand and assimilate.

With a master's degree in publicity and advertising and having a deep passion for understanding human behavior complemented with a fierce competitive PC gaming hunger have allowed Ricardo to "switch" from the creative side of the brain to the rational side very easily. This has allowed him to visualize and create technically sound web and mobile designs that are responsive, perform well, and convey the proper message through design.

Ricardo is the organizer of the CodePen Dayton meetup group. He's a member of the Dayton Web Developers and UX Dayton meetup groups. He's also one of the first members of SitePoint's Ambassadors program. He is the author of the monthly *Web Design & Development, Level Up! Newsletter*. He was also a technical reviewer for the books *Sass and Compass, Designers Cookbook* and *Sass Essentials* by Packt Publishing. He is a real-time, live one-on-one expert advisor on `https://wizpert.com/`. For several years, he was also a Flash and CorelDRAW professor at different universities in his home country, Colombia.

Ricardo has 15 years of experience in web design and 20 years of experience in visual and graphic design.

You can contact Ricardo through the following links:

Personal website: `http://ricardozea.design`

Twitter: `@ricardozea` (`https://twitter.com/ricardozea`)

Wizpert: `https://wizpert.com/ricardozea`

Acknowledgment

A huge and infinite thanks to my wife, Heather, and my beautiful son, Ricardo; they are my inspiration to be a better professional, a better person, a better husband, and a better dad.

To my mom, Socorro, who showed me the values that made me the man I am today. To my dad, Ricardo "Pinta" Zea, for giving me the determination to not only be good at what I do, but to also be the best I can be.

To God, for allowing me to share with you, the readers, my knowledge of the sometimes unforgiving world of *Responsive Web Design*.

And to you directly, the readers, for giving me the chance to help you be better web professionals.

About the Reviewers

Jean-Marc Buytaert, with an associate's degree in multimedia and web design and a bachelor's degree in fine arts in interactive media design, has been involved in a diverse array of projects since 2003, ranging from graphic design, to video production, web design, and last but not least, web development, where he found his niche.

With experience in multiple web scripting languages and having developed websites using several content management systems, Jean-Marc is now a lead web developer for Houston-based interactive marketing agency, TopSpot Internet Marketing, where he oversees a team of web developers and builds responsive websites using MODX and WordPress while implementing third-party web services using new technologies and APIs.

Tristan Denyer is a UX designer for web and mobile applications, including web apps and portals, eCommerce, online video players and widgets, games (online, iPhone, board), marketing sites, and more. He is also a UI developer and WordPress theme developer. He is currently leading the UX design for the product team at a start-up in San Francisco.

He recently wrote a book, *A Practical Handbook to WordPress Themes*, to help owners and operators of self-hosted WordPress websites get the most out of their themes.

His passions include prototyping, web security, writing, carpentry, and burritos. He can be contacted through the following links:

Twitter: @tristandenyer

GitHub: https://github.com/tristandenyer

His portfolio and blog: http://tristandenyer.com/

Alan Plotko is a software developer who works across the full stack. He loves developing applications for the Web and always makes time to attend "hackathons", weekend-long programming competitions where participants build projects from scratch to benefit the community. Alan's experience extends to Python development, various database technologies such as NoSQL, and frameworks for rapid application development. When he's not writing code, Alan spends his spare time writing stories; he is an avid writer, having previously self-published a fantasy novel and reviewed books for Packt.

J. Pedro Ribeiro is a Brazilian user interface engineer living in the heart of London. He has been working on the Web for several years, coding websites for start-ups and large companies. Currently working at RetailMeNot UK, he is responsible for creating the mobile-first experience at VoucherCodes.co.uk, focusing on performance and usability.

Website: jpedroribeiro.com

GitHub: github.com/jpedroribeiro

Marija Zaric is a web designer living in Belgrade with a focus on individual and commercial clients who demand websites that are clear, modern, creative, simple, and responsive. She works with clients from USA and all over the world, helping them present their services in a unique, yet professional, way.

She is a relentless learner. What she loves the most about web design is the constant changes in the field, especially its evolution over the last 4 years when she became inspired by its simplicity, great images, typography, and the possibility of optimizing a single website for various devices.

She redesigned and incorporated these styles into her own website and called it Creative Simplicity. Marija was a reviewer for the book *Responsive Media in HTML5* by Packt Publishing.

Her projects can be found at http://www.marijazaric.com/.

www.PacktPub.com

Support files, eBooks, discount offers, and more

For support files and downloads related to your book, please visit www.PacktPub.com.

Did you know that Packt offers eBook versions of every book published, with PDF and ePub files available? You can upgrade to the eBook version at www.PacktPub.com and as a print book customer, you are entitled to a discount on the eBook copy. Get in touch with us at service@packtpub.com for more details.

At www.PacktPub.com, you can also read a collection of free technical articles, sign up for a range of free newsletters and receive exclusive discounts and offers on Packt books and eBooks.

https://www2.packtpub.com/books/subscription/packtlib

Do you need instant solutions to your IT questions? PacktLib is Packt's online digital book library. Here, you can search, access, and read Packt's entire library of books.

Why subscribe?

- Fully searchable across every book published by Packt
- Copy and paste, print, and bookmark content
- On demand and accessible via a web browser

Free access for Packt account holders

If you have an account with Packt at www.PacktPub.com, you can use this to access PacktLib today and view 9 entirely free books. Simply use your login credentials for immediate access.

Table of Contents

Preface

Before the days of Responsive Web Design, web designers' and frontend developers' efforts were pretty much focused on translating print layouts into websites and applications. Elements and dimensions were rigid, and the need for them to adapt and scale wasn't part of the concepts we mandatorily have to account for today.

Devices come in many shapes and sizes. All sorts of screen densities, aiming our work for operating systems and browsers that support (or don't support) certain HTML, CSS and JavaScript technologies, UX principles, usability best practices, and knowing how mobile devices affect the world we live in are now an "intricate" part of what we do as web designers and frontend developers.

In this book, I provide a lot of information, technical and conceptual, about how RWD provides a pathway to better websites and web apps. Installing and using Sass, handling images and videos, and creating a solid typographic scale to building responsive e-mails are a few of the content gems you'll be able to read in this book.

Time to level up!

What this book covers

Chapter 1, *Harness the Power of Sass for Responsive Web Design*, starts with the easiest walkthrough you'll ever read on how to install Sass; then we learn how to make Sass "watch" our SCSS files. Then, there are easy-to-understand explanations about basic Sass concepts such as variables, mixins, arguments, nesting, partial files, the @import directive, source maps, and Sass comments. We also learn to automate vendor prefixing and automatically compile our SCSS files with Prepros. We talk about creating mixins to address media queries as easily as possible, considering how content defines the breakpoints.

Chapter 2, Marking Our Content with HTML5, clarifies that HTML is a markup language, not code. Then, we talk about the most used HTML5 elements that allow us to markup our content semantically. Improving the accessibility of our builds with ARIA roles is also something we address in a simple way. We also talk about the different meta tags required for RWD, and then we have an example that brings everything together.

Chapter 3, Mobile-first or Desktop-first?, demystifies why and when mobile-first or desktop-first should be used. With examples, we will learn how to retrofit a site with Adaptive Web Design, and of course, with RWD. We will learn about *Respond.js* and conditional classes in order to support legacy browsers when building mobile-first.

Chapter 4, CSS Grids, CSS Frameworks, UI Kits, and Flexbox for RWD, helps us understand what a grid is, how to use it, and why. With this understanding, we can make sound decisions when building a website or web app. We also create a custom CSS grid both with the *floats* technique and then by using Flexbox. We will use conditional classes again to address old browsers, and with the help of a small script, we can take care of the quirks from IE10 with an .ie10 specific selector.

Chapter 5, Designing Small UIs Driven by Large Finger, shows how usability and accessibility play a major role in this chapter. We also find explanations about the different sizes of our target zones, the location of our controls (links, buttons, form fields, and so on), and the touch zones in different devices. There are also three examples on how to create a menu button plus three more examples on mobile navigation patterns.

Chapter 6, Working with Images and Videos in Responsive Web Design, is one of the most interesting chapters of this book because images in RWD are a "thing". We will talk about different ways to serve different images with the <picture> element and the srcset attribute. Making videos responsive with CSS, jQuery, and JavaScript is also addressed in this chapter. We also learn about using vector-based files such as icon fonts and SVGs.

Chapter 7, Meaningful Typography for Responsive Web Design, talks about using relative units being ideal because they provide scalability, and this is what RWD is all about. The golden egg in this chapter is that we will learn how to use the Modular Scale to create a harmonious typographic scale. We will also use *Flowtype.js* to increase the legibility of our copy.

Chapter 8, Responsive E-mails, shows that e-mails are opened more on mobile devices than on desktops; that responsive e-mails have more engagement on mobile devices than nonresponsive ones; and that people click on e-mails on desktops more than on mobile. We will also create an e-mail template as an example. We'll learn to use a CSS reset block to normalize those quirky e-mail clients and learn that the best width for e-mails is not more than 600 pixels.

All these chapters have CodePen demos.

What you need for this book

There are a few considerations to follow the examples in this book: a text editor or IDE (Sublime Text is used in this book), Internet access, and admin rights to your machine to install applications.

You may also need an image editing software such as Photoshop, Fireworks, or GIMP. If you use something else, that's totally fine.

If possible, you can use one or two types of real mobile devices in order to experience the examples and demos in the right context. Otherwise, using Chrome's DevTool's *Device Mode* feature would work as well.

Who this book is for

If you already know some HTML and CSS and understand the principles of Responsive Web Design, this book is for you. There's something here for you to learn regardless of whether you're a web designer or web developer, or whether you're a beginner or a seasoned web professional.

A good understanding of HTML and CSS is required since RWD relies heavily on these technologies. Some understanding of jQuery is also recommended, but not mandatory.

Conventions

In this book, you will find a number of styles of text that distinguish between different kinds of information. Here are some examples of these styles, and an explanation of their meaning.

Code words in text, folder names, filenames, file extensions, pathnames, dummy URLs, user input, and Twitter handles are shown as follows: "The `sizes` attribute can also be used with the `<picture>` element, but we're going to focus on using the `sizes` attribute with the `<img>` tag."

A block of code is set as follows:

```
*, *:before, *:after {
    box-sizing: border-box;
}


//Moble-first Media Queries Mixin
@mixin forLargeScreens($width) {
    @media (min-width: $width/16+em) { @content }
}
```

When we wish to draw your attention to a particular part of a code block, the relevant lines or items are set in bold:

```
*, *:before, *:after {
    box-sizing: border-box;
}


//Moble-first Media Queries Mixin
@mixin forLargeScreens($width) {
    @media (min-width: $width/16+em) { @content }
}
```

Any command-line input or output is written as follows:

```
gem install sass
```

New terms and **important words** are shown in bold. Words that you see on the screen, in menus or dialog boxes for example, appear in the text like this: "clicking the **Next** button moves you to the next screen".

 Warnings or important notes appear in a box like this.

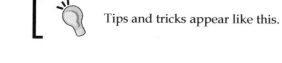 Tips and tricks appear like this.

Reader feedback

Feedback from our readers is always welcome. Let us know what you think about this book—what you liked or may have disliked. Reader feedback is important for us to develop titles that you really get the most out of.

To send us general feedback, simply send an e-mail to feedback@packtpub.com, and mention the book title via the subject of your message.

If there is a topic that you have expertise in and you are interested in either writing or contributing to a book, see our author guide on www.packtpub.com/authors.

If you have any questions, don't hesitate to look me up on Twitter via @ricardozea, I will be more than glad to help a fellow web professional wherever, whenever.

Customer support

Now that you are the proud owner of a Packt book, we have a number of things to help you to get the most from your purchase.

Downloading the example code

You can download the example code files for all Packt books you have purchased from your account at http://www.packtpub.com. If you purchased this book elsewhere, you can visit http://www.packtpub.com/support and register to have the files e-mailed directly to you.

Downloading the color images of this book

We also provide you with a PDF file that has color images of the screenshots/ diagrams used in this book. The color images will help you better understand the changes in the output. You can download this file from https://www.packtpub. com/sites/default/files/downloads/2102_0234_ImageBundle.pdf.

Errata

Although we have taken every care to ensure the accuracy of our content, mistakes do happen. If you find a mistake in one of our books—maybe a mistake in the text or the code—we would be grateful if you would report this to us. By doing so, you can save other readers from frustration and help us improve subsequent versions of this book. If you find any errata, please report them by visiting http://www.packtpub. com/submit-errata, selecting your book, clicking on the **errata submission form** link, and entering the details of your errata. Once your errata are verified, your submission will be accepted and the errata will be uploaded on our website, or added to any list of existing errata, under the Errata section of that title. Any existing errata can be viewed by selecting your title from http://www.packtpub.com/support.

Piracy

Piracy of copyright material on the Internet is an ongoing problem across all media. At Packt, we take the protection of our copyright and licenses very seriously. If you come across any illegal copies of our works, in any form, on the Internet, please provide us with the location address or website name immediately so that we can pursue a remedy.

Please contact us at copyright@packtpub.com with a link to the suspected pirated material.

We appreciate your help in protecting our authors, and our ability to bring you valuable content.

Questions

You can contact us at questions@packtpub.com if you are having a problem with any aspect of the book, and we will do our best to address it.

1
Harness the Power of Sass for Responsive Web Design

Before we dive into mastering responsive web design, we need to be on the same page as far as technologies go, in our case, CSS preprocessors and, specifically, Sass.

In this book, all CSS is going to be written in Sass in SCSS format. The way we write CSS has changed; it has improved tremendously.

CSS preprocessors such as Sass, LESS, and Stylus give the web/mobile designers and developers new superpowers. Yes, I used the word *superpowers* because that's exactly how I felt only a few hours after using Sass for the first time, and what I used was as basic as it gets:

```
.navigation-bar {
    display: flex;
    li {
        padding: 5px 10px;
    }
}
```

See the nested `li` selector? Yeah, that's Sass in action. When the preceding code is compiled, this is what it looks like:

```
.navigation-bar {
    display: flex;
}
.navigation-bar li {
    padding: 5px 10px;
}
```

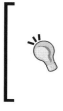

Downloading the example code

You can download the example code files from your account at `http://www.packtpub.com` for all the Packt Publishing books you have purchased. If you purchased this book elsewhere, you can visit `http://www.packtpub.com/support` and register to have the files e-mailed directly to you.

Let's see what's in store for us in this chapter:

- How does Sass work?
- The basic concepts of Sass to consider for **Responsive Web Design (RWD)**

How does Sass work?

Knowing how Sass works is a matter of understanding several basic technological concepts:

1. Sass can be based on two different technologies: Ruby or LibSass. In this book, we're going to use Sass based on Ruby.

2. Sass is a Ruby gem. Gems are packages for use in Ruby. A Ruby gem is a software that runs only on Ruby. Ruby is a programming language, just like PHP, .NET, Java, and so on.

3. We can make Sass run via the command line, but we can also run Sass with a third-party application, making the use of the command line unnecessary.

4. Sass is a programming/scripting language used to create CSS.

5. CSS is a very repetitive language. Sass allows authors to optimize those repetitive tasks and create CSS faster and more efficiently.

6. Part of the Sass workflow is when Sass is *watching* an SCSS file, for example, `book-styles.scss`. When it detects a change in that SCSS file, it then compiles it into a CSS file `book-styles.css`.

Watching an SCSS file means that the Sass watcher is running in the background looking over the SCSS file(s) for any changes.

Installing Sass

Here are the steps we're going to follow:

1. Download the Ruby installer
2. Open the command line
3. Install the Sass gem

Downloading the Ruby installer

Windows: Download the Ruby installer from the following link:

`http://rubyinstaller.org/downloads/`

Mac: Ruby comes preinstalled on all Macs, so there's no need to download anything.

Opening the command line

Windows and Mac: Open the command line.

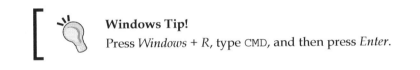

Windows Tip!
Press *Windows + R*, type CMD, and then press *Enter*.

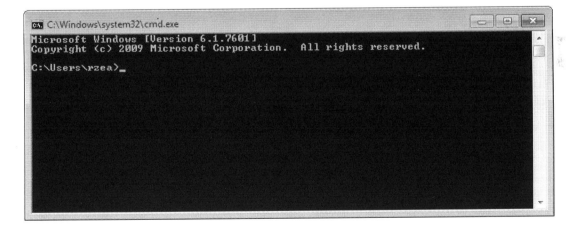

Installing the Sass gem

Type the following command into the command prompt (it doesn't matter which folder you're in):

Windows, use the following command:

```
gem install sass
```

Mac, use the following command:

```
sudo gem install sass
```

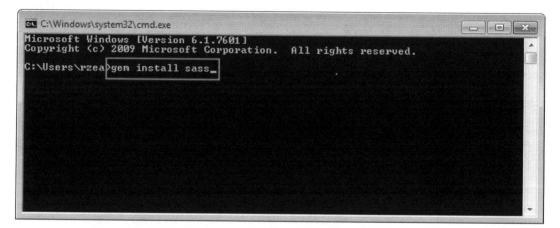

It'll take a few seconds to install Sass.

At the time of writing, the latest version of Sass was 3.4.14. The version/revisions might be different by the time the book comes out.

That's it! Sass is now installed on your machine.

Using Sass

What I'm about to show you is completely different to what any other Sass tutorial out there tells you to do. Most of those tutorials complicate things too much. This is the simplest way to use Sass you'll ever read.

The following screenshots are on Windows, but the process can be applied exactly the same regardless of platform.

In the following steps, you will see examples of how the necessary folders and files look after being created, not how to create them:

1. Create a /Demo folder anywhere on your drive:

2. Inside that folder, create two subfolders, /css and /scss:

3. Create a `.scss` file. Go into the `/scss` folder and create a file called `styles.scss`:

Name		Date modified	Type
styles.scss		12/30/2014 4:55 PM	Text Document

Notice the file extension `.scss`? This is your Sass file. Yes, right now there's nothing in it, it's empty.

4. Go back to the command line for a minute and follow these steps:
   1. In the command line, type `cd <space>`
   2. A space after `cd` means *Change Directory*. From your file manager, drag and drop the `/Demo` folder into the command prompt/terminal window and press *Enter*.

3. You should be in the /Demo folder now.

5. Make Sass *watch* your /scss and /css folders by typing this in the command line:

    ```
    sass --watch scss:css
    ```

6. Make Sass watch the /scss and /css folders.

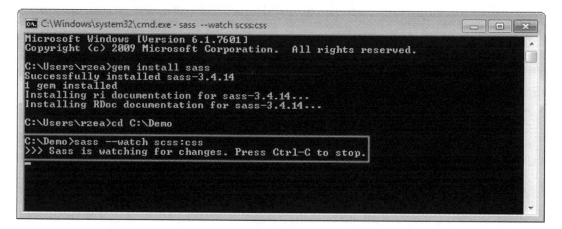

That's it! You are now using Sass!

> The --watch flag tells Sass to pay attention to the /scss and /css folders so that when we make a change to a .scss file (in our case, styles.scss), Sass will detect the change and compile the SCSS into the final CSS file we're going to use in our website or app.

7. Edit the .scss file and watch Sass compile it into a .css file:

    1. Open your text editor (I use Sublime Text).
    2. Open the styles.scss file.
    3. Add some CSS to it.
    4. Save the styles.scss file.
    5. From your command line/terminal, verify that the compiling was successful.
    6. Open your styles.css file and enjoy your new creation.

The basic concepts of Sass for RWD

For starters, Sass is a programming/scripting language. I bet you didn't see that one coming. Yes, it's a programming/scripting language focused on increasing the efficiency of web designers and web developers creating CSS. In this book, we're going to focus on the simple parts of Sass that can help us write CSS more efficiently, and more importantly, we'll have fun doing it.

Implementing RWD is time consuming: coding, testing, creating assets, browser troubleshooting, and then testing some more. The more we streamline our coding processes and the less repetitive work we do, the more efficient we become and the more value we add to a project, our team, the business and eventually, our users. Sass is going to do just that—help us streamline the coding of CSS.

Let's discuss the following concepts first:

- Sass or SCSS
- Variables
- Mixins
- Arguments
- Nesting
- Partial files
- @import
- Source maps
- Sass comments

Sass or SCSS

There are two ways we can write Sass-style CSS: the Sass syntax and the SCSS syntax.

 Make no mistake; Sass is written with capital S and the rest with lower case and SCSS is all uppercase.

The Sass syntax

The Sass syntax, also known as the *indented syntax*, was the initial and only way to write Sass. But it looked a bit too different than regular CSS, making the learning curve steeper than it really needed to be.

This syntax didn't use any braces or semicolons. In some cases, instead of colons it used the equals sign. Unlike SCSS, indentation was very strict and mandatory. Many developers weren't too fond of these aspects of the Sass syntax.

Here's a basic example:

```
.selector-a
    float: left

        .selector-b
            background: orange
```

This compiles to the following code:

```
.selector-a {
    float: left;
}

.selector-a .selector-b {
    background: orange;
}
```

The SCSS syntax

When SCSS was introduced with the release of version 3 of Sass, things got a lot easier for those of us who are not programmers but want to harness the power of Sass.

 SCSS stands for **Sassy CSS**.

If you already write CSS, you already write SCSS. All the things we already used while writing CSS are the same things we'll use when writing Sass with the SCSS syntax. So, the learning curve is initially nonexistent.

Then, you realize that you can also use bits of Sass that enhance what you already know, making learning Sass an awesome experience because you can get good at it quite fast. It honestly feels like you're gaining superpowers. I'm not kidding.

Here's the same example we saw before with the SCSS syntax:

```
.selector-a {
    float: left;
}

.selector-a, .selector-b {
    background: orange;
}
```

Wait a second! That's CSS! Yes, and it's also SCSS.

Let's see that same example in a different way using the SCSS syntax as well:

```
.selector- {
    &a {
        float: left;
    }
    &a, &b {
        background: orange;
    }
}
```

The ampersand symbol, &, in SCSS allows us to add the name of the parent selector to the nested selectors without having to type the whole thing, keeping us on the *DRY* side of things.

 DRY means Don't Repeat Yourself.

Both SCSS examples compile to the following code:

```
.selector-a {
    float: left;
}

.selector-a, .selector-b {
    background: orange;
}
```

Sass variables

Let's understand a few things first:

- A variable is simply a way to store a value for later use
- This value is usually associated with a simple *user-friendly* word
- Sass variables have to start with a dollar sign ($) symbol
- The great benefit of variables is that if we need to change the value, we would make the change in a single place rather than finding and replacing the value across the entire document

 When listing more than one variable, there should be a semicolon symbol (;) at the end of each variable. If there's only one variable, there's no need for the semicolon. However, this is a good practice to always end variables with a semicolon even if it's just one.

Here's an example of a Sass variable:

```
$brandBlue: #416e8e;
```

 I recommend you name variables using the *camelCase* style in order to differentiate them from dash-separated class names and CSS properties. This is very helpful when scanning the SCSS document, because the variables are easier to detect.

As we can see, we're storing a color value. The name we're using, `brandBlue`, is certainly more user friendly than `#416e8e`. Also, we're using the dollar sign symbol ($) and ending it with a semicolon (;) for good measure if/when we need to add more variables. Now, if we need to change the value later, all we'd need to do is change it in one location.

The variables should always be included at the top of your SCSS file so Sass knows where to go when using them. You can also include them via a partial file, but we'll talk about what partial files are later on in the chapter.

Here's an example of how to use an SCSS variable:

```
$brandBlue: #416e8e;
body {
    background: $brandBlue;
}
```

The preceding code compiles to the following:

```
body {
    background: #416e8e;
}
```

Sass mixins

Mixins are one of the most powerful features of Sass. **Mixins** are a group of CSS declarations (a property and value) that are stored for later use, just like a variable. So instead of typing all those CSS declarations over and over again, we just type the mixin's name.

A few things to consider about Sass mixins are as follows:

- They start with the @mixin directive
- A mixin is called with the @include directive
- We can store any amount of CSS/SCSS data in a mixin
- Try to use *arguments* when creating a mixin so it's more scalable

 We haven't seen what *arguments* are yet, but it's important to mention the word now so you can start getting familiar with different Sass terminology. We'll cover Sass arguments in the next section.

Let see an example of a mixin:

```
$brandBlue: #416e8e;
$supportGray: #ccc;
@mixin genericContainer {
    padding: 10px;
    border: $brandBlue 1px solid;
    background: $supportGray;
    box-shadow: 1px 1px 1px rgba(black, .3);
}
```

We call a mixin in our SCSS file as follows:

```
.selector-a {
    @include genericContainer;
}
```

When compiled, it looks like this in the CSS:

```
.selector-a {
    padding: 10px;
    border: #416e8e 1px solid;
    background: #cccccc;
    box-shadow: 1px 1px 1px rgba(0, 0, 0, 0.3);
}
```

Let's recap what we did in the mixin.

We used the @mixin directive:

```
$brandBlue: #416e8e;
$supportGray: #ccc;
@mixin genericContainer {
    padding: 10px;
    border: $brandBlue 1px solid;
    background: $supportGray;
    box-shadow: 1px 1px 1px rgba(black, .3);
}
```

We used the camelCase naming convention to differentiate the mixin's name from dash-separated class names and CSS properties:

```
$brandBlue: #416e8e;
$supportGray: #ccc;
@mixin genericContainer {
    padding: 10px;
    border: $brandBlue 1px solid;
    background: $supportGray;
    box-shadow: 1px 1px 1px rgba(black, .3);
}
```

We used Sass variables within the mixin:

```
$brandBlue: #416e8e;
$supportGray: #ccc;
@mixin genericContainer {
    padding: 10px;
    border: $brandBlue 1px solid;
    background: $supportGray;
    box-shadow: 1px 1px 1px rgba(black, .3);
}
```

We used the keyword black in the box-shadow color property instead of using the hex #000 or rgb (0, 0, 0) values:

```
$brandBlue: #416e8e;
$supportGray: #ccc;
@mixin genericContainer {
    padding: 10px;
    border: $brandBlue 1px solid;
    background: $supportGray;
    box-shadow: 1px 1px 1px rgba(black, .3);
}
```

For that matter, we could've also used our variable name like this:

```
$brandBlue: #416e8e;
$supportGray: #ccc;
@mixin genericContainer {
    padding: 10px;
    border: $brandBlue 1px solid;
    background: $supportGray;
    box-shadow: 1px 1px 1px rgba($brandBlue, .3);
}
```

We also omitted the 0 in the alpha value (.3). This is actually not a Sass feature; this is a CSS feature:

```
$brandBlue: #416e8e;
$supportGray: #ccc;
@mixin genericContainer {
    padding: 10px;
    border: $brandBlue 1px solid;
    background: $supportGray;
    box-shadow: 1px 1px 1px rgba($brandBlue, .3);
}
```

> On decimal values that start with a zero, the zero can be omitted.

Again, the preceding mixin compiles to the following CSS:

```
.selector-a {
    padding: 10px;
    border: #416e8e 1px solid;
    background: #cccccc;
    box-shadow: 1px 1px 1px rgba(65, 110, 142, 0.3);
}
```

Sass arguments

In our first mixin example, we didn't have any arguments. This is really not ideal because it doesn't allow us to use different values in the same properties. In reality, not using any arguments in a mixin isn't really any different than typing the same properties and values every time we need them. We are not really doing any DRY.

Arguments are the part(s) of a mixin in which you can put your own values depending on your needs. Arguments make a mixin worth creating.

In the mixin example mentioned earlier, let's add an argument:

```
$brandBlue: #416e8e;
$supportGray: #ccc;
@mixin genericContainer($padding) {
    padding: $padding;
    border: $brandBlue 1px solid;
    background: $supportGray;
    box-shadow: 1px 1px 1px rgba(black, .3);
}
```

The argument for `padding` allows us to set any value we want. We are not *forced* to have the padding as 10px every time.

This is how we set the value of the argument:

```
.selector-a {
    @include genericContainer(10px);
}
```

This compiles to the following:

```
.selector-a {
    padding: 10px;
    border: #416e8e 1px solid;
    background: #cccccc;
    box-shadow: 1px 1px 1px rgba(0, 0, 0, 0.3);
}
```

However, there's a potential problem with the argument; if we don't set a value for the `padding`, we're going to get an error when compiling.

So the solution here is to set a *default* value; if we don't define a value for `padding` for some reason, Sass is going to take that default value and use it when compiling without throwing an error.

Here's how we set a default value of an argument:

```
$brandBlue: #416e8e;
$supportGray: #ccc;
@mixin genericContainer($padding: 8px) {
    padding: $padding;
    border: $brandBlue 1px solid;
    background: $supportGray;
    box-shadow: 1px 1px 1px rgba(black, .3);
}
```

This is how we call the mixin, without declaring any padding value:

```
.selector-a {
    @include genericContainer;
}
```

The compiled CSS is as follows:

```
.selector-a {
    padding: 8px;
    border: #416e8e 1px solid;
    background: #cccccc;
    box-shadow: 1px 1px 1px rgba(0, 0, 0, 0.3);
}
```

How to use several arguments in the same mixin

Building on the preceding mixin, let's add a few more arguments to make it more robust and scalable:

```
@mixin genericContainer ($padding, $bdColor, $bgColor, $boxShdColor)
{
    padding: $padding;
    border: $bdColor 1px solid;
    background: $bgColor;
    box-shadow: 1px 1px 1px $boxShdColor;
}
```

This is how we declare the arguments when including our mixin:

```
.selector-a {
    @include genericContainer(2%, $brandBlue, #ccc, black);
}
```

We can use the same mixin and obtain different styles without having to type all the properties repeatedly.

The preceding mixin and its arguments compile to the following code:

```
.selector-a {
    padding: 2%;
    border: #416e8e 1px solid;
    background: #cccccc;
    box-shadow: 1px 1px 1px #000000;
}
```

Setting default values in multiple arguments

Sometimes, we need to define some default values in case we only need to declare one or a few arguments. In other words, by declaring default values in our arguments, we'll always be sure that a value is created and we don't get any errors when compiling our SCSS file.

Here's how we set default values in our arguments:

```
@mixin genericContainer ($padding: 5px, $bdColor: orange,
  $bgColor: #999, $boxShdColor: #333) {
    padding: $padding;
    border: $bdColor 1px solid;
    background: $bgColor;
    box-shadow: 1px 1px 1px $boxShdColor;
}
```

If we need to declare only the *first* property, `padding`, we can do this:

```
.selector-a {
    @include genericContainer(25px);
}
```

This compiles to the following:

```
.selector-a {
    padding: 25px;
    border: orange 1px solid;
    background: #999999;
    box-shadow: 1px 1px 1px #333333;
}
```

Some Sass compilers will turn a shorthand color hex value, #333, to a longhand value, #333333.

As we can see, only the first argument, padding, was declared. Other arguments used their default values and compiled successfully.

But let's say we still want to declare only one argument but not the padding, which is the first in the list of arguments. Let's say we want to declare the background color!

In this case, we need to declare the value by typing the name of the variable:

```scss
.selector-a { @include genericContainer($bgColor: $brandBlue); }
```

If we want to declare only a single argument that is different from the first one, we need to declare the whole argument name.

There are more advanced ways to declare arguments, but this is sufficient for the scope of this book.

Nesting in Sass

Nesting in Sass is a perfect way to make our SCSS more readable. Just like in HTML where tags get nested based on their parent elements, Sass uses exactly the same structure.

Here's an example of two-level selector nesting for a navigation bar:

```scss
$brandBlue: #416e8e;
nav {
    ul {
        display: flex;
        margin: 0;
        padding: 0;
        list-style: none;
    }

    li {
        margin: 5px;
        background: #000;
    }
```

```
a {
    display: block;
    padding: 5px 15px;
    text-decoration: none;
    color: $brandBlue;
}
}
```

Beware of deep nesting! Best practices recommend nesting a maximum of three levels. Otherwise, we will run into selector specificity and maintainability issues down the road.

Did you notice that I used the $brandBlue color variable again? The preceding SCSS for the navigation bar compiles to the following CSS:

```
nav ul {
    display: flex;
    margin: 0;
    padding: 0;
    list-style: none;
}
nav li {
    margin: 5px;
    background: #000;
}
nav a {
    display: block;
    padding: 5px 15px;
    text-decoration: none;
    color: #416e8e;
}
```

Partial files (partials) in Sass

Partial files are SCSS files we create to house SCSS snippets. Partials allow us to modularize our files, for example, _variables.scss. Partials start with the underscore symbol (_) and end with the extension .scss. The underscore symbol tells the compiler that this file and its contents do not need to be compiled into a separate CSS file.

Partials are called using the @import directive, just like it is done in CSS. The main differences are that there's no need to specify the underscore symbol and the file extension.

Let's create a partial file and put these color variables in it. We're going to call this partial file, _variables.scss. The variables (snippets) in the _variables.scss partial are as follows:

```
$brandBlue: #416e8e;
$brandRed: #c03;
$brandYellow: #c90;
```

Let's then say that our main SCSS file is named styles.scss. We now have two files: styles.scss and _variables.scss.

> The main SCSS file of a project does not start with an underscore symbol.

We call _variables.scss into styles.scss using the @import directive:

```
@import "variables";
```

Notice that the underscore symbol and file extension are not needed when referencing a partial; they can be omitted. However, if you want to add them, that's fine too. Omitting them keeps the code cleaner.

The Sass extend/inherit feature

Many professionals say extend or inherit is one of the most useful features of Sass. Others actually recommend staying away from it. This book's recommendation is: just use Sass as much as possible and experiment with different features so you can create your own opinions. When you have enough experience, you can decide which side you want to join.

Extending in Sass means that we can use a selector's properties in another selector without having to type all those properties again. This is called **inheriting**. We use the @extend directive for this.

For example, consider the following selector:

```
$brandBlue: #416e8e;
.generic-container {
    padding: 10px;
    border: $brandBlue 1px solid;
    background: #ccc;
    box-shadow: 1px 1px 1px rgba(black, .3);
}
```

Suppose we want to inherit all the properties of this selector on a different selector. We're also going to modify one property, since they are almost identical, using the @extend directive to reuse the styles of the first selector in the second one:

```
.box-customer-service {
    @extend .generic-container;
    padding: 25px;
}
```

This compiles to the following:

```
.generic-container, .box-customer-service {
    padding: 10px;
    border: #416e8e 1px solid;
    background: #cccccc;
    box-shadow: 1px 1px 1px rgba(0, 0, 0, 0.3);
}

.box-customer-service {
    padding: 25px;
}
```

Notice that .generic-container and .box-customer-service are in the same rule; this means that .box-customer-service is inheriting all the properties and values of .generic-container. Then, there's a separate rule for .box-customer-service, where only the padding property is declared since it's the only difference between the two containers.

Sass comments

Since we know that a CSS document is a valid SCSS document, using the CSS comment syntax is also valid:

```
/* This is a traditional CSS comment */
```

In Sass, there's another way. We can comment using double slashes (//) at the beginning:

```
// This is a Sass-style comment
```

The difference between the two styles is that the traditional CSS comment using /**/ syntax gets added to the compiled file, whereas the comments with Sass using // does not get added.

The comments with the Sass syntax are very helpful to document our SCSS files without having to worry about all those comments getting compiled and bloating our final CSS file. The Sass comment in the following example doesn't get compiled:

```
$brandBlue: #416e8e;
//Mixin for generic container across the app
.generic-container {
    padding: 10px;
    border: $brandBlue 1px solid;
    background: #ccc;
    box-shadow: 1px 1px 1px rgba(black, .3);
}
```

However, the traditional CSS comment does get compiled:

```
$brandBlue: #416e8e;
/* Mixin for generic container across the app */
.generic-container {
    padding: 10px;
    border: $brandBlue 1px solid;
    background: #ccc;
    box-shadow: 1px 1px 1px rgba(black, .3);
}
```

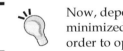 Now, depending on the options set on the compiler, the final CSS can be minimized. Thus, the traditional CSS comments will get stripped out in order to optimize file size.

Vendor prefixing

Vendor prefixing is basically adding a specific *tag* to a CSS3 property or value that hasn't been widely used by the web development industry and communities or finalized and included in the CSS3 specification.

The *vendor* part refers to the abbreviation tags that represent the names of the companies that create the browsers: Mozilla, Opera, and Microsoft.

There's one exception though, Apple. Although Apple created Safari, the vendor prefix is based on the layout engine of the browser rather than the company name.

- Mozilla: `-moz-`
- Opera: `-o-`
- Microsoft: `-ms-`
- Webkit (Apple): `-webkit-`

The *prefix* part refers to the description of adding the vendor tags *before* the CSS property or CSS value. Each vendor prefix only works in its own browser, so for the preceding list, here are the browsers they belong to:

- Mozilla: This prefix `-moz-` works in Firefox
- Opera: This prefix `-o-` works in Opera
- Microsoft: This prefix `-ms-` works in Internet Explorer
- Webkit (Apple): This prefix `-webkit-` works in Safari

If you're wondering where Google Chrome is in all this, there's a simple explanation.

Although Google created Chrome, there is no specific prefix for Chrome. In the beginning, Chrome was using the same layout engine as Safari: Webkit. Thus, the Webkit-based prefixes not only affected Safari, but also affected Chrome and other Chromium-based products.

However, Google Chrome no longer uses Webkit; it now uses its own layout engine called Blink. However, in order to maintain compatibility and avoid fragmenting the Web even more, Chrome still supports the `-webkit-` prefix.

Opera had a similar story where they had their own layout engine, Presto, and then switched to Webkit. It now uses Blink. There are other browser vendors in addition to the ones mentioned before and they use their own prefixes as well, such as the Konqueror browser with its prefix, `-k-`.

Here's an example of a vendor-prefixed CSS property:

```
-moz-box-sizing: border-box;
```

And, here's an example of a prefixed CSS value:

```
background-image: -webkit-linear-gradient(red, blue);
```

The order of vendor prefixing

The reality is that the order in which we can list the vendor prefixes doesn't matter; what matters is that we always place the nonvendor prefixed version at the end.

Staying with the example of the linear-gradient property, we should do it like this:

```
*, *:before, *:after {
    background-image: -webkit-linear-gradient(red, blue);
    background-image: -moz-linear-gradient(red, blue);
```

```
        background-image: -ms-linear-gradient(red, blue);
        background-image: -o-linear-gradient(red, blue);
        background-image: linear-gradient(red, blue);
}
```

> You can also use `background: linear-gradient(red, blue);` if you like.

The reason the nonvendor-prefixed declaration should always be last is, if the browser vendor modifies its prefix or drops the support for it, the last line will always override anything above it because of the cascade. This makes the whole CSS rule more future-proof. Plus, we won't have to rewrite our style sheets every time a vendor changes something.

Now, many CSS3 properties and values do not need all vendor prefixes. Most of the time, they only need a couple of vendor prefixes, and other times the nonvendor-prefixed - properties or values is enough.

But how do we know which CSS3 properties and values can be prefixed or not so that we can create styles that are supported by certain legacy browsers without having to memorize so much information?

The answer is *automating* the vendor prefixing process.

Automating vendor prefixing

There are several problems that come with vendor prefixing, and we can't get away from these if we want some of our CSS3 properties to work in current browsers and/ or certain legacy ones. Vendor prefixing is dirty work and we *don't* have to do it.

So how do we automate the process of vendor prefixing while keeping our work as DRY as possible? There are several ways.

Using Compass

Compass is a framework for Sass that helps us write CSS more efficiently. Compass has a massive library of mixins that we can use to leverage dealing with vendor prefixes.

The installation of Compass is outside the scope of this book, so we're going to focus on the basic usage to deal with vendor prefixes and will assume that it is already installed on your machines. Refer to the Compass site for detailed instructions on how to install it (`http://compass-style.org/`).

Once we have Compass installed, we need to import the specific module that contains the mixins we need.

Staying with the linear gradient example we used before, let's import Compass' `images` module into our SCSS file. Place this at the top of your main SCSS file:

```
@import "compass/css3/images";
```

Then, we can use the corresponding mixin:

```
header {
    @include background-image(linear-gradient(red, blue));
}
```

This will compile to the following:

```
header {
    background-image: url('data:image/svg+xml;base64,…');
    background-size: 100%;
    background-image: -webkit-gradient(linear, 50% 0%, 50% 100%,
      color-stop(0%, red), color-stop(100%, blue));
    background-image: -moz-linear-gradient(red, blue);
    background-image: -webkit-linear-gradient(red, blue);
    background-image: linear-gradient(red, blue);
}
```

There are a few new things here.

The first declaration uses a base64 embedded SVG file. This is because legacy IEs and old versions of Opera have issues rendering gradients so an SVG is their fallback. Dealing with these types of issues is completely unnecessary by today's standards:

```
header {
    background-image: url('data:image/svg+xml;base64,…');
    background-size: 100%;
    background-image: -webkit-gradient(linear, 50% 0%, 50% 100%,
      color-stop(0%, red), color-stop(100%, blue));
    background-image: -moz-linear-gradient(red, blue);
    background-image: -webkit-linear-gradient(red, blue);
    background-image: linear-gradient(red, blue);
}
```

The `background-size: 100%;` parameter is used so that the embedded SVG covers the whole container. Again, dealing with something like this is just a waste of time. Moreover, our code keeps getting bloated trying to support old technology. Consider the next block of code:

```
header {
    background-image: url('data:image/svg+xml;base64,…');
    background-size: 100%;
    background-image: -webkit-gradient(linear, 50% 0%, 50% 100%,
        color-stop(0%, red), color-stop(100%, blue));
    background-image: -moz-linear-gradient(red, blue);
    background-image: -webkit-linear-gradient(red, blue);
    background-image: linear-gradient(red, blue);
}
```

The third declaration is the old CSS linear gradient syntax that was supported only by Webkit browsers; more unnecessary code bloating in our file:

```
header {
    background-image: url('data:image/svg+xml;base64,…');
    background-size: 100%;
    background-image: -webkit-gradient(linear, 50% 0%, 50% 100%,
        color-stop(0%, red), color-stop(100%, blue));
    background-image: -moz-linear-gradient(red, blue);
    background-image: -webkit-linear-gradient(red, blue);
    background-image: linear-gradient(red, blue);
}
```

The fourth and fifth declarations are basically for old Firefox, Chrome, and Safari versions:

```
header {
    background-image: url('data:image/svg+xml;base64,…');
    background-size: 100%;
    background-image: -webkit-gradient(linear, 50% 0%, 50% 100%,
        color-stop(0%, red), color-stop(100%, blue));
    background-image: -moz-linear-gradient(red, blue);
    background-image: -webkit-linear-gradient(red, blue);
    background-image: linear-gradient(red, blue);
}
```

The last declaration is the proposed syntax without any vendor prefixes:

```
header {
    background-image: url('data:image/svg+xml;base64,…');
    background-size: 100%;
    background-image: -webkit-gradient(linear, 50% 0%, 50% 100%,
        color-stop(0%, red), color-stop(100%, blue));
    background-image: -moz-linear-gradient(red, blue);
    background-image: -webkit-linear-gradient(red, blue);
    background-image: linear-gradient(red, blue);
}
```

As we can see, Compass is a very handy tool and it allows us to customize the output. However, this may end up being more work than necessary.

A few things to consider before concluding whether Compass is the best solution for us:

- Compass needs to be installed. This is usually done via the command line.
- Once Compass is installed, we don't have to use the command line anymore to use its mixins.
- Compass has a massive library of mixins that can help deal with vendor prefixing and many other things.
- Each time we need to work with a specific CSS3 property or value, we have to import the corresponding module in our main SCSS file with the @import directive. This means that we have to spend a lot of time finding the modules we need and learn to use them.
- The learning curve of using Compass is medium, we need to be a bit knowledgeable in other technical aspects to get to use Compass even at its most basic.
- Compass has great documentation and is a project in constant development.
- There's a similar, well-known mixin library called Bourbon: http://bourbon.io/.

Using -prefix-free

-prefix-free is a JavaScript file created by Lea Verou. When the script is called by the browser, it detects it and then adds that browser's specific prefixes to the CSS. The -prefix-free file is intelligent enough to determine which prefixes are needed and only inject those.

Using -prefix-free is simple. Just add a call the JavaScript file. As per Lea Verou's recommendation, it's best to include this script after the style sheets in order to reduce the **Flash of Unstyled Content (FOUC)**.

You can visit the `-prefix-free` project at `http://leaverou.github.io/prefixfree/`.

Since our HTML is so short, we can follow the tip mentioned before:

```
<!DOCTYPE html>
<html>
<head>
    <meta charset="utf-8">
    <meta name="viewport" content="width=device-width, initial-scale=1">
    <title>Page Title</title>
    <link href="css/styles.css" rel="stylesheet">
    <script src="js/prefixfree.min.js"></script>
</head>
<body>
    Site content...
</body>
</html>
```

It's certainly tempting to use this method since calling a mere JavaScript file to deal with automating vendor prefixes sounds like the best idea ever.

Let's see a short list of things to consider before deciding to use `-prefix-free`:

- It's incredibly easy to use.
- It's an additional HTTP request. The fewer requests our site/page(s) have the faster they are, hence the better UX we provide our users. It's also beneficial for SEO.
- It's an extra file to manage. Yes, once we upload the JavaScript file we may not need to go back to it—unless we're updating it, which means we need to run extensive tests locally so that we don't break anything in production.
- It puts a bit more strain on the user's browsers to do the heavy lifting since everything happens in the browser.
- It doesn't work in files being called using the `@import` directive. This could also be seen as a good thing because if we're using `@import` to import files, we have a different and even bigger problem in our hands.
- If we're serving style sheets from a different domain than our main site, `-prefix-free` won't work on those external CSS files.
- Chrome and Opera have issues with allowing `-prefix-free` to work locally. Although this is easy to fix, it just adds another layer of complexity to our workflow.
- If there are inline styles, some unprefixed CSS values and properties won't work in IE.

With this list, we are now in a better position to make a more informed decision that will benefit the project, ourselves and our users.

Using Autoprefixer

Autoprefixer is a *CSS postprocessor* that uses the CanIUse.com database to append vendor prefixes to an already compiled CSS file.

The term *postprocessor* means that it processes the CSS *after* (post) it has been created. In other words, if we have an SCSS file called `styles.scss`, this file gets compiled into `styles.css` after we save it. At that moment, Autoprefixer takes that generated `styles.css` file, opens it, adds all the necessary vendor prefixes to each property and value, saves the file, and closes it. In addition, you can configure it to create a new separate file as well. Once this is done, we can use this file in our website/app.

The major advantage that this method has over any other automated vendor prefixing method is that it uses the CanIUse.com database; this means that as soon as a browser vendor no longer requires its prefix for a CSS property or value, all we need to do is run our CSS files through Autoprefixer and it will be up to date in seconds.

The major disadvantage of Autoprefixer is that it has so many ways to use it that it could be a bit overwhelming for some. To name a few, we can use it via the command line but we'd need to have `Node.js` installed first:

```
npm install --global autoprefixer
autoprefixer *.css
```

We can also use Autoprefixer with Compass, but we need to have Ruby installed first:

```
gem install autoprefixer-rails
```

We can use it with CodeKit on Mac and with Prepros or Koala App on Windows/Mac/Linux. We can also install plugins for Sublime Text, Brackets, or Atom Editor. There are Grunt and Gulp plugins as well.

Let's see a short list of things to consider before deciding to use Autoprefixer:

- The fact that it uses the CanIUse.com database is by far the best feature and advantage over any other automated vendor prefixing application, because we can always be sure that our CSS files have the latest prefixes, or none if the browser vendor has dropped any of them.

- It can be integrated into many applications.

- It can be a bit daunting to install for new web designers or developers.
- Autoprefixer comes preinstalled in other applications, so all we need to do is run those applications and we're automatically using Autoprefixer without having to set anything up.

Autoprefixer can be downloaded from `https://github.com/postcss/autoprefixer`.

Using Pleeease

Yes, it's *Pleeease* with three *e*. Pleeease is also a CSS postprocessor like Autoprefixer and it also depends on having `Node.js` installed. It only runs via the command line, but it's actually quite simple. Pleeease uses Autoprefixer, which means that it uses the CanIUse.com database as well to define which CSS properties and/or values need prefixing.

Once Pleeease is installed, we need to create a configuration file (a JSON file) in which the most important thing we need to define is the source CSS file and the destination CSS file:

```
{
    "in": "style.css",
    "out": "styles.fixed.css"
}
```

Once we have that configuration file set, we run this in the command line:

```
pleeease compile
```

Pleeease takes the `style.css` file, adds all necessary vendor prefixes, and creates `styles.fixed.css`, which is the file we use in production.

There are other important things that Pleeease does at this point:

- Compiles the same media queries into one `@media` block
- Inlines `@import` style sheets (this is great because we end up with one single CSS file for production)
- Minifies/compresses the final file

If you're comfortable using the command line and JSON files, Pleeease can be a very useful part of your arsenal. If you prefer to stay away from the command line, that's fine too; there are other friendlier ways to automate vendor prefixing.

Here are a few things to consider before deciding if Pleeease is the way to go to automate vendor prefixing:

- It requires the use of the command line to install and use, but the commands are quite simple.

- It uses a JSON file to configure its settings.

- It uses Autoprefixer, which means it uses the CanIUse.com database as well. This makes it incredibly powerful when it comes to knowing which properties and/or values need or don't need to be prefixed.

- It makes several other improvements to the final CSS file, such as packing the same media queries in a single @media rule, minifying the result, and so on.

- It can be integrated with the Grunt, Gulp, Brunch, and Node.js workflows.

You can download Pleeease from `http://pleeease.io/`.

Using Emmet

Emmet allows us to write CSS and HTML faster. It's a plugin for text editors such as Sublime Text, Coda, TextMate, and even Dreamweaver.

Emmet also helps us with vendor prefixing our CSS3 properties and values, which is what we're going to focus on in the following examples.

 Emmet used to be called *Zen Coding*.

Once the Emmet plugin is installed in our favorite text editor, we type this in our SCSS file:

```
.selector-a {
    -trf
}
```

-trf is the abbreviation of the CSS3 property *transform*.

Then we press *Tab* on our keyboard and the code automatically gets changed to this:

```
.selector-a {
    -webkit-transform:;
    -ms-transform:;
    -o-transform:;
    transform:;
}
```

All we need to do to add vendor prefixes is start our abbreviation with a dash (-). This tells Emmet that it needs to add the necessary vendor prefixes when hitting the key *Tab*.

 The transform values were not defined in the previous example because we want to show the result from using Emmet. Obviously, we'd have to add those values in the end.

Here are a few things to consider before deciding to use Emmet to automate vendor prefixing:

- It's up to us to define what gets prefixed and what doesn't, so we may end up prefixing properties and values that no longer need to be prefixed. Thus, we end up bloating our CSS files.
- If we forget to add a dash at the beginning of a property/value, it won't be prefixed and maybe that property/value does need prefixed. Thus, we'll spend more time troubleshooting.
- Emmet works with the most popular text editors out there, so chances are we'll be able to use it.
- The learning curve to use Emmet is incredibly low.
- Emmet does not depend on the use of the command line.
- Emmet has great documentation and it's in constant development.

You can download Emmet from `http://emmet.io/`.

Using a third-party application

As we have seen, the previous methods for automating vendor prefixing are all over the place, from methods that are used via the command line and methods that make you find a specific module to import before being able to use to JavaScript solutions.

The most important of all the features mentioned is that Autoprefixer uses the CanIUse.com database. This is pretty much what we want to use, since all we need to do is write the CSS3 properties and values and forget about vendor prefixing altogether, leaving it to Autoprefixer and CanIUse.com to add them for us.

Fortunately, there are third-party applications out there that already come with Autoprefixer installed. This means we don't have to set anything via the command line, or install a plugin, or anything like that. Just install the app, activate the Autoprefixer checkbox, and off we go!

We mentioned several applications before: CodeKit, Prepros, and the Koala app. They all do basically the same things, but they excel in two things:

- They can *watch* our SCSS files and compile them for us.
- They can automatically add vendor prefixes via Autoprefixer.

These two features have a huge impact on our workflow, allowing us to focus our energies on the important stuff, such as RWD and a better user experience.

However, there are a few things to consider before deciding if a third-party application is the best solution for vendor prefixing:

- Prepros and CodeKit are paid apps. Koala is free but supporting the author with a small donation shows appreciation for his work. However, they are not expensive by any means; the benefits are worth tens of times over when we compile a file for the first time.
- They are extremely easy to set up.
- They have great documentation, communities and are in constant development by the authors.
- For many non-frontend developers who work with CSS and HTML, these applications allow them to focus on other important things such as user experience, design, usability, and SEO—without worrying about JSON files, command line, plugins, and so on.

The recommended vendor prefixing method

This book recommends that you use CodeKit, Prepros, or Koala apps to deal with vendor prefixes. These applications not only compile the SCSS files, but also automatically run them through Autoprefixer when saving those SCSS files.

So let's take a look at Prepros, which can run on the most popular operating systems such as Windows, Linux, and Mac.

Using a third-party program to compile

Using the command line to compile our SCSS files is really not that difficult:

```
--sass watch scss:css
```

That's all we need to do in the command line to have Sass watch over the SCSS files in the `/scss` folder and compile them into the `/css` folder. It really is that simple.

The problem with the previous situation is that we need to run this command every single time we have to work on a different project. Although we can automate this in many different ways, some find the use of the command line either daunting or just unnecessary.

The Prepros app

Prepros is a tool for web designers and developers that deals with many parts of a regular workflow: compiling, CSS prefixing, live refresh, JavaScript concatenation, file minification, optimizing images, browser testing synchronization, source maps creation for compiled files, built-in server, FTP, and so on.

For the scope of this book, we're going to focus on how it can help us compile our SCSS files while adding vendor prefixes automatically.

You can download it from `https://prepros.io/`. Prepros is a paid application. However, spending $29 is not going to break the bank. I assure you that right after the first compilation, this app will have paid itself.

There is also a way to use Prepros for free and enjoy all the features of the app. However, this comes at the expense of having to keep closing the *buy the app* pop-up window about every 5 minutes.

This is the current welcome screen of Prepros (it may have changed by now):

Remember the steps in the installation of Sass where we created a /Demo folder and created two subfolders, /scss and /css, within it? We are going to drag and drop the /Demo folder onto the Prepros interface:

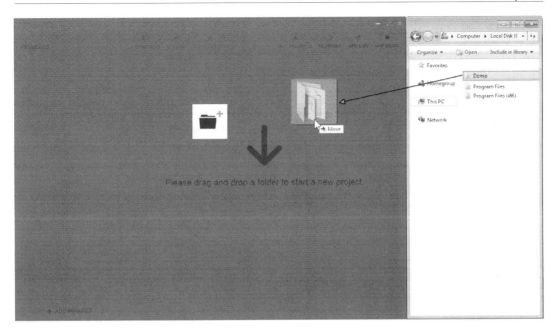

A sad face appears, letting us know that the project is empty. This is true since we haven't added any files to the /scss folder:

So, let's create a .scss file in the /scss folder:

Prepros will automatically detect the new styles.scss file and compile it to create the styles.css file, which is saved in the /css folder.

Clicking on the `styles.scss` file will bring out the file's default settings:

```
                                                                          —  ⤢  ✕

  PROJECTS          ⚡        ☁        ▦                  ▰       ▢       ✎       ▦
                 LIVE PREVIEW UPLOAD MORE OPTIONS    BUY PREPROS NETWORK APP LOG APP MENU

  ▸ ▦ Demo        ▼ ▣ CSS                                    Sass

                    ▨ styles.css                            styles.scss

                  ▼ ▣ SCSS                          OUTPUT PATH

                    ▨ styles.scss                  → /css/styles.css
                              ᕦ
                                                   FILE OPTIONS

                                                   ✓  Auto Compile

                                                   ☐  AutoPrefix CSS

                                                   ✓  Use LibSass ( Fast )

                                                   ☐  SourceMaps

                                                   ✓  Compress CSS

                                                   ☐  Compass ( Slow, No LibSass )




                                                          Process File
  ✦ ADD PROJECT
```

Let's modify some of these settings so Prepros can automatically perform the following operations:

- Add vendor prefixes.
- Create source maps.
- Not compress our compiled CSS (at least yet).

 The `source map` is a file with the `.map` extension that gets generated together with our CSS file. This map file contains the necessary information that links each line of our CSS file to their corresponding line in our SCSS files and partials. This is crucial when we need to inspect the styles of an element via the DevTools of any modern web browser.

In the **OUTPUT STYLE** section, we're going to leave the setting as **Expanded**.

The differences between the four styles of output are simple:

Expanded output

This is the traditional CSS styling where each selector, property, and value is in a separate line:

```
header {
    background: blue;
}
header .logo {
    float: left;
}
.container {
    float: right;
}
```

Nested output

You can see that the second rule is indented, which means it belongs to the header selector:

```
header {
    background: blue;
}
    header .logo {
        float: left;
    }
.container {
    float: right;
}
```

Compact output

All rules reside in a single line, as shown here:

```
header { background: blue; }
header .logo { float: left; }
.container { float: right; }
```

Compressed output

This is the minified version, which is the version we should use in production:

```
header{background:blue;}header
    .logo{float:left;}.container{float:right;}
```

That's it. We now leave Prepros running. It will add all vendor prefixes and compile the SCSS files every time we save it. Let's see this in action.

Add some CSS and let the Prepros app do the rest!

Every time we hit **Save**, Prepros will show either one of the following dialog boxes at the bottom-right corner of our screen.

Success will give us the following output:

Error will give us the following output:

Let's take our `styles.scss` file and let's add a simple CSS rule that requires some vendor prefixing.

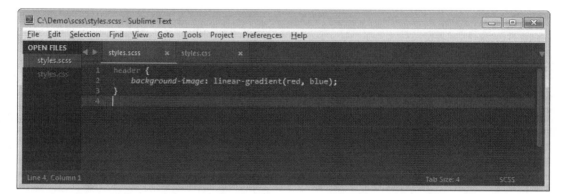

When we save the `styles.scss` file, Prepros shows the green/success dialog box and compiles our SCSS file to `styles.css`.

This is what the compiled file looks like with all the prefixes added automatically:

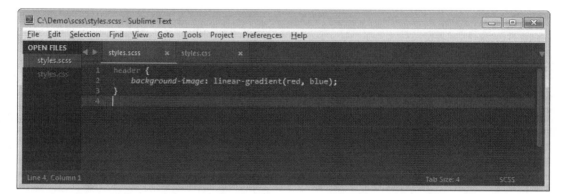

Defining how many legacy browser versions to support for prefixing

As browsers evolve, CSS3 properties and values are standardized and less of them require vendor prefixing. Our CSS files should reflect that so we don't fill our style sheets with unnecessary prefixes.

Prepros allows us to define how many legacy browser versions we want to support when applying prefixes. The steps are as follows:

1. Click on the **MORE OPTIONS** menu at the top:

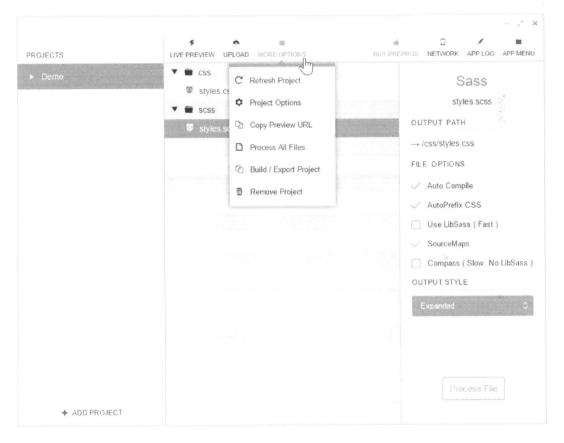

2. Click on **Project Options** from the drop-down menu:

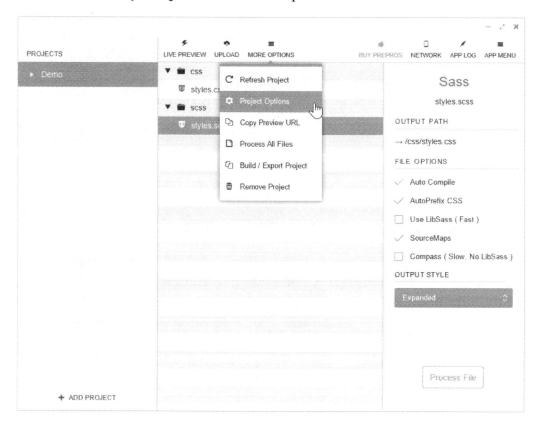

3. Click on the **CSS** menu option:

4. Scroll all the way to the bottom and type the number 2 in the **AutoPrefixer** field:

5. Once this is done, save the `styles.scss` file. We'll see that the CSS3 linear gradient property doesn't really need to be prefixed after Prepros compiles the CSS file:

> If you are not able to see the linear gradient property prefixed in the beginning, try changing the value to something very high, such as 40 so that it reads *last 40 versions*. Save your SCSS document and check your CSS file again.

That's all there is to it.

One compiler only

One very important note before we continue. So far, we've talked about using the command line via the `--watch` flag and using Prepros to compile our SCSS files. Note that *only one compiler* needs to run at any given time. Having both the CMD and Prepros compiling the same SCSS file is not necessary.

Sass mixins to house our media queries

There are many ways to create a Sass mixin to house media queries: mixins with variables only, mixins with the *No Queries* fallback for older browsers that don't support media queries, and plugins (for Compass) such as Breakpoint. There are other techniques too, such as Named Media Queries. Another technique is a simple three-line mixin that will work for anything we want.

They're all fine and very powerful. However, for the scope of this book, we're going to focus on two simple methods that will allow us to be efficient, keep things simple, and harness the power of mixins.

All that you have learned about Sass so far, especially the part about mixins, culminates in the creation of a partial file that will house our media queries for RWD.

Remember that partial files are SCSS files we create to house SCSS snippets. Their file name starts with an underscore symbol and ends with the `.scss` extension.

Media queries mixin methods

There are as many methods to name media queries and breakpoints as there are web designers and frontend developers. Everyone has their own way and style.

Regardless of the method you use, the important thing is to start using a Sass mixin to automate this process. As we build sites or apps and become better web designers / frontend developers, we'll find that other solutions may work better.

There are several ways to name your media queries mixins:

- Let the content define the breakpoints. In other words, when you resize your browser window during testing and you see that the content breaks or doesn't display in an ideal, legible way — bam! create a breakpoint (this is the recommended method).

- Name media queries using abstract names such as `small`, `medium`, and `large`, or `s`, `m`, and `l`.

- Use device-specific names (I do not recommend this method).

In this book we're going to focus only on the first and second methods mentioned in preceding list.

Let the content define the breakpoints

Since we don't know where our content is going to break and we need an initial mixin that we can add values to as we build our responsive site/app, we're going to start with a few known, width-specific values. Understand that these values may very well change and many other values will be added to this mixin.

We're going to name this file `_mediaqueries.scss`. The media queries mixin looks like this:

```
//Mobile-first
@mixin minw($point) {
    @if $point == 320 {
      @media (min-width:  20em) { @content; }
    }
    @else if $point == 640 {
      @media (min-width:  40em) { @content; }
    }
    @else if $point == 768 {
      @media (min-width:  47.5em) { @content; }
    }
}
```

This is how we use the mixin in our main SCSS file:

```
header {
    width: 50%; //Properties for small screens
    background: red;
      @include minw(640) {
          width: 100%; //Properties for large screens
          background: blue;
  }
}
```

This is what the mixin compiles to:

```
header {
    width: 50%;
    background: red;
}
@media (min-width: 40em) {
    header {
      width: 100%;
      background: blue;
    }
}
```

In the media queries examples of this book, we're going to declare the width values in em units rather than pixels. This is because using em helps scale all values better, independent of the screen densities. Let's see what's happening here.

Mixin

First, we see the Sass-style comment describing that this mixin is for a mobile-first approach:

```
//Mobile-first
```

Then, we have the opening @mixin directive. This directive contains the name of the mixin, minw, which is the abbreviation of *minimum-width*. We're going to keep this name simple because we're going to type it a lot, so it's faster to type minw than *minimum-width* while still maintaining a meaningful term.

In parenthesis, we have the ($point) argument that will store the value we specify when defining which breakpoint we're going to be using:

```
@mixin minw($point)
```

Then, we have an opening @if statement. Remember we said that Sass was a programming/scripting language? What best represents a programming language than if-else statements?

The @if statement is followed by the $point variable that equals (==) 320 pixels width. The two equals signs (==) mean that it is absolutely equal to the value, that is, 320:

```
@if $point == 320
```

After that, we have the CSS @media directive that we've seen many times before. Within this directive, we specify the width in em, in this first case, 20em.

```
@media (min-width:  20em)
```

Then, we have the `@content` directive that allows us to put any content in between the brackets:

```
@media (min-width:  20em) { @content; }
```

This is followed by the `@else` statement with the `$point` variable, the two equals (`==`) signs, and the value of 640. If the defined value is 640 instead of 320, then the mixin can go ahead and use this specific media query for 640 pixels width.

```
@else if $point == 640
```

This means that 640 pixels is `40em`:

```
@media (min-width:  40em) { @content; }
```

Finally, we have the same media query structure for 768 pixels width. 768 pixels is the same as `47.5em`.

Consider the following points before choosing the method of letting content define the breakpoints:

- The great thing about using specific width values (remember, these values are content-based) as media queries names (320, 640, or 768) is that when we use the mixin, we truly know what specific width we're targeting.

- This means that no matter how many breakpoints we have, we will always know which width we're targeting.

- We can have as many breakpoints as we need, and we'll never have to go back to the mixin to remind us which name belongs to which width.

Named media queries

This is the favorite of many frontend developers. This mixin is almost the same as the one we just saw; the difference is that instead of using specific widths and knowing that those widths will change and others will be added, this mixin uses abstract names for device-specific widths and usually there's an already defined list of breakpoints.

Here's what this mixin looks like:

```
//Mobile-first
@mixin breakpoint($point) {
    @if $point == small {
        @media (min-width:  20em) { @content; }
    }
    @else if $point == medium {
        @media (min-width:  40em) { @content; }
    }
```

```
    @else if $point == large {
        @media (min-width:  48em) { @content; }
    }
}
```

This is how we use it:

```
header {
    width: 50%; //Properties for small screens
    background: red;
    @include breakpoint(medium) {
        width: 100%; //Properties for large screens
        background: blue;
    }
}
```

And this is how it looks compiled:

```
header {
    width: 50%;
    background: red;
}
@media (min-width: 40em) {
    header {
        width: 100%;
        background: blue;
    }
}
```

Consider the following points before choosing the Named Media Queries method:

- The use of abstract names can be confusing if you have many breakpoints.
- At some point, you're either going to run out of abstract names, or have so many of them that you can't really remember which name belongs to which width.

The basic mixin

This is the recommended mixin to use when working with media queries, and it has the following advantages:

- It allows us to keep thinking in pixels when defining our widths, but the output is in relative units (em).
- It's quite simple to understand and to scale.

- If we're using the desktop-first approach, all we need to do is change the mixin name from `mobileFirst` to `desktopFirst`, and change the `min-width` keyword to `max-width`.

- If we want to use pixel-based width, we just need to remove `16` from the division: `/16+em`.

- Since it doesn't use named variables to represent different widths, there is no need to remember which named variable corresponds to which width.

- We'll never run out of named variables since it doesn't use them.

Now, considering that our recommendation is to let the content define the breakpoints, here's the mixin:

```
@mixin mobileFirst($media) {
    @media (min-width: $media/16+em) { @content; }
}
```

That's it—a mere three-line mixin. This is how we use it:

```
header {
    width: 50%; //Properties for small screens
    background: red;
    @include mobileFirst(640) {
        width: 100%; //Properties for large screens
        background: blue;
    }
}
```

This is what it compiles to:

```
header {
    width: 50%;
    background: red;
}
@media (min-width: 40em) {
    header {
        width: 100%;
        background: blue;
    }
}
```

Now, you might be asking yourselves, "where did the `em` values come from?"

It's simple. We divide the desired width by 16. The reason we're dividing by 16 is because `16px` is the default font size of all browsers. By doing this, we get our values in `em` units.

Consider the following examples if you want to use `16px` as your default font size:

- *320px/16px = 20em*
- *640px/16px = 40em*
- *768px/16px = 47.5em*

If you decide that your default font size is not going to be `16px` but rather `18px`, then the same process applies. Divide the desired width by `18px`:

- *320px/18px = 17.77em*
- *640px/18px = 35.55em*
- *768px/18px = 42.66em*

The choice is yours.

 All our examples are going to be based on a `16px` default font size.

Summary

We covered a lot in this chapter, but the best is yet to come. We learned how to install Sass and how to make it *watch* our SCSS files. We also learned that there are two different syntaxes: Sass and SCSS. We now know that any CSS file is a valid SCSS file, and if we know how to write CSS now, we also know how to write SCSS. We talked about different basic concepts of Sass like variables, mixins, arguments, nesting, partial files, the `@import` directive, source maps, and Sass comments.

We also learned what vendor prefixing is and the different ways out there that help automate this process. We decided to use Prepros for the following tasks: watch, compile the SCSS files and automate prefixing. We learned to create a partial file to house our media queries mixin called `_mediaqueries.scss`. We also learned different methods to name media queries with the basic mixin that shows us how simple dealing with media queries can be while adhering to the best practice of letting the content define the breakpoints.

In the next chapter, we're going to *dive* into HTML5 and how to mark up our content to prepare it for RWD. Get your snorkels ready!

2
Marking Our Content with HTML5

Many consider that HTML is *code*. Well, it's not. HTML—any version of it—is a *markup* language.

A markup language is a computer language that can be read and understood by humans. It uses tags to define the parts of the content. HTML and XML are markup languages.

To further help the differentiation, a coding language involves much more complex abstractions, scripting, database connections, transmission of data in some shape or form via complex protocols, and so on. Coding is truly a magical world.

HTML can do all these, but it's way less complex and a lot easier to understand.

In this chapter, we're going to focus on the science behind marking up content. Content can come in many different forms: text, images, videos, forms, error messages, success messages, iconography, and so on. Also, the way a type of content behaves in the browser or the way the user interacts with it will tell us what type of HTML element that specific content should be marked as.

For example, many web designers make an anchor link `<a href="#">Start 30 day trial</a>` *look like* a button. Many web developers make the same anchor link *behave like* a button. Why not just use the `<input type="button" value="Start 30 day trial">` element? Better yet, use the `<button>Start 30 day trial</button>` element that behaves exactly the same, is a lot easier to style, and allows the addition of HTML content if necessary.

The idea is to keep our markup as semantic as possible. Semantic markup basically means that we use HTML tags to describe what a specific piece of content is. Keeping a semantic markup has a lot of benefits:

- It's very helpful for other web designers or developers who inherit our work, because they will spend less time reverse engineering what we have done and more time enhancing it.

- It's also extremely helpful in terms of accessibility, because it allows assistive technologies to name the elements as they are: a button is actually a `<button>` and not a link `<a href="#">` styled to look like a button.

- SEO benefits greatly from semantic markup, because it allows search engines to index the content faster and more accurately.

Paying close attention to the content will go a long way for everyone in the chain—helping us during the project, helping the project itself, and eventually helping our users with and without assistive technology.

The best recommendation I can give you when marking up your content is *listen to the content*; it talks to you. It really does.

We will cover the following topics in this chapter:

- HTML5 elements in action
- Using **Web Accessibility Initiative - Accessible Rich Internet Applications (WAI-ARIA)** landmark roles to increase accessibility
- Important meta tags to consider for RWD
- A full HTML5 example page with ARIA roles and meta tags

So, which HTML elements can we use now so we're sure our websites/apps look fine in all browsers? The answer is *all elements*.

On October 28, 2014, the W3C finalized the HTML5 standard. However, all major browsers had been supporting HTML5 elements for several years.

What this means for us is that even way before the W3C finalized the HTML5 standard, we could already use any HTML5 element. So if you've been building websites/apps with HTML5, keep doing it; if you haven't started to use HTML5 yet for any specific reason, this is the time to start.

The <main> element

As per the **Mozilla Developer Network (MDN)** definition:

> *The HTML Main Element (<main>) can be used as a container for the dominant contents of the document. The main content area consists of content that is directly related to, or expands upon the central topic of a section or the central functionality of an application. This content should be unique to the document, excluding any content that is repeated across a set of documents such as sidebars, navigation links, copyright information, site logos, and search forms (unless, of course, the document's main function is as a search form). Unlike <article> and <section>, this element does not contribute to the document outline.*

Here are a few important points to remember about the <main> element:

- The top-level content of a page should be included in the <main> element.
- The content should be exclusive and unique to it.
- The <main> element should never be included inside the <header>, <footer>, <nav>, <aside>, or <article> elements.
- There can only be one <main> element per page.

Consider the following example:

```
<body>
    <main class="main-container" role="main">
      Content goes here
    </main>
</body>
```

 For good measure, use HTML entities for special characters, for example, the ampersand character (&) is & and the ellipsis character (…) is ….

The <article> element

As per the MDN definition:

> *The HTML Article Element (<article>) represents a self-contained composition in a document, page, application, or site, which is intended to be independently distributable or reusable, e.g., in syndication. This could be a forum post, a magazine or newspaper article, a blog entry, or any other independent item of content. Each <article> should be identified, typically by including a heading (h1-h6 element) as a child of the <article> element.*

Here are a few important points to remember about the `<article>` element:

- Any self-contained content should be placed inside the `<article>` element. *Self-contained* means that if we take the `<article>` element and everything inside it out into another context, all the content is self-explanatory and does not need anything else around it to be understood.

- An `<article>` can be nested inside another `<article>` element.

- There can be more than one `<article>` element in a single page.

Consider the following example:

```
<body>
    <main class="main-container" role="main">
        <article class="article-container flex-container">
            Content goes here
        </article>
    </main>
</body>
```

The `<section>` element

As per the MDN definition:

> *The HTML Section Element (`<section>`) represents a generic section of a document, i.e., a thematic grouping of content, typically with a heading. Each `<section>` should be identified, typically by including a heading (`<h1>`-`<h6>` element) as a child of the `<section>` element.*

Here are a few important points to remember about the `<section>` element:

- The `<section>` element can be used to encapsulate a group of related content. This related content doesn't necessarily have to make sense if we take it out of the page's context.

- A safe and valid way to use the `<section>` element is to place it inside an `<article>` element. You can certainly use the `<article>` element without a `<section>` element. It's recommended, although not required, to include a heading element (`<h1>`, `<h2>`, `<h3>`, and so on) when using the `<section>` element.

- It can be confusing to know when to use the `<section>` element and when to use the `<article>` element. If you're in doubt, you can choose either element.

- There can be more than one `<section>` in a single page.

Consider the following example:

```html
<body>
    <main class="main-container" role="main">
        <article class="article-container flex-container">
            <section class="main-content">
                <header>
                    <h1>The <code>&lt;main></code> element  </h1>
                </header>
                <p>As per the MDN definition:</p>
                <blockquote>
                    <p>The HTML Main Element (<code>&lt;main></code>)
                        represents&hellip;</p>
                </blockquote>
            </section>
        </article>
    </main>
</body>
```

The <aside> element

As per the MDN definition:

> *The HTML* <aside> *element represents a section of the page with content connected tangentially to the rest, which could be considered separate from that content. These sections are often represented as sidebars or inserts. They often contain the definitions on the sidebars, such as definitions from the glossary; there may also be other types of information, such as related advertisements; the biography of the author; web applications; profile information or related links on the blog.*

Here are a few important points to remember about the <aside> element:

- Content that is tangential to the main content can be included in an <aside> element. If this content was to be separated from the main content, it would still make sense on its own.
- There can be more than one <aside> in a single page.

Consider the following example:

```html
<body>
    <main class="main-container" role="main">
        <article class="article-container flex-container">
            <section class="main-content">
                <header>
```

```
                    <h1>The <code>&lt;main></code> element   </h1>
                </header>
                <p>As per the MDN definition:</p>
                <blockquote>
                    <p>The HTML Main Element (<code>&lt;main></code>)
    represents&hellip;</p>
                </blockquote>
            </section>
            <aside class="side-content" role="complementary">
                <h2>What Does "Semantic HTML" Mean?</h2>
                <p>Semantic markup basically means that we use HTML tags
    to describe what a specific piece of content is.</p>
            </aside>
        </article>
      </main>
  </body>
```

 Tangential content means that the content refers to the subject at hand, but it's not part of the main message. If this content inside the `<aside>` element is removed, the main message is not affected.

The <header> element

Usually, we think that the top section of our site/app is the header, and this is correct. The editorial name for that top section is the *masthead*.

However, from an HTML5 standpoint, there's a difference between a *masthead* and a *header*.

The masthead is the main header of our site/app and there can be only one. It usually contains the logo, some navigation, maybe a search field, and so on. The header can be considered the top area of any section and there can be more than one header.

Notice that we're not talking about the `<header>` element, at least not yet.

The masthead can be built using the `<header>` element, but the `<header>` element can also be used in other parts of the same page.

Here's the definition from MDN:

> *The HTML* <header> *Element represents a group of introductory or navigational aids. It may contain some heading elements but also other elements like a logo, wrapped section's header, a search form, and so on.*

Here are a few important points to remember about the <header> element:

- A good rule of thumb is to use a <header> element inside a <section> element.

- We can wrap a heading (h1 to h6) inside a <header> element if we think it is necessary, but this is not really a common practice or required.

- There can be more than one <header> element in a single page.

In the following example, there are two highlighted <header> sections, the masthead and a header inside a <section> element:

```
<body>
    <header class="masthead" role="banner">
        <div class="logo">Mastering RWD with HTML5 &amp; CSS3</div>
        <div class="search" role="search">
            <form>
                <label>Search:
                    <input type="text" class="field">
                    <button>Search Now!</button>
                </label>
            </form>
        </div>
    </header>
    <main class="main-container" role="main">
        <article class="article-container flex-container">
            <section class="main-content">
                <header>
                    <h1>The <code>&lt;main></code> element</h1>
                </header>
                <p>As per the MDN definition:</p>
                <blockquote>
                    <p>The HTML Main Element (<code>&lt;main></code>)
                            represents&hellip;</p>
                </blockquote>
            </section>
            <aside class="side-content" role="complementary">
                <h2>What Does "Semantic HTML" Mean?</h2>
```

```
            <p>Semantic markup basically means that we use HTML
                tags to describe what a specific piece of content
                is.</p>
        </aside>
    </article>
  </main>
</body>
```

The <footer> element

As per the MDN definition:

> *The HTML Footer Element (*`<footer>`*) represents a footer for its nearest sectioning content or sectioning root element. A footer typically contains information about the author of the section, copyright data or links to related documents.*

Here are a few important points to remember about the `<footer>` element:

- It should always contain any information about its containing parent element.
- Although the term *footer* implies the *bottom section* of a page, article, or app, the `<footer>` element doesn't necessarily have to be at the bottom.
- There can be more than one `<footer>` element in a single page.

Consider the following example:

```
<body>
    <header class="masthead" role="banner">
      <div class="logo">Mastering RWD with HTML5 &amp; CSS3</div>
      <div class="search" role="search">
         <form>
            <label>Search:
                <input type="text" class="field">
                <button>Search Now!</button>
            </label>
         </form>
      </div>
    </header>
    <main class="main-container" role="main">
      <article class="article-container flex-container">
         <section class="main-content">
            <header>
               <h1>The <code>&lt;main></code> element</h1>
            </header>
```

```
        <p>As per the MDN definition:</p>
        <blockquote>
            <p>The HTML Main Element (<code>&lt;main></code>)
                represents&hellip;</p>
        </blockquote>
    </section>
    <aside class="side-content" role="complementary">
        <h2>What Does "Semantic HTML" Mean?</h2>
        <p>Semantic markup basically means that we use HTML
            tags to describe what a specific piece of
            content is.</p>
    </aside>
</article>
<footer class="main-footer" role="contentinfo">
    <p>Copyright &copy;</p>
    <ul class="nav-container" role="navigation">
        <li><a href="#">Footer Link 1</a></li>
        <li><a href="#">Footer Link 2</a></li>
        <li><a href="#">Footer Link 3</a></li>
        <li><a href="#">Footer Link 4</a></li>
        <li><a href="#">Footer Link 5</a></li>
    </ul>
</footer>
</main>
</body>
```

The <nav> element

As per the MDN definition:

> *The HTML Navigation Element (<nav>) represents a section of a page that links to other pages or to parts within the page: a section with navigation links.*

Here are a few important points to remember about the <nav> element:

- It is used to group a list or collection of links. The links can either point to external resources or to other pages within the site/app.
- It's common practice to use an unordered list <ul> inside the <nav> element to structure the links, because it's easier to style.
- Including a <nav> in the <header> element is also a common practice but not required.

- Not all groups of links have to be inside a <nav> element. If we have a list of links inside a <footer> tag, then its isn't really necessary to include those links in a <nav> as well.

- There can be more than one <nav> element in a single page, for example, a main navigation, a utility navigation, and a <footer> navigation.

Consider the following example:

```
<body>
    <header class="masthead" role="banner">
      <div class="logo">Mastering RWD with HTML5 &amp; CSS3</div>
      <div class="search" role="search">
        <form>
           <label>Search:
              <input type="text" class="field">
              <button>Search Now!</button>
           </label>
        </form>
      </div>
    </header>
    <nav class="main-nav" role="navigation">
      <ul class="nav-container">
         <li><a href="#">Link 1</a></li>
         <li><a href="#">Link 2</a></li>
         <li><a href="#">Link 3</a></li>
         <li><a href="#">Link 4</a></li>
      </ul>
    </nav>
    <main class="main-container" role="main">
      <article class="article-container flex-container">
        <section class="main-content">
           <header>
              <h1>The <code>&lt;main></code> element</h1>
           </header>
           <p>As per the MDN definition:</p>
           <blockquote>
              <p>The HTML Main Element (<code>&lt;main></code>)
                    represents&hellip;</p>
           </blockquote>
        </section>
        <aside class="side-content" role="complementary">
           <h2>What Does "Semantic HTML" Mean?</h2>
```

```
        <p>Semantic markup basically means that we use HTML
            tags to describe what a specific piece of
            content is.</p>
    </aside>
 </article>
 <footer class="main-footer" role="contentinfo">
    <p>Copyright &copy;</p>
    <ul class="nav-container" role="navigation">
        <li><a href="#">Footer Link 1</a></li>
        <li><a href="#">Footer Link 2</a></li>
        <li><a href="#">Footer Link 3</a></li>
        <li><a href="#">Footer Link 4</a></li>
        <li><a href="#">Footer Link 5</a></li>
    </ul>
 </footer>
 </main>
 </body>
```

Using WAI-ARIA landmark roles to increase accessibility

One of the most neglected aspects of the web is accessibility, unless you are part of a group dedicated to this subject. As web designers and web developers, we rarely think about handicapped users accessing the web and using our websites or apps with screen readers and other assistive technologies. We actually think first about supporting legacy browsers rather than increasing the accessibility of our products.

In this chapter, we're going to touch on what **WAI-ARIA landmark roles** are and how they can be easily implemented in our markup, enhancing the semantics of our documents to provide those users with assistive technology a better and pleasant experience when they navigate our websites/apps with their keyboards on any modern browser.

> WAI-ARIA stands for **Web Accessibility Initiative – Accessible Rich Internet Applications**.

WAI-ARIA landmark roles

WAI-ARIA landmark roles can also be referred to as *ARIA roles*, so that's the term we're going to use.

An ARIA role looks like this when implemented in an HTML5 element:

```
<header role="banner">
```

There are really multiple ARIA roles at our disposal, but in this book we're going to focus on the ones that are easier to implement and that will enhance the accessibility of our websites/apps efficiently.

The banner role

Here are a few important points to remember:

- This role is usually applied to the top `<header>` of the page.
- The header region contains the most prominent heading or title of a page.
- Usually, the content that has `role="banner"` appears constantly across the site rather than in a single specific page.
- Only one `role="banner"` is allowed per page/document.

Consider the following example:

```
<header class="masthead" role="banner">
    <div class="logo">Mastering RWD with HTML5 &amp; CSS3</div>
    <div class="search" role="search">
      <form>
        <label>Search:
          <input type="text" class="field">
          <button>Search Now!</button>
        </label>
      </form>
    </div>
</header>
```

The navigation role

Here are a few important points to remember:

- This role is usually applied to the `<nav>` element, but it can also be applied to other containers such as `<div>` or `<ul>`.

- It describes a group of navigational elements/links. These links can be either to navigate the site or the page they appear on.

- There can be more than one role="navigation" per page.

Consider the following example where the role is applied to the main <nav> element:

```
<nav class="main-nav" role="navigation">
    <ul class="nav-container">
      <li><a href="#">Link 1</a></li>
      <li><a href="#">Link 2</a></li>
      <li><a href="#">Link 3</a></li>
      <li><a href="#">Link 4</a></li>
    </ul>
</nav>
```

Consider the following example where the role is applied to the <ul> element of the footer navigation:

```
<footer class="main-footer" role="contentinfo">
    <p>Copyright &copy;</p>
    <ul class="nav-container" role="navigation">
      <li><a href="#">Footer Link 1</a></li>
      <li><a href="#">Footer Link 2</a></li>
      <li><a href="#">Footer Link 3</a></li>
      <li><a href="#">Footer Link 4</a></li>
      <li><a href="#">Footer Link 5</a></li>
    </ul>
</footer>
```

There is no particular preference as to which element we add the navigation role to. It's the same if we add it to the <nav> element or the <ul> element.

The main role

Here are a few important points to remember:

- This role is usually applied to the <main> element of the page.

- The container of the main/central subject of the page should be marked with this role.

- Only one role="main" is allowed per page/document.

Consider the following example:

```
<body>
    <main class="main-container" role="main">
        Content goes here
    </main>
</body>
```

The contentinfo role

Here are a few important points to remember:

- This role is usually applied to the main `<footer>` element of the page.

- This is the section that contains information about the document/site/app.

- If the section contains, for example, a copyright link, footnotes, links to privacy statement, or terms and conditions, it's a good candidate for `role="contentinfo"`.

- Only one `role="contentinfo"` is allowed per page/document.

Consider the following example:

```
<footer class="main-footer" role="contentinfo">
    <p>Copyright &copy;</p>
    <ul class="nav-container" role="navigation">
      <li><a href="#">Footer Link 1</a></li>
      <li><a href="#">Footer Link 2</a></li>
      <li><a href="#">Footer Link 3</a></li>
      <li><a href="#">Footer Link 4</a></li>
      <li><a href="#">Footer Link 5</a></li>
    </ul>
</footer>
```

The search role

Here are a few important points to remember:

- This role is usually applied to the `<form>` element that belongs to the search feature of the page/app.

- If the search form is wrapped inside a `<div>` element, this role can also be applied to that `<div>` element. If this is the case, then there's no need to add it to the child `<form>` element.

- There can be more than one `role="search"` per page as long as the control is an actual search feature. For example, using the `role="search"` on a contact form is incorrect and unsemantic.

Consider the following example where the role is applied to the site's search `<form>` element:

```
<div class="search">
    <form role="search">
        <label>Search:
            <input type="text" class="field">
            <button>Search Now!</button>
        </label>
    </form>
</div>
```

The form role

Here are a few important points to remember:

- This role is usually applied to a `<div>` element that contains some type of form, *except* the main search form of the site/app, for example, contact forms, registration forms, payment forms, and so on.

- It should *not* be applied to the actual `<form>` element, because this element already has default role semantics that assist technology support.

Consider the following example:

```
<div class="contact-form" role="form">
    <header>
      <h2>Have Questions About HTML5?</h2>
    </header>
    <form>
      <div class="flex-container">
        <label class="label-col">Name: <input type="text"
class="field name" id="name" required></label>
        <label class="label-col">Email: <input type="email"
            class="field email" id="email" required></label>
      </div>
      <label for="comments">Comments:</label>
      <textarea class="comments" id="comments" cols="50"
            required></textarea>
      <button>Send Question!</button>
    </form>
</div>
```

The complementary role

Here are a few important points to remember:

- This role is usually applied to an `<aside>` element.

- It should be used on a region that contains supporting content; if separated from the content, it can still make sense on its own. This is pretty much the description of the `<aside>` element.

- There can be more than one `role="complementary"` per page.

Consider the following example:

```
<aside class="side-content" role="complementary">
    <h2>What Does "Semantic HTML" Mean?</h2>
    <p>Semantic markup basically means that we use HTML tags
        to describe what a specific piece of content is.</p>
</aside>
```

> **WAI-ARIA roles explained**
>
> If you're curious about the list of ARIA roles, you can visit the Web Platform website where the explanations are simple and very easy to understand: `https://specs.webplatform.org/html-aria/webspecs/master/#docconformance`

Important meta tags to consider for RWD

There are many ways web designers and developers use meta tags, but those extensive explanations are outside the scope of this book, so we're going to focus on the bits and pieces that are relevant and work as intended for RWD.

The following meta tags are very important for our responsive site/app. These meta tags are not just for HTML5 pages, they will work with any version of HTML.

Let's get started.

The viewport meta tag

The `viewport` meta tag is the most important meta tag for RWD. It was introduced by Apple in their mobile Safari browser. Now, other mobile browsers support it as well. Oddly enough, this meta tag is not part of any web standards of any kind, yet it is mandatory if we want our responsive sites/apps to display correctly on small screens.

The recommended syntax of this meta tag is as follows:

```
<meta name="viewport" content="width=device-width,
initial-scale=1">
```

Here are a few important points to remember:

- The `name="viewport"` directive describes the type of meta tag.
- The `content="width=device-width, initial-scale=1"` directive does several things:
  - The `width` property defines the size of the `viewport` meta tag. We can also use specific pixel widths, for example, `width=960`.
  - The `device-width` value is the width of the screen at 100 percent zoom in CSS pixels.
  - The `initial-scale` value defines the zoom level the page should be shown at when it's first loaded. 1 equals 100 percent zoom and 1.5 equals 150 percent zoom.
- With this syntax, users will be able to zoom in if they want to. This is a UX best practice.

 This book strongly discourages the use of the following `viewport` properties: `maximum-scale=1` and `user-scalable=no`. By using these `viewport` properties, we deny the users the ability to zoom in our website/app. We never know when zooming may be important for anyone, so it's best to steer away from including those viewport properties.

To help websites that are not responsive (yet) display a bit better on small screens, add the specific pixel width the site was built at. For example, if a website is as wide as 960px, add this `viewport` meta tag to it:

```
<meta name="viewport" content="width=960">
```

If you're interested in reading in more detail about the `viewport` meta tag, MDN explains it very well: `https://developer.mozilla.org/en/docs/Mozilla/Mobile/Viewport_meta_tag`.

The X-UA-Compatible meta tag

The X-UA-Compatible meta tag targets only Internet Explorer and its Compatibility View feature. As we all know, Microsoft introduced Compatibility View in IE8.

The recommended syntax of this meta tag looks like this:

```
<meta http-equiv="X-UA-Compatible" content="IE=edge">
```

Here are a few important points to remember:

- The http-equiv="X-UA-Compatible" directive tells IE that a certain rendering engine needs to be used to render a page.
- The content="IE=edge" directive tells IE that it should use its latest rendering HTML and JavaScript engines.
- Using this meta tag to trigger IE's latest HTML and JavaScript engines is very good, because the latest version of IE always has the latest security updates and support for many more features.

There's no need to use the chrome=1 value anymore, since Chrome Frame was retired in February 2014.

Google Chrome Frame was a plugin for old versions of IE. When installed, it would replace certain modules within IE, such as rendering and JavaScript engines, thus improving the user experience. In other words, it was like installing a small version of Google Chrome on top of IE.

The charset meta tag

The charset meta tag tells the browser which character set to use to interpret the content. Some say it isn't that important to include because the server itself sends the character set to the browsers via HTTP headers anyway. But it's always a good measure to include it in our pages as well.

If charset is not declared in the HTML and the server doesn't send the character set to the browser, it's likely that some special characters may display incorrectly.

The recommended syntax of this meta tag in HTML5 is like this:

```
<meta charset="utf-8">
```

Here are a few important points to remember:

- This meta tag was created exclusively for HTML5 documents. The main benefit is that there's less code to write.

- For HTML 4 and XHTML, you should use the following syntax:

```
<meta http-equiv="Content-Type" content="text/html;
charset=UTF-8">
```

- Another common value is ISO-8859-1, but UTF-8 is more widely used because there is a better chance of the browser interpreting the content correctly.

 UTF-8 stands for **Unicode Transformation Format-8**.

A full HTML5 example page with ARIA roles and meta tags

Now that we have gone through a few essential HTML5 elements, the ARIA roles they can be applied to, and the proper meta tags for display, let's visualize all of them in a full HTML5 page:

```html
<!DOCTYPE html>
<html>
<head>
    <meta charset="utf-8">
    <meta http-equiv="X-UA-Compatible" content="IE=edge">
    <meta name="viewport" content="width=device-width,
        initial-scale=1">
    <title>Mastering RWD with HTML5 &amp; CSS3</title>
    <link rel="stylesheet" href="css/site-styles.css">
</head>
<body>
<header class="masthead" role="banner">
    <div class="logo">Mastering RWD with HTML5 &amp; CSS3</div>
    <div class="search" role="search">
      <form>
        <label>Search:
            <input type="text" class="field">
            <button>Search Now!</button>
        </label>
      </form>
```

```
        </div>
</header>
    <nav class="main-nav" role="navigation">
      <ul class="nav-container">
          <li><a href="#">Link 1</a></li>
          <li><a href="#">Link 2</a></li>
          <li><a href="#">Link 3</a></li>
          <li><a href="#">Link 4</a></li>
        </ul>
    </nav>
    <main class="main-container" role="main">
      <h1>Chapter 2: Marking Our Content with HTML5</h1>
      <p>Many consider that HTML is "code". Well, it's not. HTML,
            any version of it, is a "markup" language. </p>
      <article class="article-container flex-container">
        <section class="main-content">
          <header>
            <h1>The <code>&lt;main></code> element  </h1>
          </header>
          <p>As per the MDN definition:</p>
          <blockquote>
            <p>The HTML Main Element (<code>&lt;main></code>)
                represents&hellip;</p>
          </blockquote>
        </section>
        <aside class="side-content" role="complementary">
          <h2>What Does "Semantic HTML" Mean?</h2>
          <p>Semantic markup basically means that we use HTML
                tags to describe what a specific piece of
                content is.</p>
        </aside>
      </article>
      <div class="contact-form" role="form">
        <header>
          <h2>Have Questions About HTML5?</h2>
        </header>
        <form>
          <div class="flex-container">
            <label class="label-col">Name: <input type="text"
                class="field name" id="name"
                required></label>
            <label class="label-col">Email: <input type="email"
  class="field email" id="email" required></label>
          </div>
          <label for="comments">Comments:</label>
```

```
            <textarea class="comments" id="comments" cols="50"
                        required></textarea>
            <button>Send Question!</button>
        </form>
    </div>
    <footer class="main-footer" role="contentinfo">
        <p>Copyright &copy;</p>
        <ul class="nav-container" role="navigation">
            <li><a href="#">Footer Link 1</a></li>
            <li><a href="#">Footer Link 2</a></li>
            <li><a href="#">Footer Link 3</a></li>
            <li><a href="#">Footer Link 4</a></li>
            <li><a href="#">Footer Link 5</a></li>
        </ul>
    </footer>
    </main>
</body>
</html>
```

As a bonus, let's take a look at the SCSS that ties all this together into a nice responsive page.

 The following SCSS code was built using a desktop-first approach, since we are going to progress methodically into mobile-first as we move along in the book.

Here's the SCSS:

```
//Media Query Mixin - Desktop-first
@mixin forSmallScreens($media) {
    @media (max-width: $media/16+em) { @content; }
}
//Nav
.main-nav {
    max-width: 980px;
    margin: auto;
    padding: 10px 5px;
    background: #555;
    @include forSmallScreens(420) {
        padding: 5px 0;
    }
}
```

```scss
//All Navigations
.nav-container {
    display: flex;
    justify-content: center;
    list-style-type: none;
    margin: 0;
    padding: 0;
    @include forSmallScreens(420) {
        flex-wrap: wrap;
    }
    li {
        display: flex;
        width: 100%;
        margin: 0 5px;
        text-align: center;
        @include forSmallScreens(420) {
            display: flex;
            justify-content: center;
            flex-basis: 45%;
            margin: 5px;
        }
    }
    a {
        @extend %highlight-section;
        display: flex;
        justify-content: center;
        align-items: center;
        width: 100%;
        padding: 10px;
        color: white;
    }
}

//Header
.masthead {
    display: flex;
    justify-content: space-between;
    max-width: 980px;
    margin: auto;
    padding: 10px;
    background: #333;
    border-radius: 3px 3px 0 0;
    @include forSmallScreens(700) {
        display: block;
```

```scss
            text-align: center;
        }
    }

    .logo {
        @extend %highlight-section;
        padding: 0 10px;
        color: white;
        line-height: 2.5;
        @include forSmallScreens(420) {
            font-size: .85em;
        }
    }

    //Search field
    .search {
        @extend %highlight-section;
        padding: 5px;
        color: white;
        @include forSmallScreens(420) {
            font-size: .85em;
        }
        .field {
            width: auto;
            margin: 0 10px 0 0;
        }
        button {
            @include forSmallScreens(420) {
                width: 100%;
                margin-top: 10px;
            }
        }
    }

    //Main Container
    .main-container {
        max-width: 980px;
        margin: auto;
        padding: 10px;
        background: #999;
        border-radius: 0 0 3px 3px;
    }

    //Article
```

[77]

```scss
.article-container {
    @extend %highlight-section;
    margin-bottom: 20px;
    padding: 10px;
}


    //Main Content of the Page
    .main-content {
        @extend %highlight-section;
        width: 75%;
        margin-right: 10px;
        padding: 10px;
        @include forSmallScreens(600) {
            width: 100%;
        }
        h1 {
            margin: 0;
        }
    }


    //Side Content
    .side-content {
        @extend %highlight-section;
        width: 25%;
        padding: 10px;
        font-size: .8em;
        background: #999;
        @include forSmallScreens(600) {
            width: 100%;
            margin-top: 12px;
        }
        h2 {
            margin: 0;
        }
        ol {
            padding-left: 20px;
        }
        a {
            color: #eee;
        }
    }

//Contact Form
.contact-form {
    @extend %highlight-section;
    width: 540px;
    margin: 0 auto 20px;
```

```scss
    padding: 20px;
    @include forSmallScreens(600) {
        width: 100%;
    }
    h2 {
        margin-top: 0;
    }
    label, button {
        display: block;
    }
    .comments {
        height: 100px;
    }
    .flex-container {
        justify-content: space-between;
        @include forSmallScreens(600) {
            display: flex;
        }
        @include forSmallScreens(400) {
            display: block;
        }
    }
    .label-col {
        width: 48%;
        @include forSmallScreens(400) {
            width: 100%;
        }
    }
}

//Form Elements
.field,
.comments {
    width: 100%;
    margin-bottom: 10px;
    padding: 5px;
    @include forSmallScreens(420) {
        width: 100%;
    }
}

//Footer
.main-footer {
    color: white;
    padding: 10px;
    background: #333;
    p {
```

```
        margin-top: 0;
    }
}

//Placeholder
%highlight-section {
    border: white 1px solid;
    border-radius: 3px;
    background: rgba(white, .1);
}

//Helper Classes
.flex-container {
    display: flex;
    @include forSmallScreens(600) {
        display: block;
    }
}

//General
*,
*:before,
*:after {
    box-sizing: border-box;
}

body {
    font-family: Arial, "Helvetica Neue", Helvetica, sans-serif;
}

blockquote {
    font-style: italic;
}
```

Output screenshots for desktop and mobile

The following screenshots represent a prototype/demo both in the wireframe and styled modes. You'll be able to see both the desktop (980-pixels wide) as well as mobile (320-pixels wide) outputs.

In the wireframe screenshots, the white outlines and the gray backgrounds in different tones are basically visual cues to help you understand where the boundaries of each element are without having to use a browser's DevTools.

The styled screenshots, on the other hand, show you what can be accomplished with a small does of CSS. Both the wireframe and styled pages use exactly the same markup.

The demos of the pages can be seen here:

- Visit `http://codepen.io/ricardozea/pen/717c6ab2dab9646f814f04291 53a6777` for the wireframe page

- Visit `http://codepen.io/ricardozea/pen/244886bac2434369bd038294d f72fdda` for the styled page

Let's see the screenshots.

The desktop output [wireframe] is as follows:

The desktop output [styled] is as follows:

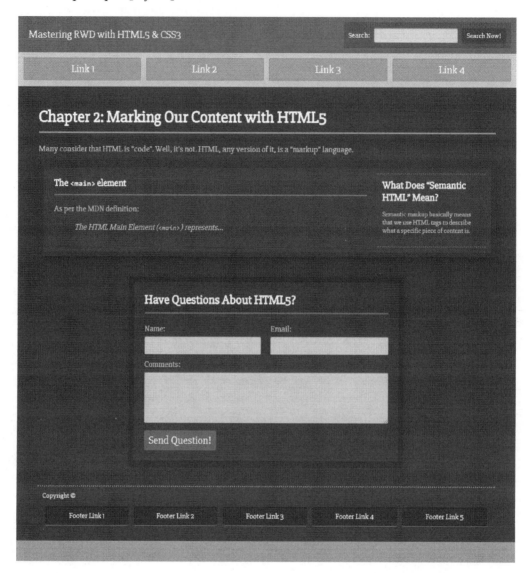

The mobile output [wireframe] is as follows:

The mobile output [styled] is as follows:

Summary

This was a short chapter but it was certainly full of important information.

We learned that HTML is markup and not code. We also saw various HTML5 elements in action. This will help us understand which HTML5 elements can be used to markup the content we are provided with.

We also learned how to mark your HTML with ARIA roles to make our sites/apps more accessible for users with assistive technologies.

We also addressed a few important meta tags that will help your pages and markup display correctly on different devices, and trigger the latest HTML and JavaScript engines in Internet Explorer.

Finally, we saw all the aforementioned topics implemented in an actual full HTML5 example together with its SCSS. The example was built using the desktop-first approach; this will allow us to methodically transition our mental model to the mobile-first technique.

The next chapter is going to be about *demystifying* when and how to use the mobile-first and/or desktop-first approaches, and how to work with each methodology. Take out your crystal balls!

3
Mobile-first or Desktop-first?

In my years of experience designing and building responsive websites, I've found that in order to have a better view of the content and the messages, it's easier to visualize things with a desktop-first approach during the wireframe and design phases.

As we are able to see more content in a given layout with a desktop-first approach, it allows us to translate the hierarchy of the content that was provided to us into a layout that represents said hierarchy. Doing this in a small canvas of 320 pixel width is more difficult than it needs to be.

When you accomplish that hierarchy, it will remain the same on small-screen devices, and the only thing that changes is the layout.

Best practices recommend building mobile-first, but many web professionals don't really know why we build *mobile-first* in the first place. Pun intended.

So, let's clear it up. The reason we build mobile-first is because of three principles mentioned by Luke Wroblewski, the author who actually coined the term *mobile-first* in 2009. You will notice that none of those principles are related to HTML, CSS, and/or JavaScript. In other words, you don't build mobile-first because of any advantage with HTML, CSS, or JavaScript. For more information, visit `http://www.lukew.com/ff/entry.asp?933`.

Consider the following points:

- **Mobile is exploding**: Well, mobile has already exploded. This basically means that it's a lot easier, faster, and more convenient for people to use their mobile devices to access the web. So if you build your website to be compatible with mobile devices first, there's a better chance of providing a better user experience and being viewed by more people than if you have a desktop-only website/app.

- **Mobile forces you to focus**: Since there's a lot less space on a mobile device's screen than on a desktop screen, there's a mandatory need to prioritize. This means that the most important tasks and/or messages need to be visible right away.

- **Mobile extends your capabilities**: Mobile devices have features that a desktop device doesn't have: GPS, accelerometer, multitouch inputs, voice recognition, front and rear cameras, and so on. When going mobile-first, you can use these advanced technologies to create richer, more exciting experiences.

Now that you have a final design, you now need to implement that design into HTML, CSS, and JavaScript. For this phase, you should use the mobile-first approach and take into account the three reasons we mentioned earlier:

- Building mobile-fist means your website/app can be seen by more people
- It makes you prioritize the content
- If you need to, it will allow you to use the advanced features and capabilities of mobile devices

In this chapter, we will cover the following topics:

- Create your designs in a desktop-first view, but implement them with mobile-first.
- Sass mixins for mobile-first and desktop-first media queries.
- Dealing with legacy browsers.
- How to deal with high-density screens.
- Why RWD is sometimes not necessarily the right solution.
- Retrofitting an old website with RWD.

Create your designs in a desktop-first view, but implement them with mobile-first

Let's look at some terminology so that we're on the same page:

- **Wireframe**: This is a very basic visual representation of a layout using only outlines, in other words, in black and white. There are no colors, no branding, and no defined styles of any kind.

- **Design/Comp**: This is a *fleshed out* wireframe with colors, branding, and styles. It's a very close representation (usually, say, 95 percent close to the final product) of the final page/site/app without going into markup or coding of any kind.

- **HTML mockup or HTML template**: This is when the design has been implemented into an actual HTML page with CSS and — sometimes — JavaScript. It can only be viewed in the browser. It's practically an exact representation (99 percent close to the final product) of how the page/site/ web app will look and work like.

With the terminology clear, let's continue.

Some professionals, including me, recommend using more modern and efficient techniques to create visual assets in order to optimize the time spent during the process of wireframing and creating designs/comps. Techniques such as style tiles, mood boards, element collages, and atomic design differentiate themselves from traditional wireframing and designs/comps methodologies. They offer the opportunity to explore layouts and styles, independent of screen widths, technologies, and even content creation.

For the scope of this book, we are going to focus on how a few things of the traditional wireframing and designs/comps methodologies can still be harnessed while maximizing the use of our time in these initial stages of mastering **Responsive Web Design (RWD)** with HTML5 and CSS3.

Why create designs in a desktop-first view?

The reason behind creating designs in a desktop-first view is simple: real estate (space).

As designers, we are required to reflect the hierarchy of the content in a visual way. To accomplish this, we use many design principles such as rhythm, proximity, whitespace, patterns, contrast, balance, grid, symmetry, and so on.

When the canvas on which we're creating a wireframe or design/comp is big enough to try different arrangements and layouts, we have the necessary flexibility to explore different ways that can represent the said content hierarchy.

For example, we're using a 12-column grid and the content we were provided with dictates the following content hierarchy:

- The business wants users to be able to provide their e-mail IDs to receive our newsletter.
- We want to display a *featured post* chosen by the editorial department.

With the preceding content hierarchy, we can immediately start picturing different layouts to convey this hierarchy:

- For users to provide their e-mail addresses, we'll create a form with a heading, a paragraph, an input type e-mail, and a button. This form will be on the top-left corner below the header and it could have a width of three to four columns. I'm thinking that maybe four columns is too wide though, but let's wireframe it and see how that feels and what usability, accessibility, and legibility issues or benefits this could have.

- For the *featured post*, we'll use the remaining columns. If the e-mail form is three-column wide, we'll use the remaining nine; if the e-mail form is four-column wide, we'll just use the remaining eight columns. The featured post has a lot more content, such as the heading, author, date, category, snippet, thumbnail, and a link to the full post.

With a wide canvas in our design/wireframing application, we can play with these different approaches and eventually end with a proposed layout that's sound and represents the content hierarchy as required by the business or stakeholders.

Creating a layout like this one with a mobile-first approach with a small canvas is practically impossible. The small real estate screen is incredibly restrictive and limited. But when things start to grow, we would need to make this exploration process each time we think of a specific breakpoint.

[
　　Actually, we shouldn't be thinking about breakpoints at this point (no pun intended), because the content—not specific device widths—is what dictates where a new breakpoint needs to be added.
]

Once we have a layout defined that reflects the content hierarchy, we will be in a good spot because when that content is rearranged on smaller screens, no matter which widths, the hierarchy will remain intact.

Why implement with mobile-first?

Let's clarify a term first: *implement* means create an HTML mockup with CSS and, if necessary, JavaScript, based on a wireframe or design/comp.

The reasons mentioned at the beginning of this chapter are the answer to the question *why implement with mobile-first?* Remember: mobile is exploding (well, it already did), mobile forces you to focus and mobile extends your capabilities.

None of those reasons could be accomplished with a desktop-first implementation, except maybe (that's a huge *maybe*) the second premise.

Let's change gears and move on to a subject a bit more technical that will help us understand how Sass mixins can help us master RWD for the mobile-first and desktop-first methodologies.

So, let's recap. Use desktop-first to create your designs and wireframes. Having a large canvas allows us to explore different layouts and properly arrange the hierarchy of the content. When it's time to implement (create HTML mockups), use mobile-first.

Sass mixins for the mobile-first and desktop-first media queries

For our examples, there are two types of Sass mixins we're going to use in this book: a mobile-first mixin that uses the `min-width` property and a desktop-first mixin that uses the `max-width` property. We already saw the following mixins and how they worked in *Chapter 1, Harness the Power of Sass for Responsive Web Design*, but here's a refresher.

The mobile-first mixin

We're going to use the following mobile-first mixin:

```
@mixin forLargeScreens($media) {
    @media (min-width: $media/16+em) { @content; }
}
```

This is how we use it:

```
header {
   //Properties for small screens
   width: 50%;
   background: red;
   @include forLargeScreens(640) {
     //Properties for large screens
      width: 100%;
      background: blue;
   }
}
```

This compiles to the following:

```
header {
    width: 50%;
    background: red;
}

@media (min-width: 40em) {
    header {
        width: 100%;
        background: blue;
    }
}
```

The desktop-first mixin

Here's the desktop-first mixin we're going to use:

```
@mixin forSmallScreens($media) {
    @media (max-width: $media/16+em) { @content; }
}
```

This is how we use it:

```
header {
    //Properties for large screens
    width: 100%;
    background: purple;
    @include forSmallScreens(640) {
      //Properties for small screens
        width: 50%;
        background: yellow;
    }
}
@include forSmallScreens
```

This compiles to the following:

```
header {
    width: 100%;
    background: purple;
}

@media (max-width: 40em) {
    header {
        width: 50%;
        background: yellow;
    }
}
```

> The great thing about using these mixins is that it's incredibly easy
> to find out which approach is being used, because we can see either
> the term `forLargeScreens` or `forSmallScreens` is repeated all
> over our SCSS file. If someone else were to edit any of the work we
> initially did, they will get a clear idea of which approach we used
> to build our site/app just by scanning the SCSS file.

Dealing with legacy browsers

Within the question "mobile-first or desktop-first?" there's an area that we need
to cover about legacy browsers. Each project, each client, and their corresponding
analytics (if they have any, which they should) have different requirements that
affect how we are supposed to deal with those older browsers.

If you're building with a desktop-first approach, your current workflow should
remain the same as this is pretty much what we've been doing since before RWD
became practically mandatory.

This means that you would still use something like this:

```
header {
    //Desktop-first declaration
    width: 50%;
    @include forSmallScreens(768) {
      //Target small screens (mobile devices)
      width: 100%; }
}
```

This compiles to the following:

```
header {
    width: 50%;
}

@media (max-width: 48em) {
    header {
      width: 100%;
      }
}
```

IE7 and IE8 do not support media queries, but the preceding code will work just fine because the `header { width: 50%; }` rule is not inside a media query.

However, if you're doing mobile-first, then `header { width: 50%; }` is going to be inside a media query so that IE7 and IE8 won't be able to see that rule:

```
.article {
    //Mobile-first declaration
    width: 100%;
    //IE7 and IE8 won't be able to see this rule.
    @include forLargeScreens(768) {
      width: 50%;
      }
}
```

This compiles to the following:

```
header {
    width: 100%;
}

@media (min-width: 48em) {
    header {
      width: 50%;
      }
}
```

What do you do then? The solution is quite simple: use the `Respond.js` script.

How to use Respond.js for RWD

`Respond.js` is a type of script called a *polyfill*. A polyfill, according to the one who coined the term in the first place, Remy Sharp, is a piece of code that provides the technology that we, web developers, expect browsers to provide natively.

In web design and development, polyfills are more abundant as JavaScript implementations, in our case, Scott Jehl's `Respond.js`. But we could also say that there are polyfills in CSS too, for example, the well-known `reset.css` from Eric Meyer and `Normalize.css` from Nicolas Gallagher and Jonathan Neal.

The `Respond.js` script is a polyfill that makes legacy browsers (IE6/7/8) support a particular CSS feature they were never made to support: media queries.

You can download `Respond.js` from `https://github.com/scottjehl/Respond`.

 Although I'm suggesting the use of a polyfill, we need to be mindful of the additional HTTP request the site/app needs to make in order to fetch this JavaScript file. The fewer requests our sites/apps make, the faster they are going to be creating many benefits such as improved user experience and positive SEO impact.

So, here's what you need to do:

- Make sure the call to `Respond.js` is *after* the call to your CSS file(s) (hopefully it is just one CSS file).
- Call the `Respond.js` script.

Performance best practices recommend placing nonessential scripts at the bottom of the markup right before the closing `</body>` tag. Since `Respond.js` is aimed at legacy browsers, let's go ahead and do that. Another benefit of placing scripts at the bottom of the markup is that it helps to avoid blocking the rendering of the page.

Here's our example HTML:

```
<!DOCTYPE html>
<html>
<head>
    <meta charset="utf-8">
    <title>Mastering RWD with HTML5 &amp; CSS3</title>
    <link href="styles.css" rel="stylesheet">
</head>
```

```
<body>
    <header>Logo goes here...</header>
    <article>Content goes here...</article>
    <script src="js/respond.min.js"></script>
</body>
</html>
```

In our `styles.scss` file, we type the following lines:

```
//Mobile-first declaration
article { background: red;
    //Target screens 640px wide and larger
    @include forLargeScreens(640) {
        & { background: green; }
    }
}
```

This compiles to the following:

```
article {
    background: red;
}

@media (min-width: 40em) {
    article {
        background: green;
    }
}
```

So, when you resize an IE7 or IE8 browser window, it will be able to display a red background if the window width is 640 pixels or less, and a green background if the window is 641 pixels or more.

The days of an IE-specific style sheet are dead

I've avoided creating IE-specific style sheets since I started writing CSS. The reasons for this are simple:

- **File management**: The fewer files there are to manage when going to production, the smoother every process goes; not to mention being less prone to errors.

- **Scalability**: If you need to add, remove, or edit a style, you and your team know that the final change(s) needs to end up in your main and only CSS file, in our case, the SCSS file.

- **Organization**: Keep everyone on the same page when adding, removing, or editing IE-specific styles in the right CSS file(s), in our case, SCSS file(s).

- **Performance**: One less HTTP request is a good thing, a very good thing. Anything we can do for performance, no matter how small, can go a long way for a good user experience; not to mention a fast website is good for SEO.

Other benefits of not using an IE-specific style sheet

In legacy browsers, page rendering is not blocked when they try to download the IE-specific style sheet. Also, troubleshooting is easier. So what do we use then?

There are several ways to deal with IE by keeping everything in one style sheet:

- Use CSS hacks (not recommended).
- Use `Modernizr.js`.
- Use conditional classes in the `<html>` tag.

Let's talk a bit more about a popular method, using conditional classes.

Use conditional classes in the <html> tag

Paul Irish's 2008 article (`http://www.paulirish.com/2008/conditional-stylesheets-vs-css-hacks-answer-neither/`) specifies a method that I recommend for several reasons:

- It's easy to implement; it's just a matter of copying and pasting this block of markup at the top of our HTML file.

- It's not intrusive, since there's no need for anyone in the chain (users, browsers, servers, and us) to deal with additional files.

- It doesn't require JavaScript to work; if a visitor has JavaScript unavailable or disabled, everything will still work.

This is the one I use:

```
<!--[if IE 8]> <html class="no-js ie8" lang="en"> <![endif]-->
<!--[if IE 9]> <html class="no-js ie9" lang="en"> <![endif]-->
<!--[if gt IE 9]><!--><html class="no-js" lang="en">
<!--<![endif]-->
```

IE10 and above does not support *conditional comments* anymore, that's why there isn't any mention of IE10 in the conditional classes markup.

With the preceding conditional classes in place, targeting a specific IE (IE7 in this example) looks like this:

```
.ie7 nav li {
    float: left;
}
```

If we need to target all IEs, we would do this:

```
.ie7, .ie8, .ie9 {
    nav li {
        float: left;
    }
}
```

This compiles to the following:

```
.ie7 nav li,
.ie8 nav li,
.ie9 nav li {
    float: left;
}
```

For all other browsers, we would do this:

```
nav {
    display: flex;
}
```

It doesn't matter which of the methods you use, `Modernizr.js` or conditional classes, it's all personal preference. You'll be doing *the right thing* by using either of those two methods.

Remember, avoid CSS hacks at all costs. As web designers and web developers, we have a moral responsibility of creating a better web for everyone.

How to deal with high-density screens

There are many articles on the Web that explain what **Dots Per Inch (DPI)**, **Pixels Per Inch (PPI)**, and **Density-independent Pixel (DP/DiP)** are. Although it may be important to understand the intricate details of such technologies and terms, let's keep the scope of the book in the realms of what the basis of high density screens is and what we need to understand to create sound responsive designs.

Bitmaps or vectors for high-density screens?

Vectors like SVGs, Icon Fonts, or regular fonts are a visual representation of mathematical equations, thus they never lose quality, no matter their size.

In order for bitmap images to display well on high-density screens, we have to export a high-resolution version of the *normal-quality* image. This means that we need to create two files (or more) for every bitmap image we plan to use: one normal-quality image for non-high-density screens (standard LCD displays, old TFT monitors, some TVs, and so on) and one (or more) high-quality image for high-density screens (any *retina* devices and Super AMOLED displays, for example).

This is where good design judgment comes into play, because sometimes we may not necessarily need to export two (or more) bitmap images every time.

There are several techniques that we can use to deal with images when we have to consider high-density screens. These techniques are explained in detail in *Chapter 6, Working with Images and Videos in Responsive Web Design*.

Sometimes RWD is not necessarily the right solution

Take, for example, the booking section of most travel sites. The sheer amount and type of information a site like this manages makes it quite difficult to have a responsive site. When visiting the eight highest ranked travel sites in Google's search results, this is what I saw:

- http://www.kayak.com/
  - **Homepage**: Responsive
  - **Booking page**: Not responsive

- http://www.expedia.com/
  - **Homepage**: Responsive
  - **Booking page**: Responsive

- https://www.hotwire.com/
  - **Homepage**: Not responsive
  - **Booking page**: Responsive

- http://www.travelocity.com/
  - ° **Homepage**: Responsive
  - ° **Booking page**: Responsive

- http://www.orbitz.com/
  - ° **Homepage**: Not responsive
  - ° **Booking page**: Not responsive

- http://www.priceline.com/
  - ° **Homepage**: Not responsive
  - ° **Booking page**: Not responsive

- http://www.tripadvisor.in/
  - ° **Homepage**: Not responsive
  - ° **Booking page**: Not responsive

- https://www.hipmunk.com/
  - ° **Homepage**: Not responsive
  - ° **Booking page**: Not responsive

Here is a brief list of our findings:

- Since Expedia acquired Travelocity, they share the same platform. The difference is in the branding; thus, I will consider these two sites as one.
- The homepages of five out of seven sites (71 percent) are not responsive.
- The booking pages of five out of seven sites (71 percent) are not responsive.
- Only one site (Expedia/Travelocity) out of seven (14 percent) is fully responsive.
- Four out of seven sites (57 percent) have no RWD whatsoever.

We can conclude that the most popular travel sites have not fully embraced RWD yet, but some are hybrids between fixed width and responsive layouts. That's why all of those sites have separate mobile apps. For them, RWD may not be a priority, so they rely on their mobile apps to balance this deficiency.

Although very rare these days, sometimes we may need to build a site or page that is not responsive. Actually, there are some pages out there today that are not responsive.

CodePen is one of the most popular frontend sandboxes out there and the editor of CodePen is not responsive. Why? Because it doesn't need to be. It's very unlikely that a developer would go to CodePen to write HTML, Sass, and JavaScript using their phone.

With that being said, if you ever need to build a site/page that doesn't need to be responsive, there are two good options as far as CSS grid systems go:

- Use our old friend, the 960 Grid System (`http://960.gs/`).
- Use the 1140 Grid System (`http://www.1140px.com/`).

There are a few things to consider:

- The 960 Grid System is aimed at screens 1024px wide.
- The 1140 Grid System is aimed at screens 1280px wide.
- The 1140 Grid System includes media queries by default, so we need to take this into account and decide whether it's best to leave them or if it's best to delete them to reduce file size and selector limitations in IE6-IE9.

Because I always thought that the 10px padding on the left and right of the 960 Grid System left the content too close to the edges of the main container, I added 10 more pixels to each side, increasing the padding to 20px—turning the 960 Grid System into a 980 Grid System. From now on, we will refer to it as the 980GS.

Retrofitting an old website with RWD

If and when the moment comes, we need to be prepared to make a nonresponsive or fixed-width site/app responsive.

There are two ways of retrofitting a nonresponsive or fixed-width site/app. One way is using the **Adaptive Web Design (AWD)** technique that uses absolute units (that is, pixels). The other way is using RWD and transforming all pixel values to percentages with a very simple formula.

Regardless of which techniques we use, we are going to have to use a desktop-first approach since the site we're dealing with was built for wide screens only. This means that we're going to use the `max-width` property in our media queries.

Before we look at both retrofitting techniques, we need a base page to start with.

The base page

The graphic you see here is proportional to a 12-column 980GS layout. The browser window is 1024px wide and the page is 980px wide:

> Our main container in gray, which is 980px wide, already has 10px padding to the left and right. This means that the sections inside always need to add up to **960px**.

The following are the container's components:

- The main container in gray is 980px wide with 10px padding on the left and right.

- The **Header** in green and **Footer** in red are 960px or 12-column wide each: 940px with a 10px margin on the left and right.

- The **Nav** section in blue is 240px or 3-column wide: 220px with 10px left margin and right margins.

- The **Content** section in yellow is 710px or 9-column wide: 700px with 10px right margin.

- The gutter in white is 20px wide, that is, a 10px right margin from **Nav** and a 10px left margin from **Content**.
- So, *220px Nav + 710px Content + 20px gutter + 10px margins = 960px.*

HTML

Here's the markup that represents our base page:

```
<!DOCTYPE html>
<html>
<head>
    <meta charset="utf-8">
    <title>Retrofitting with Adaptive Web Design</title>
    <link href="css/styles.css" rel="stylesheet">
</head>
<body>
    <main class="container_12 clear">
      <header class="grid_12">Header</header>
      <nav class="grid_3">Nav</nav>
      <section class="grid_9">Content</section>
      <footer class="grid_12">Footer</footer>
    </main>
</body>
</html>
```

CSS/SCSS

Regarding our CSS/SCSS, we are only going to need to create one partial, the _980gs.scss file that contains the fixed-width grid.

Then, we're going to create a styles.scss file with which we are going to perform the following operations:

- Import the _980gs.scss file.
- Include our simple desktop-first Sass mixin to handle the media queries.
- Create all the necessary media queries using the max-width property.
- Compile it to styles.css and use it in our page.

Creating the _980gs.scss file

The `_980gs.scss` file contains the basic grid and looks like this:

```scss
//Globals
*, *:before, *:after {
    box-sizing: border-box;
}

//Container
.container_12 {
    width: 980px;
    padding: 0 10px;
    margin: auto;
}

//Grid >> Global
.grid {
    &_1, &_2, &_3, &_4, &_5, &_6, &_7, &_8, &_9, &_10,
    &_11, &_12 {
      float: left;
      margin: 0 10px;
    }
}

//Grid >> 12 Columns
.container_12 {
    .grid_1  { width: 60px;  }
    .grid_2  { width: 140px; }
    .grid_3  { width: 220px; }
    .grid_4  { width: 300px; }
    .grid_5  { width: 380px; }
    .grid_6  { width: 460px; }
    .grid_7  { width: 540px; }
    .grid_8  { width: 620px; }
    .grid_9  { width: 700px; }
    .grid_10 { width: 780px; }
    .grid_11 { width: 860px; }
    .grid_12 { width: 940px; }
}

//Clear Floated Elements - http://davidwalsh.name/css-clear-fix
.clear, .row {
    &:before,
```

```
    &:after { content: ''; display: table; }
    &:after { clear: both; }
}

//Use rows to nest containers
.row { margin-bottom: 10px;
    &:last-of-type { margin-bottom: 0; }
}
//Legacy IE
.clear { zoom: 1; }
```

Retrofitting with AWD

Unlike RWD where the widths are fluid and elastic (ems and percentages), hence the term *relative units*, in AWD, the widths are fixed (pixels). Hence, we use the term *absolute units* and elements will *snap* to these fixed widths when we resize our browser window.

In AWD, we use pixels for practically every width, even our media queries.

Creating the styles.scss file

The first thing we're going to do in the styles.scss file is to import the partial _980gs.scss file:

```
//Retrofitting with Adaptive Web Design
@import "980gs";
```

Then, we're going to include our simple desktop-first mixin to handle the media queries. However, remember I mentioned before how this is mixin is scalable and we could make it compile pixel-based values if we wanted to? All we need to do is remove the value /16+em from the division $media/16+em:

```
//Retrofitting with Adaptive Web Design
@import "980gs";

//Desktop-first Media Query Mixin
@mixin forSmallScreens($media) {
    @media (max-width: $media) { @content; }
}
```

The following rules are merely for styling purposes in order to accomplish the same design we saw in the screenshot before:

```
//Retrofitting with Adaptive Web Design
@import "980gs";

//Desktop-first Media Query Mixin
@mixin forSmallScreens($media) {
    @media (max-width: $media) { @content; }
}

//Basic styling
.container_12 {
    background: #aaa;
    font-size: 30px;
    text-shadow: 0 1px 1px rgba(black,.5);
}
header { background: #429032; }
nav { background: #2963BD; }
section { background: #c90; }
footer { background: #c03; }

//Give heights to elements for better perception of sections
header, footer { height: 150px; }
nav, section { height: 440px; }
```

At this point, our page is 980px wide and it looks like the screenshot we initially saw.

Let's define the widths at which we are going to make our base page *snap* to:

- At 980px, we're going to snap the page to 768px.
- At 768px, we're going to snap the page to 640px.
- At 640px, we're going to snap the page to 480px.
- At 480px, we're going to snap the page to 320px.

This is where the fun begins. Let's start retrofitting this page by creating the media queries for each section.

980px to 768px (AWD)

The following media queries are aimed at 768px:

```
.container_12 {
  @include forSmallScreens(980px) {
      width: 768px;
  }
    .grid_12 { //Header and Footer sections
      @include forSmallScreens(980px) {
```

```
        width: 728px;
      }
    }
    .grid_3 { //Nav section
      @include forSmallScreens(980px) {
        width: 200px;
      }
    }
    .grid_9 { //Content section
      @include forSmallScreens(980px) {
        width: 508px;
      }
    }
  }
}
```

Admittedly, it is a bit hard to perceive the difference in the book from 980px to 768px, but believe me, the following screenshot fully represents a browser window 980px wide and a page 768px wide:

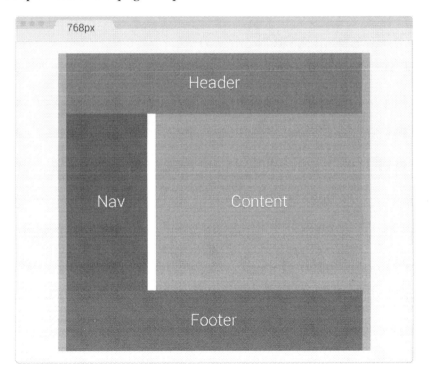

As you can see, the moment the screen is 980px, the width of our main container (.container_12) goes from 980px to 768px. Our main container has 10px padding to the left and the right, so the widths of all other sections should add up to match 748px.

Let's take a look.

Our **Header** and **Footer** that use the same class .grid_12 are now 728px wide. So if we add: *728px + 10px left margin + 10px right margin = 748px*.

If we add the widths of our **Nav** (.grid_3) and **Content** (.grid_9) sections:

- *200px Nav + 508px Content = 708px*
- *708px + 20px gutter = 728px*
- *728px + 10px left margin on Nav + 10px right margin on Content = 748px*

Stay with me, I promise this will be very interesting.

768px to 640px (AWD)

The following media queries are aimed at 640px:

```
.container_12 {
    @include forSmallScreens(980px) {
        width: 768px;
    }
    @include forSmallScreens(768px) {
        width: 640px;
    }
    .grid_12 { //Header and Footer sections
        @include forSmallScreens(980px) {
            width: 728px;
        }
        @include forSmallScreens(768px) {
            width: 600px;
        }
    }
    .grid_3 { //Nav section
        @include forSmallScreens(980px) {
            width: 200px;
        }
        @include forSmallScreens(768px) {
            width: 160px;
        }
    }
```

```scss
.grid_9 { //Content section
  @include forSmallScreens(980px) {
    width: 508px;
  }
  @include forSmallScreens(768px) {
    width: 420px;
  }
}
```

Ok, this layout is now a single column page. We're starting to see some results. Nice!

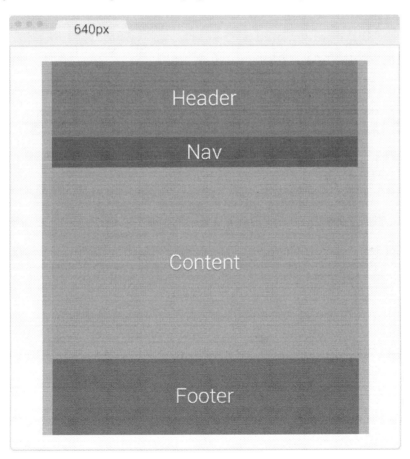

Again, remember that our main container has 10px padding to the left and the right, thus the widths of all other sections should add up to match 620px.

Let's make sure our numbers add up:

Our **Header** and **Footer** that use the same class .grid_12 are now 600px wide. So if we add: *600px + 10px left margin + 10px right margin = 620px*.

If we add the widths of our **Nav** (.grid_3) and **Content** (.grid_9) sections:

- *160px Nav + 420px Content = 580px*
- *580px + 20px gutter = 600px*
- *600px + 10px left margin on Nav + 10px right margin on Content = 620px*

Let's make this page even smaller!

640px to 480px (AWD)

The following media queries are aimed at 480px:

```
.container_12 {
    @include forSmallScreens(980px) {
      width: 768px;
    }
    @include forSmallScreens(768px) {
      width: 640px;
    }
    @include forSmallScreens(640px) {
      width: 480px;
    }
    .grid_12 { //Header and Footer sections
      @include forSmallScreens(980px) {
        width: 728px;
      }
      @include forSmallScreens(768px) {
        width: 600px;
      }
    }
    .grid_3 { //Nav section
      @include forSmallScreens(980px) {
        width: 200px;
      }
      @include forSmallScreens(768px) {
        width: 160px;
      }
    }
    .grid_9 { //Content section
      @include forSmallScreens(980px) {
        width: 508px;
      }
      @include forSmallScreens(768px) {
```

```
        width: 420px;
      }
    }
    .grid_3,
    .grid_9,
    .grid_12 {
      @include forSmallScreens(640px) {
        width: 440px;
      }
    }
  }
```

We're making some well-deserved progress! Here, the browser window is 640px wide and the page is 480px wide:

Remember that our main container has 10px padding to the left and the right, thus the widths of all other sections should add up to match 460px.

Now, we are going to change from a 2-column to a 1-column layout. This means that all sections now have the exact same width.

This also means that in our SCSS file, we can create a single media block for all three classes:

```scss
.grid_3,
.grid_9,
.grid_12 {
    @include forSmallScreens(640px) {
      width: 440px;
    }
}
```

Now, let's make sure our numbers add up:

Our **Header**, **Nav**, **Content**, and **Footer** sections are now 440px wide, stacked one on top of the other. So if we add: *440px of all sections + 10px left margin + 10px right margin = 460px*.

Here we go, the last piece of this puzzle!

480px to 320px (AWD)

The following media queries are aimed at 320px:

```scss
.container_12 {
    @include forSmallScreens(980px) {
      width: 768px;
    }
    @include forSmallScreens(768px) {
      width: 640px;
    }
    @include forSmallScreens(640px) {
      width: 480px;
    }
    @include forSmallScreens(480px) {
      width: 320px;
      padding: 0;
    }
```

```scss
.grid_12 { //Header and Footer sections
  @include forSmallScreens(980px) {
    width: 728px;
  }
  @include forSmallScreens(768px) {
    width: 600px;
  }
}
.grid_3 { //Nav section
  @include forSmallScreens(980px) {
    width: 200px;
  }
  @include forSmallScreens(768px) {
    width: 160px;
  }
  @include forSmallScreens(640px) {
    height: 50px; //This is only for styling
  }
}
.grid_9 { //Content section
  @include forSmallScreens(980px) {
    width: 508px;
  }
  @include forSmallScreens(768px) {
    width: 420px;
  }
}
.grid_3,
.grid_9,
.grid_12 {
  @include forSmallScreens(640px) {
    width: 440px;
  }
  @include forSmallScreens(480px) {
    width: 300px;
  }
}
}
```

There we go! In this screenshot, the browser window is 320px wide — the content is 320px wide as well and fits very nicely:

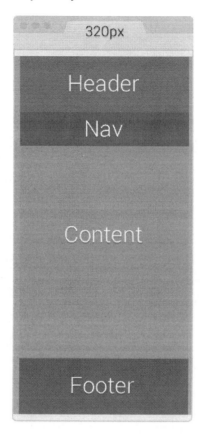

We already know that our main container has 10px padding to the left and the right. In this case, we are going to remove that padding to gain those 20 pixels, since our screen real estate is now very small:

```
@include forSmallScreens(480px) {
    width: 320px;
    padding: 0;
}
```

The 10px spacing on the left and right are now going to be created by the left and right margins from the other sections. This means that the width of each section should be 300px.

Adding the new 320px breakpoint is easy:

```scss
.grid_3,
.grid_9,
.grid_12 {
    @include forSmallScreens(640px) {
      width: 440px;
    }
    @include forSmallScreens(480px) {
      width: 300px;
    }
}
```

Now, let's make sure our numbers add up:

Our **Header**, **Nav**, **Content**, and **Footer** sections are now 300px wide, stacked one on top of the other. So if we add: *300px of all sections + 10px left margin + 10px right margin = 320px*.

That's it. We have now retrofitted a fixed-width page to be responsive with the AWD technique.

The final SCSS is as follows:

```scss
.container_12 {
    @include forSmallScreens(980px) {
      width: 768px;
    }
    @include forSmallScreens(768px) {
      width: 640px;
    }
    @include forSmallScreens(640px) {
      width: 480px;
    }
    @include forSmallScreens(480px) {
      width: 320px; padding: 0;
    }
    .grid_12 { //Header and Footer sections
      @include forSmallScreens(980px) {
        width: 728px;
      }
```

```scss
    @include forSmallScreens(768px) {
      width: 600px;
    }
  }
  .grid_3 { //Nav section
    @include forSmallScreens(980px) {
      width: 200px;
    }
    @include forSmallScreens(768px) {
      width: 160px;
    }
    @include forSmallScreens(640px) {
      height: 50px; //This is only for styling
    }
  }
  .grid_9 { //Content section
    @include forSmallScreens(980px) {
      width: 508px;
    }
    @include forSmallScreens(768px) {
      width: 420px;
    }
  }
  .grid_3, .grid_9, .grid_12 {
    @include forSmallScreens(640px) {
      width: 440px;
    }
    @include forSmallScreens(480px) {
      width: 300px;
    }
  }
}
```

It compiles to the following CSS:

```css
@media (max-width: 980px) {
    .container_12 {
      width: 768px;
    }
}
@media (max-width: 768px) {
    .container_12 {
      width: 640px;
    }
}
```

```
@media (max-width: 640px) {
    .container_12 {
        width: 480px;
    }
}
@media (max-width: 480px) {
    .container_12 {
        width: 320px;
        padding: 0;
    }
}
@media (max-width: 980px) {
    .container_12 .grid_12 {
        width: 728px;
    }
}
@media (max-width: 768px) {
    .container_12 .grid_12 {
        width: 600px;
    }
}
@media (max-width: 980px) {
    .container_12 .grid_3 {
        width: 200px;
    }
}
@media (max-width: 768px) {
    .container_12 .grid_3 {
        width: 160px;
    }
}
@media (max-width: 640px) {
    .container_12 .grid_3 {
        height: 50px;
    }
}
@media (max-width: 980px) {
    .container_12 .grid_9 {
        width: 508px;
    }
}
@media (max-width: 768px) {
    .container_12 .grid_9 {
        width: 420px;
```

```
        }
    }
    @media (max-width: 640px) {
        .container_12 .grid_3,
        .container_12 .grid_9,
        .container_12 .grid_12 {
          width: 440px;
        }
    }
    @media (max-width: 480px) {
        .container_12 .grid_3,
        .container_12 .grid_9,
        .container_12 .grid_12 {
          width: 300px;
        }
    }
}
```

> As you can see, several breakpoints are repeated in our final CSS file. This is an issue with Sass. However, it's really not an issue or something we need to worry about because when this file is gzipped by the server, it will compress it at its maximum. If we minimize the final output (which we should anyhow), we'll be compressing the file even more. The repeated @media breakpoints have very little if any impact on performance.

Now, let's see how retrofitting the same page looks when using percentages and RWD.

Retrofitting with RWD

We just saw how using AWD is accomplished, using pixels. With RWD and a very simple equation, we can retrofit a site using relative units, in our case percentages. Not to mention it will be a lot easier than using AWD.

The RWD magic formula

Discovered/created by Ethan Marcotte, who coined the term *Responsive Web Design*, the RWD magic formula is a very simple equation:

$$(target \div context) \times 100 = result \%$$

Before we start turning pixels into percentages, we need to see which width our *context* is going to be.

The main container

Our context is going to be the main container of the page `.container_12`, which has a maximum width of 980px. However, there's a catch involving the main container and the columns that will turn this 980px context into 960px. Notice the 10px left-right padding on the `.container_12` section and the 10px left-right margin in the `.grid` rules:

```
.container_12 {
    width: 980px;
    padding: 0 10px;
    margin: auto;
}
.grid {
    &_1, &_2, &_3, &_4, &_5, &_6, &_7, &_8, &_9, &_10,
    &_11, &_12 {
        float: left;
        margin: 0 10px;
    }
}
```

The 10px left-right margin in the `.grid` rule means that the widths of all the columns have an additional 20px. So, for example, the header and footer that are 940px wide are really 960px wide. The `box-sizing: border-box;` property only accounts for subtracting what's inside the box model (padding), not what's outside (margin).

One solution would be to remove the 10px left-right padding on `.container_12` and increase the left-right margin in the `.grid` rule to 20px in order to keep the gutters; otherwise, the columns would touch.

Now, the gutters become wider and this may not be intended for design purposes, and—believe it or not—somehow an extra 1px is added to the widest containers. In our case, it is added to the header and footer.

As a designer, I know I do not want to deal with any of those issues if I don't have to.

The second solution is simpler: make the context 960px. This way, we can remove the 10 extra pixels globally without affecting the integrity of the main container and the columns, and the resulting values are almost the same since we're getting percentages.

In other words: *(960px ÷ 980px) x 100 = 97.95918367346939% (97.95%)*

It's practically the same as: *(940px ÷ 960px) x 100 = 97.91666666666667% (97.91%)*

In the second solution, the 1px issue does happen, but happens at random widths when resizing the browser. However, the 1px issue is permanent with the first solution, regardless of the browser's width.

With this part clear, we are then going to turn all pixel-based widths into percentages using 960px as their context.

The Header and Footer sections

Both the **Header** and **Footer** sections have the same width, 940px. Knowing that their context is 960px, let's go ahead and find their widths in percentages using the magic formula: *(940px ÷ 960px) x 100 = 97.91666666666667%*.

You might be asking yourselves, "are that many decimals necessary?" Not all of them, but at least two are recommended.

So we end up with the **Header** and **Footer** sections of 97.91 percent.

Some developers recommend using all the decimals and letting the browser decide how many it wants to use. In the past, I decided to challenge this recommendation and use only two decimals to see what happened. Since I started using two decimals, I haven't experienced any unwanted behavior or width issues whatsoever in any browser.

Firefox and IE11 trim the excess decimals to two. Chrome, on the other hand, leaves all the decimals. I recommend using no less than two decimals, which is what we're going to use in the book to keep things simple and short. However, if you prefer to use all the decimals, by all means, go for it! At this point, it is a matter of personal preference.

> Avoid rounding up the values, and let the browsers deal with the decimals as they are. Doing this also keeps you focused on what matters most: being efficient and trying to create something memorable for the users.

The Nav section

To find the width of the **Nav** section in percentages, we use 960px as its context as well: *(220px ÷ 960px) x 100 = 22.91666666666667%*.

Using two decimals, we end up with a **Nav** section of 22.91 percent.

The Content section

To find out the width of the **Content** section in percentages, our formula looks almost identical. The only difference is that we are changing the first value which corresponds to the width of the **Content** section in pixels: *(700px ÷ 960px) x 100 = 72.91666666666667%*.

Using only two decimals, our final value is a **Content** section of 72.91 percent.

This is what our initial retrofitting RWD SCSS file starts to look like:

```
.container_12 {
    .grid_12 { //Header and Footer sections
      width: 97.91%;
    }
    .grid_3 { //Nav section
      width: 22.91%;
    }
    .grid_9 { //Content section
        width: 72.91%;
    }
}
```

Now, let's take a step back and address a few other pixel-based widths before we continue. Remember the 10px padding to the left and the right of the main container .container_12? We need to turn those 10px into percentages as well.

With our magic formula, we do it like this:

(10px ÷ 960px) x 100 = 1.041666666666667%.

Using only two decimals, our final value is a left and right padding of 1.04 percent.

Let's add this value to our SCSS:

```
.container_12 {
    width: 980px;
    padding: 0 1.04%;
    margin: auto;
}
.container_12 {
    .grid_12 { //Header and Footer sections
      width: 97.91%;
    }
```

```
.grid_3 { //Nav section
  width: 22.91%;
}
.grid_9 { //Content section
   width: 72.91%;
}
}
```

Also, all our columns have a 10px margin to the left and right. Since we already know that 10px is 1.04 percent, let's add this value to all our columns in our SCSS:

```
.container_12 {
    width: 980px;
    padding: 0 1.04%;
    margin: auto;
}
.grid {
    &_1, &_2, &_3, &_4, &_5, &_6, &_7, &_8, &_9, &_10, &_11, &_12 {
      float: left;
      margin: 0 1.04%;
    }
}
.container_12 {

    .grid_12 { //Header and Footer sections
      width: 97.91%;
    }
    .grid_3 { //Nav section
      width: 22.91%;
    }
    .grid_9 { //Content section
       width: 72.91%;
    }
}
```

Now, we have a browser window 1024px wide, a layout 980px wide, and all the columns at their corresponding percentage values. In reality, this is practically impossible without looking at the code to visually tell the differences between the fixed width and the percentage-based layouts.

We're doing good here!

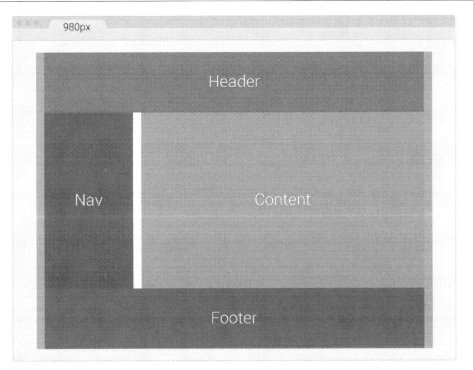

Let the fun begin. Let's add our first media query.

980px to 768px (RWD)

The following media query is aimed at 768px:

```
.container_12 {
    width: 980px;
    padding: 0 1.04%;
    margin: auto;
}
.grid {
    &_1, &_2, &_3, &_4, &_5, &_6, &_7, &_8, &_9, &_10,
    &_11, &_12 {
        float: left;
        margin: 0 1.04%;
    }
}
```

```
.container_12 {
  @include forSmallScreens(980px) {
    width: 768px;
  }
  .grid_12 { //Header and Footer sections
    width: 97.91%;
  }
  .grid_3 { //Nav section
    width: 22.91%;
  }
  .grid_9 { //Content section
      width: 72.91%;
  }
}
```

Since the widths of the **Header**, **Footer**, **Nav**, and **Content** sections, their paddings, and their margins are set in percentages now, we don't have to declare any media queries for them—at least not yet because the layout hasn't changed.

When we resize our browser window, the **Header**, **Footer**, **Nav**, and **Content** sections automatically respond, shrink proportionally, snap properly, and fit the new width of the main container `.container_12` without breaking the layout. This is shown in the following screenshot:

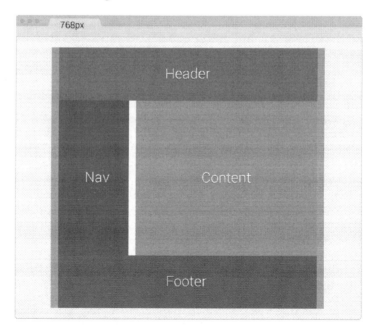

This is awesome!

Let's add another breakpoint.

768px to 640px (RWD)

In the following breakpoint (640px), our layout is going to change to a single column. So we are going to add a new media query that will make the **Nav** and **Content** sections as wide as the **Header** and **Footer** sections, and make them stack on top of each other.

The following media query is aimed at 640px and makes the **Nav** and **Content** sections full width:

```
.container_12 {
    width: 980px;
    padding: 0 1.04%;
    margin: auto;
}
.grid {
    &_1, &_2, &_3, &_4, &_5, &_6, &_7, &_8, &_9, &_10,
    &_11, &_12 {
        float: left;
        margin: 0 1.04%;
    }
}
.container_12 {
    @include forSmallScreens(980px) {
        width: 768px;
    }

    @include forSmallScreens(768px) {
        width: 640px;
    }
    .grid_12 { //Header and Footer sections
      width: 97.91%;
    }
    .grid_3 { //Nav section
      width: 22.91%;
    }
    .grid_9 { //Content section
      width: 72.91%;
    }
```

```
.grid_3, .grid_9 { //Nav and Content sections
    @include forSmallScreens(640px) {
        width: 97.91%;
    }
}
```

Ok, we now have a single-column layout. Not bad, not bad!

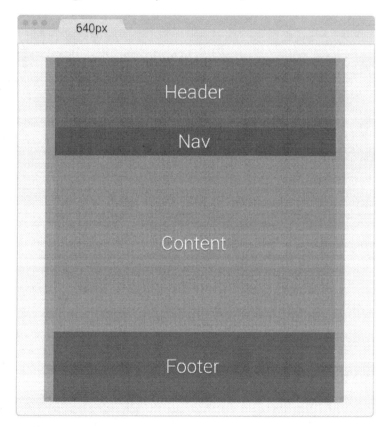

640px to 480px (RWD)

We are now going as small as 480px and the one-column layout won't change, only the widths of all the containers will change.

The following media query is aimed at 480px:

```
.container_12 {
  width: 980px;
  padding: 0 1.04%;
```

```scss
    margin: auto;
}
.grid {
    &_1, &_2, &_3, &_4, &_5, &_6, &_7, &_8, &_9, &_10,
    &_11, &_12 {
      float: left;
      margin: 0 1.04%;
    }
}
.container_12 {
    @include forSmallScreens(980px) {
      width: 768px;
    }
    @include forSmallScreens(768px) {
      width: 640px;
    }
    @include forSmallScreens(640px) {
      width: 480px;
    }
    .grid_12 { //Header and Footer sections
      width: 97.91%;
    }
    .grid_3 { //Nav section
      width: 22.91%;
      @include forSmallScreens(640px) {
        height: 50px; //This is only for styling
      }
    }
    .grid_9 { //Content section
        width: 72.91%;
    }
    .grid_3, .grid_9 { //Nav and Content sections
      @include forSmallScreens(640px) {
        width: 97.91%;
      }
    }
}
```

Our layout is getting narrower and all we needed to do was add a new media query and that was it! No need to mess around with the other containers; they all adapt perfectly to any width we define.

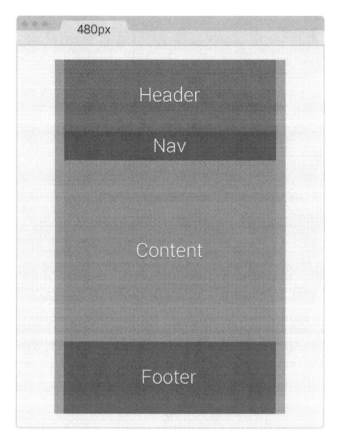

480px to 320px (RWD)

Finally, we address the 320px width without modifying the one-column layout. We remove the padding on .container_12 to make use of all the available screen real estate.

The following media query is aimed at 320px:

```
.container_12 {
    width: 980px;
    padding: 0 1.04%;
    margin: auto;
}
.grid {
```

```
    &_1, &_2, &_3, &_4, &_5, &_6, &_7, &_8, &_9, &_10,
    &_11, &_12 {
    float: left;
    margin: 0 1.04%;   }
  }
.container_12 {
    @include forSmallScreens(980px) {
      width: 768px;
    }
    @include forSmallScreens(768px) {
      width: 640px;
    }
    @include forSmallScreens(640px) {
      width: 480px;
    }
    @include forSmallScreens(480px) {
      width: 320px; padding: 0;
    }
    .grid_12 { //Header and Footer sections
      width: 97.91%;
    }
    .grid_3 { //Nav section
      width: 22.91%;
      @include forSmallScreens(640px) {
        height: 50px; //This is only for styling
      }
    }
    .grid_9 { //Content section
      width: 72.91%;
    }
    .grid_3, .grid_9 {
      @include forSmallScreens(640px) {
        width: 97.91%;
      }
    }
  }
```

Once more, we do not have to add anything to the **Header**, **Footer**, **Nav**, and **Content** sections, since all of them are now 97.91 percent wide. This makes them responsive and we don't have to worry about anything else.

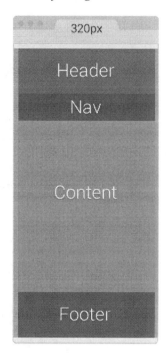

The final SCSS, combining all breakpoints and widths, is as follows:

```
.container_12 {
    width: 980px;
    padding: 0 1.04%;
    margin: auto;
}
.grid {
    &_1, &_2, &_3, &_4, &_5, &_6, &_7, &_8, &_9, &_10,
    &_11, &_12 {
        float: left;
        margin: 0 1.04%;
    }
}
.container_12 {
    @include forSmallScreens(980px) {
```

```
            width: 768px;
        }
        @include forSmallScreens(768px) {
            width: 640px;
        }
        @include forSmallScreens(640px) {
            width: 480px;
        }
        @include forSmallScreens(480px) {
            width: 320px; padding: 0;
        }
        .grid_12 { //Header and Footer sections
          width: 97.91%;
        }
        .grid_3 { //Nav section
          width: 22.91%;
        }
        .grid_9 { //Content section
          width: 72.91%;
        }
        .grid_3, .grid_9 { //Nav and Content sections
            @include forSmallScreens(640px) {
                width: 97.91%;
            }
        }
    }
}
```

It compiles to the following CSS:

```
.container_12 {
    width: 980px;
    padding: 0 1.04%;
    margin: auto;
}

.grid_1, .grid_2, .grid_3, .grid_4, .grid_5, .grid_6, .grid_7,
.grid_8, .grid_9, .grid_10, .grid_11, .grid_12 {
    float: left;
```

```
        margin: 0 1.04%;
    }

    @media (max-width: 980px) {
        .container_12 {
          width: 768px;
        }
    }
    @media (max-width: 768px) {
        .container_12 {
          width: 640px;
        }
    }
    @media (max-width: 640px) {
        .container_12 {
          width: 480px;
        }
    }
    @media (max-width: 480px) {
        .container_12 {
          width: 320px;
          padding: 0;
        }
    }
    .container_12 .grid_12 {
        width: 97.91%;
    }
    .container_12 .grid_3 {
        width: 22.91%;
    }
    .container_12 .grid_9 {
        width: 72.91%;
    }
    @media (max-width: 640px) {
        .container_12 .grid_3, .container_12 .grid_9 {
          width: 97.91%;
        }
    }
```

As you can see, it's a lot less code using RWD than AWD to retrofit a site. Granted, these examples are an extreme simplification of a site/app layout, but now you are aware of the basic concepts of each technique when the time to make the call of using AWD or RWD knocks on your door.

Summary

We discussed a lot of interesting stuff in this chapter, for sure. We saw how using desktop-first to create our designs and wireframes is beneficial because having a large canvas allows us to explore different layouts and properly arrange the hierarchy of the content.

When creating HTML mockups, using mobile-first is better because a mobile-friendly site will have more reach, allow focused content, and leverage mobile devices' technologies.

We were able to retrofit with AWD and RWD a fixed-width site using the magic formula. We also discussed the benefits of RWD, since it required a lot less code. However, the analysis of the travel sites clearly shows us that RWD sometimes isn't the right solution.

We also saw how `Respond.js` can be used to make legacy browsers support media queries if we are building with a mobile-first approach. Using conditional classes is a good technique because it's not intrusive, it's very easy to implement, and it has no JavaScript dependencies.

In the next chapter, we're going to talk about some of the most interesting subjects in the world of RWD: CSS grids, CSS frameworks, and the power of Flexbox.

Let's do this!

4
CSS Grids, CSS Frameworks, UI Kits, and Flexbox for RWD

Responsive Web Design (RWD) has introduced a new layer of work for everyone building responsive websites and apps. When we have to test our work on different devices and in different dimensions, wherever the content breaks, we need to add a breakpoint and test again.

This can happen many, many times. So, building a website or app will take a bit longer than it used to.

To make things a little more interesting, as web designers and developers, we need to be mindful of how the content is laid out at different dimensions and how a grid can help us structure the content to different layouts.

Now that we have mentioned grids, have you ever asked yourself, "what do we use a grid for anyway?"

To borrow a few terms from the design industry and answer that question, we use a grid to allow the content to have rhythm, proportion, and balance. The objective is that those who use our websites/apps will have a more pleasant experience with our content, since it will be easier to scan (rhythm), easier to read (proportion) and organized (balance).

In order to speed up the design and build processes while keeping all the content properly formatted in different dimensions, many authors and companies have created CSS frameworks and CSS grids that contain not only a grid but also many other features and styles than can be leveraged by using a simple class name.

As time goes by and browsers start supporting more and more CSS3 properties, such as Flexbox, it'll become easier to work with layouts. This will render the grids inside CSS frameworks almost unnecessary.

Let's see what CSS grids, CSS frameworks, UI kits, and Flexbox are all about and how they can help us with RWD.

In this chapter, we're going to cover the following topics:

- What is a grid?
- CSS grids
- The pros and cons of CSS grids for RWD
- CSS frameworks
- UI kits
- The pros and cons of CSS frameworks for RWD
- Creating a custom CSS grid
- Building a sample page with the custom CSS grid
- Using Flexbox
- Building a sample page with Flexbox

What is a grid?

A grid is a set of visual guidelines (vertical, horizontal, or both, hence the term *grid*) that help define where elements can be placed. Once the elements have been placed, we end up with a *layout*.

The benefit of using a grid is that the elements placed on it will have a harmonious flow along the pages, enhancing the user experience in terms of legibility, layout consistency, and good proportions between the elements.

CSS grids

A CSS grid is basically a compound of vertical guidelines that form columns. The properties of these columns are defined in a CSS file. This file contains a list of classes with specific widths that match the amount of columns that a specific grid is built for.

We've seen this before in *Chapter 3, Mobile-first or Desktop-first?* when we used the **980 Grid System (980GS)** to retrofit an old, fixed-width site. Here's the SCSS file again:

```scss
*, *:before, *:after {
    box-sizing: border-box;
}

//Container
.container-12 {
    width: 980px;
    padding: 0 10px;
    margin: auto;
}
//Grid >> Global
.grid {
    &-1, &-2, &-3, &-4, &-5, &-6, &-7, &-8, &-9, &-10, &-11, &-12 {
        float: left;
        margin: 0 10px;
    }
}
//Grid >> 12 Columns
.container-12 {
    .grid-1  { width: 60px; }
    .grid-2  { width: 140px; }
    .grid-3  { width: 220px; }
    .grid-4  { width: 300px; }
    .grid-5  { width: 380px; }
    .grid-6  { width: 460px; }
    .grid-7  { width: 540px; }
    .grid-8  { width: 620px; }
    .grid-9  { width: 700px; }
    .grid-10 { width: 780px; }
    .grid-11 { width: 860px; }
    .grid-12 { width: 940px; }
}
//Clear Floated Elements - http://davidwalsh.name/css-clear-fix
.clear, .row {
    &:before,
    &:after { content: ''; display: table; }
    &:after { clear: both; }
}
//Use rows to nest containers
.row { margin-bottom: 10px;
    &:last-of-type { margin-bottom: 0; }
}
//Legacy IE
.clear { zoom: 1; }
```

Remember that we turned 960GS into 980GS because the content would look too close to the edge of the main container with only 10px gutters on the left and right of that main container. So, we added 10px more to each side and made the main container 980px wide.

Because we are mastering RWD with HTML5 and CSS3, let's look at that same 980GS with percentages to make it fluid.

The RWD magic formula is *(target ÷ context) x 100 = result %*.

Our context in this case is 980px, as shown here:

```
//Container
.container-12 {
    width: 100%;
    max-width: 980px;
    padding: 0 1.02%;
    margin: auto;
}
//Grid >> Global
.grid {
    &-1, &-2, &-3, &-4, &-5, &-6, &-7, &-8, &-9, &-10, &-11, &-12 {
        float: left;
        margin: 0 1.02%;
    }
}
//Grid >> 12 Columns
.container-12 {
    .grid-1  { width: 6.12%; }
    .grid-2  { width: 14.29%; }
    .grid-3  { width: 22.45%; }
    .grid-4  { width: 30.61%; }
    .grid-5  { width: 38.78%; }
    .grid-6  { width: 46.94%; }
    .grid-7  { width: 55.10%; }
    .grid-8  { width: 63.27%; }
    .grid-9  { width: 71.43%; }
    .grid-10 { width: 79.59%; }
    .grid-11 { width: 87.76%; }
    .grid-12 { width: 95.92%; }
}
//Clear Floated Elements - http://davidwalsh.name/css-clear-fix
.clear, .row {
```

```
  &:before,
  &:after { content: ''; display: table; }
  &:after { clear: both; }
}
//Use rows to nest containers
.row { margin-bottom: 10px;
  &:last-of-type { margin-bottom: 0; }
}
//Legacy IE
.clear { zoom: 1; }
```

In web design, grids are usually made with 12 or 16 columns. 960GS is pretty much one of the most famous ones, albeit it's always been a fixed-width grid. But other authors have ported it to make it fluid, such as the *Fluid 960 Grid System*, but not responsive. The 960GS also has the option of 24 columns, but it's not as popular as the 12 column version.

There are other grids for web design that do not have a defined frame width or number of columns, instead these grids can have an infinite amount of columns, such as the *Frameless Grid*, which is based on **Adaptive Web Design** (**AWD**). This means that the width of the main container *snaps* to a specific breakpoint calculated by the number of columns that fit in it.

The pros and cons of CSS grids for RWD

The idea behind listing pros and cons of CSS grids for RWD is that we should be able to make the most informed decision when we plan to use a certain type of grid. It helps clarify the clients' expectations and ours, because using a certain grid will impact the timeline, design, layout, and many UX factors.

The advantages are as follows:

- Laying out elements is a lot easier because the columns serve as guidelines for placement.

- If using a prebuilt CSS grid, there's no need to do any of the math to deal with the column and gutter widths. It's already taken care of by the author of the grid.

- We can build faster, since all we need to do is add specific classes to our containers in our HTML and—for the most part—the layout will happen instantly.

- Understanding grids in web design is relatively simple, so enhancing/editing someone else's markup and code in an already built project is less painful than if they hadn't used a CSS grid at all.

- If the grid is responsive or adaptive, we don't have to worry too much about the breakpoints.

- If we are using a third-party CSS grid, any cross-browser issues have already been addressed.

The disadvantages are as follows:

- Some CSS grids have a steeper learning curve than others.

- With many CSS grids, we are locked into using the name conventions the author created.

- We may have to change/adapt the way we write our HTML.

- There are so many CSS grids to choose from that it can be overwhelming for some.

- If our content breaks at certain points the grid doesn't support, we have to spend time amending the original grid to fit each individual situation.

CSS frameworks

A CSS framework is a group of prebuilt features that basically help speed up frontend development for the Web. A lot of the small but important details have already been taken care of by the authors of these CSS frameworks, so those who decide to use them can focus on their tasks at hand while leaving a lot of the decisions to the CSS frameworks themselves.

Many developers and designers believe (I do too) that the true value of any CSS framework is their CSS grids, and sometimes we go to great lengths to extract the CSS grid and customize it to fit our needs.

In this book, we're going to focus on the CSS grids to master RWD rather than stripping one out from a CSS framework or UI kit (if it happens to offer one). We'll get to this shortly.

The following list describes some of the features and characteristics of CSS frameworks:

- CSS frameworks are focused solely on web-based development, not native mobile apps.

- CSS frameworks always offer a CSS grid.

- Many of them also offer user interface components as well (just like a UI kit), for example, sliders, paginations, navigation bars, typography, buttons, and so on in the form of HTML and CSS.

- Both CSS frameworks and web-oriented UI kits can be called *frontend frameworks*.

UI kits

Similar to CSS frameworks, there is another type of frontend framework called UI kits. However, UI kits can be a breed of their own.

Truth be told, sometimes differentiating between a CSS framework and a UI kit is difficult. But don't delve too much into which one is which, the important thing is to understand why we're using them in the first place and how they can help us build better and faster responsive sites and apps.

The following list describes some of the features and characteristics of UI kits:

- There are basically two types of UI kits: those that are built with web technologies (HTML and CSS) and can be used to prototype web-based applications, and those that are made of (usually) Photoshop (PSD) files to help mock up and design native mobile apps.
- Very few web-oriented UI kits offer a grid of some sort.
- UI kits are focused on providing user interface components such as sliders, paginations, navigation bars, dialog boxes, overlays/modals, buttons, typography, tooltips, lists, accordions, tab systems, carousels/slideshows, forms, and so on.
- In a web-oriented UI kit, the architecture is very modular. This means that each component can be incorporated into any CSS framework.

The pros and cons of CSS frameworks for RWD

With RWD as our main driver for any decisions we make in terms of layout versus screen real estate, let's take a look at what the good and not so good things are about CSS frameworks:

The advantages are as follows:

- They are very useful to rapidly build responsive prototypes rather than showing static wireframes.
- Cross-browser issues are already taken care of.
- They force you, in a good way, to create grid-based layouts.
- They offer a solid starting point to build on top of.

- The modularity allows you to handpick the components you want. For example, you can just use the CSS grid module or you can use the `forms` module.
- Changing the styling to fit your design(s) is relatively easy.
- If you aren't too good at CSS, you can still use a CSS framework to implement your own designs.

The disadvantages are as follows:

- They can bloat your project(s) with CSS that you will never use.
- They have a large footprint if you decide to use the entire CSS framework.
- You might need to change your habits and the way you write your HTML and CSS to fit the CSS framework you're using.
- They can be opinionated, so if you don't like the way things are named you have very little choice for customization.
- Customizing a CSS framework is doable, but it can be very time consuming and dangerous. Change a name to something else and there's almost no way to know what the impact is going to be on other parts of the framework.
- If the default styling is not changed to fit your brand/designs, your site or app will not be unique and will look like everyone else's, losing credibility in front of users.
- If you need to build something simple, using a CSS framework is overkill.
- Every website/app or project is different, so you may end up spending a lot of time changing and overriding properties for every single project.
- They try to solve every frontend problem.

Now that we've seen the pros and cons of CSS grids, CSS frameworks and UI kits it's time to make a decision and answer this question: which methodology is best for RWD?

The answer isn't the most encouraging, I admit it, but it's the truth: it depends.

If we're freelancing and doing everything ourselves, or working in a very small group, it may not be necessary to use any frameworks at all. We can custom build something based on the same principles major frameworks have been built on. Obviously, we would want to automate any repetitive processes so we use our time efficiently.

But if we're working in a large team, a melting pot of web professional with in-house and off-shore resources, maybe using a framework can be helpful. This is because everyone will need to adhere to the framework's structures so that all things are consistent.

Creating a custom CSS grid

Since we're mastering RWD, we have the luxury of creating our own CSS grid. However, we need to work smart, not hard. So what we're going to do is leverage the *Variable Grid System* app and combine its result with our own approach, making a mobile-first, fluid, custom build, and solid CSS grid from which we can create robust responsive designs.

Let's lay out our CSS grid requirements:

- It should have 12 columns.
- It should be 1200px wide to account for 1280px screens.
- It should be fluid, with relative units (percentages) for the columns and gutters.
- It should use the mobile-first approach.
- It should use the SCSS syntax.
- It should be reusable for other projects.
- It should be simple to use and understand.
- It should be easily scalable.

Here's what our 1200 pixel wide and 12-column width 20px grid looks like:

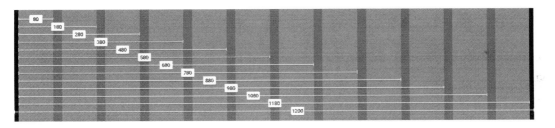

The left and right padding in black are 10px each. We'll convert those 10px into percentages at the end of this process.

Doing the math

We're going to use the RWD magic formula: *(target ÷ context) x 100 = result %*.

Our context is going to be 1200px. So let's convert one column: *80 ÷ 1200 x 100 = 6.67%*.

For two columns, we have to account for the gutter that is 20px. In other words, we can't say that two columns are exactly 160px. That's not entirely correct.

Two columns are: *80px + 20px + 80px = 180px.*

Let's now convert two columns: *180 ÷ 1200 x 100 = 15%.*

For three columns, we now have to account for two gutters:
80px + 20px + 80px + 20px + 80px = 280px.

Let's now convert three columns: *280 ÷ 1200 x 100 = 23.33%.*

Can you see the pattern now? Every time we add a column, all that we need to do is add 100 to the value. This value accounts for the gutters too!

Check the screenshot of the grid we saw moments ago, you can see the values of the columns increment by 100.

So, all the equations are as follows:

```
1    column:     80 ÷ 1200 x 100 =  6.67%
2    columns:   180 ÷ 1200 x 100 =  15%
3    columns:   280 ÷ 1200 x 100 =  23.33%
4    columns:   380 ÷ 1200 x 100 =  31.67%
5    columns:   480 ÷ 1200 x 100 =  40%
6    columns:   580 ÷ 1200 x 100 =  48.33%
7    columns:   680 ÷ 1200 x 100 =  56.67%
8    columns:   780 ÷ 1200 x 100 =  65%
9    columns:   880 ÷ 1200 x 100 =  73.33%
10   columns:   980 ÷ 1200 x 100 =  81.67%
11   columns:  1080 ÷ 1200 x 100 =  90%
12   columns:  1180 ÷ 1200 x 100 =  98.33%
```

Let's create the SCSS for the 12-column grid:

```scss
//Grid 12 Columns
.grid {
    &-1   { width:6.67%; }
    &-2   { width:15%; }
    &-3   { width:23.33%; }
    &-4   { width:31.67%; }
    &-5   { width:40%; }
    &-6   { width:48.33%; }
    &-7   { width:56.67%; }
    &-8   { width:65%; }
    &-9   { width:73.33%; }
    &-10  { width:81.67%; }
    &-11  { width:90%; }
    &-12  { width:98.33%; }
}
```

Using hyphens (-) to separate words allows for easier selection of
the terms when editing the code.

Adding the UTF-8 character set directive and a Credits section

Don't forget to include the UTF-8 encoding directive at the top of the file to let
browsers know the character set we're using. Let's spruce up our code by adding
a Credits section at the top. The code is as follows:

```scss
@charset "UTF-8";

/*
    Custom Fluid & Responsive Grid System
    Structure: Mobile-first (min-width)
    Syntax: SCSS
    Grid: Float-based
    Created by: Your Name
    Date: MM/DD/YY
*/

//Grid 12 Columns
.grid {
    &-1   { width:6.67%; }
    &-2   { width:15%; }
    &-3   { width:23.33%; }
    &-4   { width:31.67%; }
    &-5   { width:40%; }
    &-6   { width:48.33%; }
    &-7   { width:56.67%; }
    &-8   { width:65%; }
    &-9   { width:73.33%; }
    &-10  { width:81.67%; }
    &-11  { width:90%; }
    &-12  { width:98.33%; }
}
```

Notice the Credits are commented with CSS style comments: /* */.
These types of comments, depending on the way we compile our SCSS
files, don't get stripped out. This way, the Credits are always visible
so that others know who authored the file. This may or may not work
for teams. Also, the impact on file size of having the Credits display is
imperceptible, if any.

Including the box-sizing property and the mobile-first mixin

Including the `box-sizing` property allows the browser's box model to account for
the padding inside the containers; this means the padding gets subtracted rather
than added, thus maintaining the defined width(s).

Since the structure of our custom CSS grid is going to be mobile-first, we need to
include the mixin that will handle this aspect:

```
@charset "UTF-8";

/*
    Custom Fluid & Responsive Grid System
    Structure: Mobile-first (min-width)
    Syntax: SCSS
    Grid: Float-based
    Created by: Your Name
    Date: MM/DD/YY
*/

*, *:before, *:after {
    box-sizing: border-box;
}

//Moble-first Media Queries Mixin
@mixin forLargeScreens($width) {
    @media (min-width: $width/16+em) { @content }
}

//Grid 12 Columns
.grid {
    &-1  { width:6.67%; }
    &-2  { width:15%; }
    &-3  { width:23.33%; }
    &-4  { width:31.67%; }
```

```scss
    &-5   { width:40%; }
    &-6   { width:48.33%; }
    &-7   { width:56.67%; }
    &-8   { width:65%; }
    &-9   { width:73.33%; }
    &-10  { width:81.67%; }
    &-11  { width:90%; }
    &-12  { width:98.33%; }
}
```

The main container and converting 10px to percentage value

Since we're using the mobile-first approach, our main container is going to be 100% wide by default; but we're also going to give it a maximum width of 1200px since the requirement is to create a grid of that size.

We're also going to convert 10px into a percentage value, so using the RWD magic formula: *10 ÷ 1200 x 100 = 0.83%*.

However, as we've seen before, 10px, or in this case 0.83%, is not enough padding and makes the content appear too close to the edge of the main container. So we're going to increase the padding to 20px: *20 ÷ 1200 x 100 = 1.67%*.

We're also going to horizontally center the main container with `margin: auto;`.

 There's no need to declare zero values to the top and bottom margins to center horizontally. In other words, `margin: 0 auto;` isn't necessary. Just declaring `margin: auto;` is enough.

Let's include these values now:

```scss
@charset "UTF-8";

/*
    Custom Fluid & Responsive Grid System
    Structure: Mobile-first (min-width)
    Syntax: SCSS
    Grid: Float-based
    Created by: Your Name
    Date: MM/DD/YY
*/
```

```scss
*, *:before, *:after {
    box-sizing: border-box;
}

//Moble-first Media Queries Mixin
@mixin forLargeScreens($width) {
    @media (min-width: $width/16+em) { @content }
}

//Main Container
.container-12 {
    width: 100%;
    //Change this value to ANYTHING you want, no need to edit
      anything else.
    max-width: 1200px;
    padding: 0 1.67%;
    margin: auto;
}

//Grid 12 Columns
.grid {
    &-1   { width:6.67%;  }
    &-2   { width:15%;    }
    &-3   { width:23.33%; }
    &-4   { width:31.67%; }
    &-5   { width:40%;    }
    &-6   { width:48.33%; }
    &-7   { width:56.67%; }
    &-8   { width:65%;    }
    &-9   { width:73.33%; }
    &-10  { width:81.67%; }
    &-11  { width:90%;    }
    &-12  { width:98.33%; }
}
```

 In the padding property, it's the same if we type 0.83% or .83%. We can omit the zero. It's always a good practice to keep our code as streamlined as possible. This is the same principle as when we use hexadecimal shorthand values: #3336699 is the same as #369.

Making it mobile-first

On small screens, all the columns are going to be 100% wide. Since we're working with a single column layout, we don't use gutters; this means we don't have to declare margins, at least yet.

At 640px, the grid will kick in and assign corresponding percentages to each column, so we're going to include the columns in a 40em (640px) media query and float them to the left. At this point, we need gutters. Thus, we declare the margin with .83% to the left and right padding.

 I chose 40em (640px) arbitrarily and only as a starting point. Remember to create content-based breakpoints rather than device-based ones.

The code is as follows:

```scss
@charset "UTF-8";

/*

    Custom Fluid & Responsive Grid System
    Structure: Mobile-first (min-width)
    Syntax: SCSS
    Grid: Float-based
    Created by: Your Name
    Date: MM/DD/YY
*/

*, *:before, *:after {
    box-sizing: border-box;
}

//Moble-first Media Queries Mixin
@mixin forLargeScreens($width) {
    @media (min-width: $width/16+em) { @content }
}

//Main Container
.container-12 {
    width: 100%;
    //Change this value to ANYTHING you want, no need to edit
      anything else.
    max-width: 1200px;
    padding: 0 1.67%;
```

```scss
        margin: auto;
    }

    //Grid
    .grid {
        //Global Properties - Mobile-first
        &-1, &-2, &-3, &-4, &-5, &-6, &-7, &-8, &-9, &-10, &-11, &-12 {
            width: 100%;
        }
        @include forLargeScreens(640) { //Totally arbitrary width, it's
            only a starting point.
        //Global Properties - Large screens
        &-1, &-2, &-3, &-4, &-5, &-6, &-7, &-8, &-9, &-10, &-11, &-12 {
            float: left;
            margin: 0 .83%;
        }
        //Grid 12 Columns
        .grid {
            &-1   { width:6.67%; }
            &-2   { width:15%; }
            &-3   { width:23.33%; }
            &-4   { width:31.67%; }
            &-5   { width:40%; }
            &-6   { width:48.33%; }
            &-7   { width:56.67%; }
            &-8   { width:65%; }
            &-9   { width:73.33%; }
            &-10 { width:81.67%; }
            &-11 { width:90%; }
            &-12 { width:98.33%; }
        }
    }
}
```

Adding the row and float clearing rules

If we use rows in our HTML structure or add the class `.clear` to a tag, we can declare all the float clearing values in a single nested rule with the `:before` and `:after` pseudo-elements.

It's the same thing to use single or double colons when declaring pseudo-elements. The double colon is a CSS3 syntax and the single colon is a CSS2.1 syntax. The idea was to be able to differentiate them at a glance so a developer could tell which CSS version they were written on. However, IE8 and below do not support the double-colon syntax.

The float clearing technique is an adaptation of David Walsh's CSS snippet (http://davidwalsh.name/css-clear-fix).

We're also adding a rule for the rows with a bottom margin of 10px to separate them from each other, while removing that margin from the last row to avoid creating unwanted extra spacing at the bottom. Finally, we add the clearing rule for legacy IEs.

Let's include these rules now:

```scss
@charset "UTF-8";

/*
    Custom Fluid & Responsive Grid System
    Structure: Mobile-first (min-width)
    Syntax: SCSS
    Grid: Float-based
    Created by: Your Name
    Date: MM/DD/YY
*/

*, *:before, *:after {
    box-sizing: border-box;
}

//Moble-first Media Queries Mixin
@mixin forLargeScreens($width) {
    @media (min-width: $width/16+em) { @content }
}

//Main Container
.container-12 {
    width: 100%;
    //Change this value to ANYTHING you want, no need to edit
      anything else.
    max-width: 1200px;
    padding: 0 1.67%;
    margin: auto;
}

//Grid
.grid {
    //Global Properties - Mobile-first
    &-1, &-2, &-3, &-4, &-5, &-6, &-7, &-8, &-9, &-10, &-11, &-12 {
```

```scss
        width: 100%;
    }
    @include forLargeScreens(640) { //Totally arbitrary width,
      it's only a starting point.
    //Global Properties - Large screens
    &-1, &-2, &-3, &-4, &-5, &-6, &-7, &-8, &-9, &-10, &-11, &-12 {
        float: left;
        margin: 0 .83%;
    }
    //Grid 12 Columns
    .grid {
        &-1   { width:6.67%; }
        &-2   { width:15%; }
        &-3   { width:23.33%; }
        &-4   { width:31.67%; }
        &-5   { width:40%; }
        &-6   { width:48.33%; }
        &-7   { width:56.67%; }
        &-8   { width:65%; }
        &-9   { width:73.33%; }
        &-10  { width:81.67%; }
        &-11  { width:90%; }
        &-12  { width:98.33%; }
    }
}


//Clear Floated Elements - http://davidwalsh.name/css-clear-fix
.clear, .row {
    &:before,
    &:after { content: ''; display: table; }
    &:after { clear: both; }
}

//Use rows to nest containers
.row { margin-bottom: 10px;
    &:last-of-type { margin-bottom: 0; }
}

//Legacy IE
.clear { zoom: 1; }
```

Let's recap our CSS grid requirements:

- **12 columns**: Starting from `.grid-1` to `.grid-12`.

- **1200px wide to account for 1280px screens**: The `.container-12` container has `max-width: 1200px;`

- **Fluid and relative units (percentages) for the columns and gutters**: The percentages go from 6.67% to 98.33%.

- **Mobile-first**: We added the mobile-first mixin (using `min-width`) and nested the grid inside of it.

- **The SCSS syntax**: The whole file is Sass-based.

- **Reusable**: As long as we're using 12 columns and we're using the mobile-first approach, we can use this CSS grid multiple times.

- **Simple to use and understand**: The class names are very straightforward. The `.grid-6` grid is used for an element that spans 6 columns, `.grid-7` is used for an element that spans 7 columns, and so on.

- **Easily scalable**: If we want to use 980px instead of 1200px, all we need to do is change the value in the `.container-12 max-width` property. Since all the elements are using relative units (percentages), everything will adapt proportionally to the new width—to *any* width for that matter. Pretty sweet if you ask me.

Building a sample page with the custom CSS grid

Here's the HTML we're going to use in this example:

```
<!DOCTYPE html>
<html>
<head>
    <meta charset="utf-8">
    <meta http-equiv="X-UA-Compatible" content="IE=edge">
    <meta name="viewport" content="width=device-width,
        initial-scale=1">
    <title>Mastering RWD with HTML5 &amp; CSS3</title>
    <link rel="stylesheet" href="css/site-styles.css">
    <!--[if lt IE 9]>
    <script src="//html5shiv.googlecode.com/svn/trunk/html5.js">
    </script>
    <![endif]-->
</head>
```

```
<body>
    <h1>Basic Layout Using a Custom CSS Grid</h1>
    <main class="container-12 clear" role="main">
    <header class="grid-12" role="banner">Header
        (.grid-12)</header>
        <nav class="grid-4" role="navigation">Nav (.grid-4)</nav>
        <section class="grid-8">
          <div class="row">
              <div class="grid-6 black">.grid-6</div>
              <div class="grid-6 black">.grid-6</div>
          </div>
          <div class="row">
              <div class="grid-4 black">.grid-4</div>
              <div class="grid-4 black">.grid-4</div>
              <div class="grid-4 black">.grid-4</div>
          </div>
          <div class="row">
              <div class="grid-3 black">.grid-3</div>
              <div class="grid-3 black">.grid-3</div>
              <div class="grid-3 black">.grid-3</div>
              <div class="grid-3 black">.grid-3</div>
          </div>
          <div class="row">
              <div class="grid-2 black">.grid-2</div>
              <div class="grid-7 black">.grid-7</div>
              <div class="grid-3 black">.grid-3</div>
          </div>
          <p>Content (.grid-8)</p>
        </section>
    <footer class="grid-12" role="contentinfo">Footer
        (.grid-12)</footer>
    </main>
</body>
```

Nested containers

Notice that there are several nested containers inside their own row (black background). The idea here is to highlight the nested content sections that add up to 12 columns.

Nesting columns are a major advantage of any grid system. In this book, we are harnessing this power so we don't limit the design in any way.

We're using the HTML5 Shiv polyfill to add HTML5 support to IE8 and below.

On small screens (320px wide), this is what the container looks like:

```
                    320px

        Header (.grid-12)


         Nav (.grid-4)

            .grid-6
            .grid-6

            .grid-4
            .grid-4
            .grid-4

            .grid-3
            .grid-3
            .grid-3
            .grid-3

            .grid-2
            .grid-7
            .grid-3

        Content (.grid-8)


        Footer (.grid-12)
```

On large screens starting at 40em (640px) wide, this is what the layout looks like:

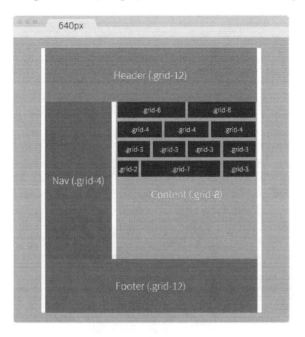

You can see the demo I created on CodePen at `http://codepen.io/ricardozea/` `pen/d6ab6e0293be9b6bac2e16ad37942ed5`.

Stop using CSS grids, use Flexbox!

I bet you didn't see this one coming, ha!

Indeed, Flexbox is one amazing CSS property that opens the layout possibilities to new horizons. Here are a few things about Flexbox:

- Its browser support is perfect in modern browsers.

- IE8 and IE9 don't support it. But no worries, addressing these two browsers is very simple using the conditional classes technique mentioned in *Chapter 3, Mobile-first or Desktop-first?*

- IE10 only supports the 2012 syntax, but Autoprefixer (within Prepros) takes care of this old vendor prefixing automatically for us.

- We need to be careful when using Flexbox because the old `display: box;` syntax causes the browser to do a multi-pass in the layout, deteriorating the performance.

- In contrast, the new/current syntax `display: flex;` has no impact on performance whatsoever. Browser performance issues have now been addressed since the old syntax, so we should be in good shape.

 Paul Irish and Ojan Vafai explain this very well in the post **Flexbox layout isn't slow**, which can be found at `http://updates.html5rocks.com/2013/10/Flexbox-layout-isn-t-slow`.

Let's get down to it, shall we?

Building a sample page with Flexbox

In the following example, we are going to build the same layout we built using the custom CSS grid but using the Flexbox property. This will help us better understand the power of Flexbox and eventually *detach* us from using CSS grids altogether, while keeping a more semantic structure in our HTML.

 A great article by Chris Coyer, **A Complete Guide to Flexbox**, can be found at `https://css-tricks.com/snippets/css/a-guide-to-flexbox/`.

A few things to note about the sample page:

- We're including the conditional classes in the `<html>` element to support legacy browsers and save one request to the server from using a JavaScript file dependency.

- Since we're not using a CSS grid, the nested containers are just going to have to the term **Content**, display in them.

- We're going to use the HTML5 Shiv polyfill to have IE8 support for all the necessary HTML5 tags.

- Since IE10 has some math calculation issues with Flexbox, we need to target it with an `.ie10` class added to the `<html>` element. We're going to accomplish this by using a simple script created by Louis Lazaris inside an IE-excluding Conditional Comment so that IE8/9 doesn't run the script. All the information about this script can be found in the article at `http://www.impressivewebs.com/ie10-css-hacks/`.

The script we're using to target IE10 is not using User Agent sniffing. UA sniffing isn't considered a good practice. The script is using a Conditional Compilation statement. More information about the `@cc_on` statement can be found in the **Microsoft Developer Network (MSDN)**: `https://msdn.microsoft.com/en-us/library/8ka90k2e(v=vs.94).aspx`.

This is what the Flexbox layout looks like on small screens (320px wide):

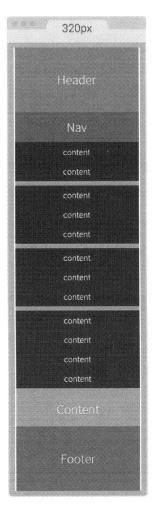

This is what it looks like on large screens. This screen is 768px wide but the content is 40em (640px):

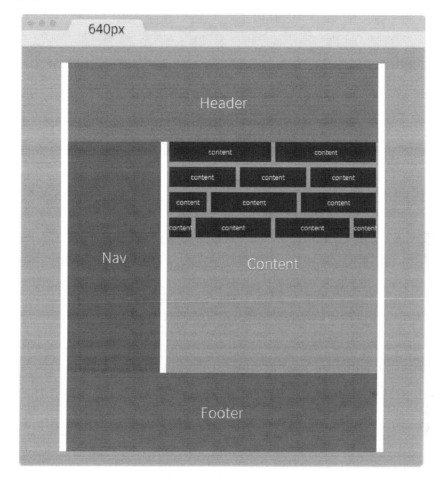

The HTML

Here's the markup we're going to use in the sample page:

```
<!DOCTYPE html>
<!--[if IE 8]> <html class="no-js ie8" lang="en"> <![endif]-->
<!--[if IE 9]> <html class="no-js ie9" lang="en"> <![endif]-->
<!--[if gt IE 9]><!--><html class="no-js"
        lang="en"><!--<![endif]-->
<head>
    <meta charset="utf-8">
    <meta name="viewport" content="width=device-width,
        initial-scale=1">
```

```html
    <meta http-equiv="X-UA-Compatible" content="IE=edge">
    <title>Basic Layout Using Flexbox</title>
    <!--[if lt IE 9]>
      <script
src="http://html5shiv.googlecode.com/svn/trunk/html5.js">
      </script>
    <![endif]-->
    <!--[if !IE]><!-->
      <script>
        if (/*@cc_on!@*/false && document.documentMode === 10) {
          document.documentElement.className+=' ie10';
        }
      </script>
    <!--<![endif]-->
  </head>
<body>
    <h1>Basic Layout Using Flexbox</h1>
    <main class="main-container" role="main">
        <header role="banner">Header</header>
        <!-- Flexible elements need to be wrapped in
            a container -->
        <div class="flex-container">
            <nav role="navigation">Nav</nav>
            <section>
                <div class="flex-container row-1">
                    <div class="level-1">content</div>
                    <div class="level-1">content</div>
                </div>
                <div class="flex-container row-2">
                    <div class="level-1">content</div>
                    <div class="level-1">content</div>
                    <div class="level-1">content</div>
                </div>
                <div class="flex-container row-3">
                    <div class="level-1">content</div>
                    <div class="level-1">content</div>
                    <div class="level-1">content</div>
                    <div class="level-1">content</div>
                </div>
                <div class="flex-container row-4">
                    <div class="level-1 content-a">content</div>
                    <div class="level-1 content-b">❦content</div>
                    <div class="level-1 content-c">content</div>
                </div>
                <p>Content</p>
```

```
            </section>
        </div>
        <footer role="contentinfo">Footer</footer>
    </main>
</body>
</html>
```

The SCSS

The SCSS code has a few sections similar to the code used in the CSS grid. However, there are important differences.

Let's take it apart.

We're going to start by creating the Credits section, the box-sizing: border-box; parameter to account for the padding inside the containers rather than outside, the mobile-first mixin, and the main container properties:

```
/*
    Custom Fluid & Responsive Grid System
    Structure: Mobile-first (min-width)
    Syntax: SCSS
    Grid: Flexbox-based
    Created by: Your Name
    Date: MM/DD/YY
*/
*, *:before, *:after {
  box-sizing: border-box;
}
//Moble-first Media Queries Mixin
@mixin forLargeScreens($media) {
    @media (min-width: $media/16+em) { @content }
}
//Main container
.main-container {
    width: 100%;
    //Change this value to ANYTHING you want,
      //no need to edit anything else
    max-width: 1200px;
    //Any value you want
    padding: 0 1.67%;
    margin: auto;
}
```

Adding the Flexbox container

Now, let's add the properties for the Flexbox container that acts somewhat similar to the .row in the CSS grid. The code is as follows:

```scss
/*
    Custom Fluid & Responsive Grid System
    Structure: Mobile-first (min-width)
    Syntax: SCSS
    Grid: Flexbox-based
    Created by: Your Name
    Date: MM/DD/YY
*/
*, *:before, *:after {
    box-sizing: border-box;
}
//Moble-first Media Queries Mixin
@mixin forLargeScreens($media) {
    @media (min-width: $media/16+em) { @content }
}
//Main container
.main-container {
    width: 100%;
  //Change this value to ANYTHING you want,
      no need to edit anything else
    max-width: 1200px;
    //Any value you want
    padding: 0 1.67%;
    margin: auto;
}
//Flexbox container
.flex-container {
    margin-bottom: 10px;
    //Remove the margin from the last flexbox container
    &:last-of-type {
        margin-bottom: 0;
    }
    @include forLargeScreens(640) {
        display: flex;
    }
}
```

As you can see, we're adding margin-bottom: 10px; to separate the content rows. However, we're removing that margin on the last Flexbox container so that it doesn't generate unwanted extra padding at the end.

Then we're including the mobile-first mixin that targets a screen width of 640px (40em). This means that we're **only** going to use Flexbox for large screens, but for small screens, we are not going to use it.

 There's no need to use Flexbox if all the columns have equal width. In our example columns are 100% wide in small screens.

DIVs inside the Flexbox container

Now, let's add the .83% left and right margins to the columns on large screens. On small screens, the columns have no margins. Remember that *10px = 0.83%*.

We are going to use the attribute selector with the star/asterisk so we can target all the DIVs that contain at least one value with the term level- in their class name. We're also going to remove the left margin on the first container and the right margin on the last container, so our DIVs are flushed to the edges of their parent containers. The code is as follows:

```
/*
    Custom Fluid & Responsive Grid System
    Structure: Mobile-first (min-width)
    Syntax: SCSS
    Grid: Flexbox-based
    Created by: Your Name
    Date: MM/DD/YY
*/
*, *:before, *:after {
    box-sizing: border-box;
}
//Moble-first Media Queries Mixin
@mixin forLargeScreens($media) {
    @media (min-width: $media/16+em) { @content }
}
//Main container
.main-container {
    width: 100%;
    //Change this value to ANYTHING you want, no need to edit
        anything else
    max-width: 1200px;
    //Any value you want
    padding: 0 1.67%;
    margin: auto;
}
```

```scss
//Flexbox container
.flex-container {
    margin-bottom: 10px;
    //Remove the margin from the last flexbox container
    &:last-of-type {
        margin-bottom: 0;
    }
    @include forLargeScreens(640) {
        display: flex;
    }
}
//DIVs inside the flex container
[class*="level-"] {
    width: 100%;
    @include forLargeScreens(640) {
        margin: 0 .83%;
    }
    &:first-of-type { margin-left: 0; }
    &:last-of-type { margin-right: 0; }
}
```

The Header, Footer, Nav, and Section Containers

Now, the Header and Footer sections are 100% wide on both small and large screens, so they don't need any specific rules. This example, however, adds a few properties to both the Header and Footer sections but only for styling reasons, not really for layout. Nonetheless, the Nav and Section containers do have particular widths depending on the available screen width.

On small screens, the Nav and Section containers are 100% wide, while on large screens they stay side by side; The Nav container is 33% wide with a right margin to create the gutter of 1.67% (which equals 20px). The Section container is 65.33% wide on large screens. Here's the formula: *33% + 1.67% + 65.33 = 100%*.

Let's go ahead and define those properties for the Nav and Section containers:

```scss
/*
    Custom Fluid & Responsive Grid System
    Structure: Mobile-first (min-width)
    Syntax: SCSS
    Grid: Flexbox-based
    Created by: Your Name
    Date: MM/DD/YY
*/
*, *:before, *:after {
```

```scss
        box-sizing: border-box;
}
//Moble-first Media Queries Mixin
@mixin forLargeScreens($media) {
    @media (min-width: $media/16+em) { @content }
}
//Main container
.main-container {
    width: 100%;
    //Change this value to ANYTHING you want,
        no need to edit anything else
    max-width: 1200px;
    //Any value you want
    padding: 0 1.67%;
    margin: auto;
}
//Flexbox container
.flex-container {
    margin-bottom: 10px;
    //Remove the margin from the last flexbox container
    &:last-of-type {
        margin-bottom: 0;
    }
    @include forLargeScreens(640) {
        display: flex;
    }
}
//DIVs inside the flex container
[class*="level-"] {
    width: 100%;
    @include forLargeScreens(640) {
        margin: 0 .83%;
    }
    &:first-of-type { margin-left: 0; }
    &:last-of-type { margin-right: 0; }
}
//Nav
nav {
    width: 100%;
    @include forLargeScreens(640) {
        width: 33%;
        margin-right: 1.67%;
    }
}
```

```scss
//Content area
section {
    width: 100%;
    @include forLargeScreens(640) {
        width: 65.33%;
    }
}
```

Nested containers

Finally, for this example, we're going to define widths for different content sections with a black background so you can have a clear idea about how to nest containers.

What we're basically doing is assigning specific but different widths to both `.content-a` and `.content-c`, which are the first and third content areas of that row. There's no need to assign a width to the second content area, unless we wanted to. Flexbox will make that second container fully occupy all the remaining space between the first and third content areas.

 IE10 has issues calculating the nested containers values, so we need to create specific widths to those containers. We are going to include the widths for IE10 in the same rule we're going to create for IE8 and IE9.

The reason I'm using arbitrary values such as 30% and 42% is to show you that we can play with these values all we want and Flexbox will always try to maintain these proportions as long as there's space available.

Let's add those properties now for the different nested containers:

```scss
/*
    Custom Fluid & Responsive Grid System
    Structure: Mobile-first (min-width)
    Syntax: SCSS
    Grid: Flexbox-based
    Created by: Your Name
    Date: MM/DD/YY
*/
*, *:before, *:after {
    box-sizing: border-box;
}
//Moble-first Media Queries Mixin
@mixin forLargeScreens($media) {
    @media (min-width: $media/16+em) { @content }
```

```scss
}
.main-container {
    //Change this value to ANYTHING you want,
        no need to edit anything else.
    width: 100%;
    max-width: 1200px;
    //Any value you want
    padding: 0 1.67%;
    margin: auto;
}
//Flexbox container
.flex-container {
    margin-bottom: 10px;
    //Remove the margin from the last flexbox container
    &:last-of-type {
        margin-bottom: 0;
    }
    @include forLargeScreens(640) {
        display: flex;
    }
}
//DIVs inside the flex container
[class*="level-"] {
    width: 100%;
    @include forLargeScreens(640) {
        margin: 0 .83%;
    }
    &:first-of-type { margin-left: 0; }
    &:last-of-type { margin-right: 0; }
}
//Nav
nav {
    width: 100%;
    @include forLargeScreens(640) {
        width: 33%;
        margin-right: 1.67%;
    }
}
//Content area
section {
    width: 100%;
    @include forLargeScreens(640) {
        width: 65.33%;
    }
```

```scss
}
//Different width containers
.content- {
    @include forLargeScreens(640) {
        &a { width: 30%; }
        &c { width: 42%; }
    }
}
```

Supporting old IEs

Using Flexbox doesn't come with its caveats regarding IE8, IE9 and IE10 as well.

As with legacy browsers, it's a matter of tweaking values and testing to get the best results. And remember that websites do not have to look exactly the same in every browser.

Let's clarify a few things. The classes .ie8 and .ie9 come from the Conditional Classes in the <html> element. The class .ie10 comes from the script inside an IE-excluding Conditional Comment. Therefore, IE8 and IE9 are unable to run this script. But no need to fret, the solutions are simple, you'll see. Let's check them out.

One rule to rule them all

The first thing we do is create a rule for all three: IE8, IE9 and IE10. In this rule, we're going to declare the widths of the nested containers in percentages. Truth be told, we could declare these widths in pixels as well, but we're going to use percentages for consistency reasons with all other responsive examples.

Here's the one rule that... well, rules them all:

```scss
/*
    Custom Fluid & Responsive Grid System
    Structure: Mobile-first (min-width)
    Syntax: SCSS
    Grid: Flexbox-based
    Created by: Your Name
    Date: MM/DD/YY
*/
*, *:before, *:after {
    box-sizing: border-box;
}
//Moble-first Media Queries Mixin
@mixin forLargeScreens($media) {
    @media (min-width: $media/16+em) { @content }
```

```scss
}
.main-container {
    //Change this value to ANYTHING you want,
        no need to edit anything else.
    width: 100%;
    max-width: 1200px;
    //Any value you want
    padding: 0 1.67%;
    margin: auto;
}
//Flexbox container
.flex-container {
    margin-bottom: 10px;
    //Remove the margin from the last flexbox container
    &:last-of-type {
        margin-bottom: 0;
    }
    @include forLargeScreens(640) {
        display: flex;
    }
}
//DIVs inside the flex container
[class*="level-"] {
    width: 100%;
    @include forLargeScreens(640) {
        margin: 0 .83%;
    }
    &:first-of-type { margin-left: 0; }
    &:last-of-type { margin-right: 0; }
}
//Nav
nav {
    width: 100%;
    @include forLargeScreens(640) {
        width: 33%;
        margin-right: 1.67%;
    }
}
//Content area
section {
    width: 100%;
    @include forLargeScreens(640) {
        width: 65.33%;
    }
```

```scss
}
//Different width containers
.content- {
    @include forLargeScreens(640) {
        &a { width: 30%; }
        &c { width: 42%; }
    }
}
//All IEs
.ie8, .ie9, .ie10 {
    //Exact values (desired width - 0.83% = result %) are
      commented, but they need tweaked to have one value for all IEs
    section {
        .row-1 .level-1 { width: 49.17%; }
        //Exact value is 32.17%
        .row-2 .level-1 { width: 32.20%; }
        //Exact value is 24.17%
        .row-3 .level-1 { width: 23.75%; }
        .row-4 {
          .content-a { width: 19.17%; }
          .content-b { width: 49.17%; }
          //Exact value is 29.17%
          .content-c { width: 28.3%; }
        }
    }
}
```

Rules for both IE8 and IE9

We will now declare the rule that will handle the values for IE8 and IE9. We declare overflow: hidden; to clear the floats in their parent container, the .flex-container DIVs. We then float left to the Nav and Content sections and give them a height; this height is merely for styling purposes.

We give the Nav section a width and a margin right of 1% to keep things simple. We assign a width to the Content section as well. Then, we use the Footer to clear the floating Nav and Content sections with both the clear: both; and zoom: 1; parameters for good measure.

Here's the SCSS for IE8/9:

```scss
/*
    Custom Fluid & Responsive Grid System
    Structure: Mobile-first (min-width)
    Syntax: SCSS
    Grid: Flexbox-based
```

```scss
      Created by: Your Name
      Date: MM/DD/YY
*/
*, *:before, *:after {
    box-sizing: border-box;
}
//Moble-first Media Queries Mixin
@mixin forLargeScreens($media) {
    @media (min-width: $media/16+em) { @content }
}
.main-container {
    //Change this value to ANYTHING you want,
        no need to edit anything else.
    width: 100%;
    max-width: 1200px;
    //Any value you want
    padding: 0 1.67%;
    margin: auto;
}
//Flexbox container
.flex-container {
    margin-bottom: 10px;
    //Remove the margin from the last flexbox container
    &:last-of-type {
        margin-bottom: 0;
    }
    @include forLargeScreens(640) {
        display: flex;
    }
}
//DIVs inside the flex container
[class*="level-"] {
    width: 100%;
    @include forLargeScreens(640) {
        margin: 0 .83%;
    }
    &:first-of-type { margin-left: 0; }
    &:last-of-type { margin-right: 0; }
}
//Nav
nav {
    width: 100%;
    @include forLargeScreens(640) {
        width: 33%;
```

```scss
            margin-right: 1.67%;
        }
    }
    //Content area
    section {
        width: 100%;
        @include forLargeScreens(640) {
            width: 65.33%;
        }
    }
    //Different width containers
    .content- {
        @include forLargeScreens(640) {
            &a { width: 30%; }
            &c { width: 42%; }
        }
    }
    //All IEs
    .ie8, .ie9, .ie10 {
        //Exact values (desired width - 0.83% = result %) are
        commented, but they need tweaked to have one value for all IEs
        section {
            .row-1 .level-1 { width: 49.17%; }
            //Exact value is 32.17%
            .row-2 .level-1 { width: 32.20%; }
            //Exact value is 24.17%
            .row-3 .level-1 { width: 23.75%; }
            .row-4 {
              .content-a { width: 19.17%; }
              .content-b { width: 49.17%; }
              //Exact value is 29.17%
              .content-c { width: 28.3%; }
            }
        }
    }
    //IE8/9
    .ie8, .ie9 {
        .flex-container { overflow: hidden; }
        nav, section { float: left; min-height: 440px; }
        nav { width: 29%; margin-right: 1%; }
        section { width: 70%; }
        footer { clear: both; zoom: 1; }
    }
```

Specific rules for IE8 and IE9

Finally, we seal the deal for legacy browsers with a couple of rules: one for IE8 and another one for IE9 using the attribute selector for all the nested containers.

For IE8, we give the nested containers `display: inline-block;` rather than `float: left;` to make the groups of nested containers centered in their corresponding rows. If we don't do this, there are going to be weird gaps on the right side of all the rows. We're also going to declare a left and right margin of .2%. After testing, any larger value makes the nested containers wrap.

For IE9, we're going to float the nested containers to the left.

Let's check these two rules out:

```scss
/*
  Custom Fluid & Responsive Grid System
    Structure: Mobile-first (min-width)
    Syntax: SCSS
    Grid: Flexbox-based
    Created by: Your Name
    Date: MM/DD/YY
*/
*, *:before, *:after {
    box-sizing: border-box;
}
//Moble-first Media Queries Mixin
@mixin forLargeScreens($media) {
    @media (min-width: $media/16+em) { @content }
}
.main-container {
    //Change this value to ANYTHING you want, no need to edit anything
else.
    width: 100%;
    max-width: 1200px;
    //Any value you want
    padding: 0 1.67%;
    margin: auto;
}
//Flexbox container
.flex-container {
    margin-bottom: 10px;
    //Remove the margin from the last flexbox container
    &:last-of-type {
        margin-bottom: 0;
    }
```

```scss
    @include forLargeScreens(640) {
        display: flex;
    }
}
//DIVs inside the flex container
[class*="level-"] {
    width: 100%;
    @include forLargeScreens(640) {
        margin: 0 .83%;
    }
    &:first-of-type { margin-left: 0; }
    &:last-of-type { margin-right: 0; }
}
//Nav
nav {
    width: 100%;
    @include forLargeScreens(640) {
        width: 33%;
        margin-right: 1.67%;
    }
}
//Content area
section {
    width: 100%;
    @include forLargeScreens(640) {
        width: 65.33%;
    }
}
//Different width containers
.content- {
    @include forLargeScreens(640) {
        &a { width: 30%; }
        &c { width: 42%; }
    }
}
//All IEs
.ie8, .ie9, .ie10 {
    //Exact values (desired width - 0.83% = result %)
    are commented, but they need tweaked to have
    one value for all IEs
```

```
section {
    .row-1 .level-1 { width: 49.17%; }
    //Exact value is 32.17%
    .row-2 .level-1 { width: 32.20%; }
    //Exact value is 24.17%
    .row-3 .level-1 { width: 23.75%; }
    .row-4 {
      .content-a { width: 19.17%; }
      .content-b { width: 49.17%; }
      //Exact value is 29.17%
      .content-c { width: 28.3%; }
    }
  }
}
//IE8/9
.ie8, .ie9 {
    .flex-container { overflow: hidden; }
    nav, section { float: left; min-height: 440px; }
    nav { width: 29%; margin-right: 1%; }
    section { width: 70%; }
    footer { clear: both; zoom: 1; }
}
//IE8
.ie8 {
    [class*="level-"] {
        display: inline-block;
        margin: 0 .2%;
    }
}
//IE9
.ie9 {
    [class*="level-"] { float: left; }
}
```

Summary

A lot to digest in this chapter, eh?

However, we now know what a grid is and what it's used for, something many of us have never really questioned before. We also understand more about CSS grids, CSS frameworks, and UI kits; use them as you please, as long as you are clear about how they help us be more efficient when building sound responsive sites and apps.

Creating our custom CSS with the traditional *floats* technique was a matter of identifying the pattern where the addition of a new column was a matter of increasing the value by 100. Now, we can create a 12-column grid at any width we want.

With the help of Flexbox, we now understand where the future of responsive and fluid layouts is. With such great browser support, there's no question Flexbox is a major contender for the traditional CSS grids. Using Conditional Classes is a good option to support our complex layouts in legacy browsers. In addition, for IE10 we need to use the Conditional Compilation script that only IE10 is capable of seeing. Therefore, we can target IE10 with an `.ie10` specific selector.

In the next chapter, we're going to dive into the world of usability and UX when we talk about building responsive interfaces for our large fingers on small screens. Time to put those big fingers to the test!

5

Designing Small UIs Driven by Large Finger

The intense popularity of touchscreen devices is nothing new to us — the web/ mobile designers and developers. So we're not going to talk about market shares, statistics, or analytics numbers. Instead, we're going to talk about the things we need to consider to build a usable interface, such as target sizes, navigation patterns, navigation icons, best practices and mobile device ergonomics.

In this chapter, we're going to cover the following topics:

- The ideal target sizes on small UIs.
- The posture patterns and the touch zones.
- The basic guidelines to consider for RWD.
- The navigation patterns for RWD.

The ideal target sizes on small UIs

All vendors have different sets of rules and guidelines regarding the ideal size of targets on small screen devices. Some of them refer to these sizes in pixels, others in points, and others in units such as inches, millimeters, or centimeters.

Regardless of the units these vendors use, they all agree on one basic concept: make your target size big enough to avoid accidental taps. This goes in hand with Fitts's law, which states that *the smaller the target, the longer the user will take to reach it.*

Obviously, as web designers, we have to be mindful of what *large* means in the context of our designs, so we need to balance the target size recommendations with good design principles. Our aim is that the messages should reach the users and they should be able to comfortably use our interfaces.

One thing to keep in mind is that the guidelines for target sizes for RWD are mostly based on mobile apps design patterns. Let's get right to it.

The average width of an adult's index finger is about 16 mm to 20 mm. This is close to 45px to 57px.

According to *Apple's iOS Human Interface Guidelines*, the recommended minimum target size is 44pt x 44pt.

> The reason some user interface guidelines use points and millimeters as their measuring units is to provide a consistent scale that is device independent. That's because 1px in one device may not necessarily mean exactly 1px in another device. Nonetheless, some vendors do provide guidelines on pixels, but mostly so we can get an idea of how an element's proportions relate to one another.

In the past, Apple did recommend their target sizes in pixels, 44px x 44px, but when retina displays were introduced, 1 pixel from the iPhone 3 turned into 4 pixels on the iPhone 4. There wasn't a 1:1 ratio anymore.

This means that 44pt x 44pt in non-retina devices is actually 44px x 44px, but on retina devices it is 88px x 88px. These pixel values change again every time Apple releases a new device with an even higher density screen.

Having a good understanding of the screen density of Apple's devices, or any device for that matter, is a must in the RWD world. This way, we can always account for these technicalities when creating our designs so we don't hinder the user experience and the usability of our websites and apps.

On the other hand, *Microsoft's Windows 8 Touch Guidance* documentation recommends an ideal target size of 7 mm x 7 mm (40px x 40px). If accuracy is crucial, because of serious consequences such as close or delete, the *Windows 8 Touch Guidance* guidelines recommend target sizes of 9 mm x 9 mm (50px x 50px). Also, when screen real estate is scarce and things need to fit, the minimum recommended target size is 5 mm x 5 mm (30px x 30px).

These dimensions are for non high-density screens.

The *Windows 8 Touch Guidance* guidelines go as far as recommending a minimum padding between elements: 2 mm (10px), regardless of the target size (and this is good).

The *Android Developers* guidelines recommend a minimum target size of 48dp, which is about 9 mm. The minimum and maximum recommended target sizes are 7 mm and 10 mm, respectively.

The Android Developers guidelines also recommend a minimum spacing between elements of 8dp.

> Here, **dp** means density-independent pixels. This means that 1dp is the same as 1px in *normal* density screens. Just like Apple with the use of points (pt), they are trying to define a unit that is global and screen density independent.

There is also the *Ubuntu* documentation recommending that interface elements shouldn't be smaller than 1 cm (about 55px).

As we can see, the recommended minimum and maximum target sizes vary from vendor to vendor. However, they are not that far apart.

We can safely conclude from all the target sizes mentioned, that the proper dimensions are (in low density screens):

- The recommended target size is 48dp × 48dp = 48px × 48px.
- The minimum target size is 5 mm x 5 mm = 30px × 30px.
- The maximum target size is 10 mm x 10 mm = 55px × 55px.
- The padding between any element is 2 mm = 10px.

The posture patterns and the touch zones

No matter how usable the sizes of our touch targets are, if they are not placed in the right location, all our efforts are pretty much worthless.

We can't talk about small UIs and large fingers without mentioning the extensive work of Luke Wroblewski in his article *Responsive Navigation: Optimizing for Touch Across Devices* (http://www.lukew.com/ff/entry.asp?1649).

The posture patterns

In his article, Luke talks about the patterns of posture most users have when holding their smartphones, tablets, and touch-enabled laptops:

Posture Patterns

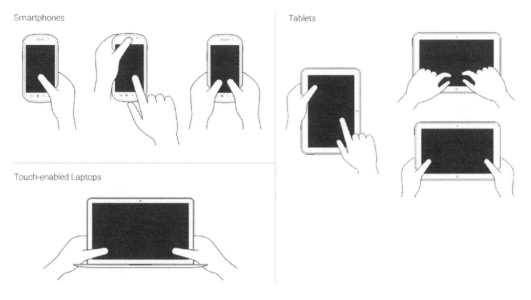

These patterns allow us to define the best way to lay out our content in order to be easily usable and accessible.

Understanding the posture patterns of our users will allow us to understand when our targets can be the right size or even a bit smaller if there isn't enough screen real estate, or a bit larger if precision is needed, since it's different when someone uses their thumbs as opposed to their index fingers.

The touch zones

Luke also talks about *touch zones*, which are basically the areas of a device that are either easy or hard to reach, depending on the posture.

In all major styles of devices, smartphones, tablets and touch-enabled laptops, the ideal touch zones are in dark green, the *ok* touch zones are in lighter green, and the hard-to-reach zones are in yellow:

Touch Zones

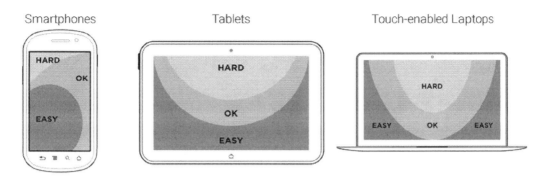

In RWD, it's a bit hard to drastically change the layout of a single page, let alone many pages (at least yet) like a standalone app, without an exorbitant amount of work. Also, there is a very high probability of negatively impacting the user experience and maintaining the content hierarchy.

RWD is strongly coupled with content strategy, so the content hierarchy needs to be preserved regardless of the device our site/app is being viewed on. We need to make sure the elements themselves are big enough for someone with large fingers to use properly. These elements are, to name a few, links, buttons, form fields, navigation items, controls of any sort like paginations, open/collapse controls in accordions, tab systems, and so on.

Now, there is one website/app element that is quite versatile in RWD: the menu button.

In order to trigger the navigation, there is a very particular element that the UX communities have very strong opinions about: The *hamburger* icon (≡). For now, we're going to call it something more generic: the *nav* icon. I'm calling it the *nav* icon because it doesn't necessarily have to be a hamburger icon/graphic, it can be another type of icon or a word.

The location, behavior, and design of the navigation icon and the navigation items themselves have as many variations as there are designers. What works for others may not necessarily work for us, and vice versa. So, testing becomes the go-to methodology to decide what our users feel comfortable with.

Nonetheless, there are a few UX guidelines for the nav icon that are worth mentioning and that we're going to see next.

The nav icon – basic guidelines to consider for RWD

The nav icon can be represented in many ways. RWD takes patterns from mobile apps since small screens apps and websites have many similar metaphors.

Let's take a look at the common navigation icon patterns:

- The hamburger icon.
- The word *Menu*.
- The hamburger icon plus the word *Menu*.

The hamburger icon

This is by far the most popular icon used to represent the navigation button: ≡.

The *hamburger* icon was created by Norm Cox in 1981. Norm's intention with this icon was to "*...mimic the look of the resulting displayed menu list.*" (`http://gizmodo.com/who-designed-the-iconic-hamburger-icon-1555438787`).

In other words, the hamburger icon's real name is the *list* icon.

Now, if we think about it, the hamburger icon is semantically correct because it represents exactly what is displayed when it's triggered: a list of items. However, some UX studies have revealed that the hamburger icon isn't as effective as we may think, and yet we see it all over the place in both responsive sites and mobile apps.

Although the hamburger icon has several cons, it's a matter of time before practically everyone is able to recognize this icon as a representation of navigation.

The bottom line is that there's nothing wrong with using the hamburger icon as long as we follow the target size recommendations and make the links inside the navigation bar easy to tap on small screens.

The advantages are as follows:

- It's easily recognized by certain demographics, especially young ones.
- It takes up very little space in a design.
- It's not language dependent.
- It's easy to make using the Unicode character 2261 (≡), which has a global support of 96 percent.

The disadvantages are as follows:

- It's not easily recognized by some demographics, especially older ones.

- Although very popular, a lot of people have a hard time understanding that the hamburger icon represents a menu.

- It promotes low discoverability since a site's navigation will usually be hidden.

If you plan to use the hamburger icon, don't bother using images of any kind or any CSS techniques with borders or box shadows. Keep it simple. All you need to do is use the Unicode character 2261 (≡).

In the following examples, we are going to use a well-known technique to hide content (with a few variations to fit our demos): the Kellum Method. This method is not in any way a hack or anything similar; we are not trying to deceive our users or the search engines with this approach. We're actually being quite mindful of the improved accessibility the navigation icons gain by leaving the text in the markup so that users with assistive technologies can still access the menus. Consider the following example.

The HTML is as follows:

```
<button class="hamburger-icon"><span>Menu</span></button>SCSS
//Hamburger Icon
.hamburger-icon  {
    //Basic styling, modify if you want
    font-size: 40px;
    color: #666;
    background: #efefef;
    padding: 0 10px;
    border-radius: 3px;
    cursor: pointer;
    //Hamburger Icon
    &:before {
        content: '≡';
    }
    //Hide the term Menu from displaying without
    //sacrificing accessibility
    span {
        display: inline-block;
        width: 0;
```

```
        height: 0;
        text-indent: -100%;
        overflow: hidden;
        white-space: nowrap;


    }
}
```

The result is this one:

> The word *Menu* should always be included in the markup for accessibility reasons. When users with **assistive technology** (**AT**) will focus on the hamburger icon, the screen reader will read the word *Menu*. Also, enclosing the word *Menu* in `<span>` tags allows us to hide the word from being displayed in the browser without hurting the accessibility of the link.

The word Menu

Some informal tests on the web have yielded that using the word *Menu* is the most trusted solution to the drawbacks of the hamburger icon.

However, it's important to note that the studies and tests done by many authors where they compare the hamburger icon versus the word *Menu* can be misleading, since they are testing different visual languages: an icon versus a word.

For these tests to be fully reliable, they would have to test icon versus icon, and word versus word. For example, testing the hamburger icon against an arrow pointing down or the word *Menu* against the word *Nav*.

Let's look at the pros and cons of the word *Menu*.

The advantages are as follows:

- It's self-explanatory.
- Virtually anyone from any demographic can understand what it means.
- It can be used in any language.
- It takes up very little space in the design.

The disadvantage is as follows:

- It may clash with an iconography system since it's a word.

Consider the following example.

Here's the HTML:

```
<button class="word-menu">Menu</button>
```

And here's the CSS:

```
//Word "Menu"
.word-menu {
    //Basic styling, modify if you want
    display: inline-block;
    padding: 16px 8px;
    color: #666;
    font: 12px Arial, "Helvetica Neue", Helvetica, sans-serif;
    background: #efefef;
    border-radius: 3px;
    cursor: pointer;
}
```

And this is the result:

 In this example, I used the class name .word-menu to explicitly represent my intent for this book, but this is not the proper way to name your elements for production. Use more meaningful and universal naming conventions, for example, something like .menu-trigger could be an alternative. Using a generic class name will allow us to use any design for the navigation icon without altering the markup.

The hamburger icon plus the word Menu

One alternative to the hamburger icon versus the word *Menu* discussion is to use both at the same time. Some argue that we may get the best of both worlds by doing this.

The advantages are:

- It's self-explanatory.
- Virtually anyone from any demographic can understand what it means.
- It can be used in any language.
- It can still take up very little space in the design.
- It is easy to make using the Unicode character 2261 (≡), which has a global support of 96 percent.

The disadvantage is:

- Depending on the design, the word *Menu* could be too small.

Let's look at two styles that we can use to represent this pattern.

Consider the following example.

The HTML is as follows:

```
<button class="hamburger-icon-plus-menu style-1">Menu</button>
```

The SCSS is as follows:

```
//Hamburger Icon Plus Word "Menu" - Style 1
.hamburger-icon-plus-menu {
    //Basic styling, modify if you want
    display: inline-block;
    font-family: Arial, "Helvetica Neue", Helvetica, sans-serif;
    background: #efefef;
    color: #666;
    border-radius: 3px;
    cursor: pointer;
}
.style-1 {
    padding: 16px 8px;
    font-size: 16px;
    //Hamburger Icon
    &:before {
        content: '≡ ';
    }
}
```

The result is as follows:

Notice the space after the '≡', that's what separates the icon from the word "Menu" without having to use margins of any kind.

Consider the following example.

The HTML is:

```html
<button class="hamburger-icon-plus-menu style-2">Menu</button>
```

The SCSS is:

```scss
//Hamburger Icon plus Word "Menu" - Style 2
.hamburger-icon-plus-menu {
    //Basic styling, modify if you want
    display: inline-block;

    font-family: Arial, "Helvetica Neue", Helvetica, sans-serif;
    background: #efefef;
    color: #666;
    border-radius: 3px;
    cursor: pointer;
}
.style-2 {
    padding: 4px 12px 6px;
    font-size: 10px;
    line-height: .8;
    text-align: center;
    //Hamburger Icon
    &:before {
        display: block;
        content: '≡';
        font-size: 40px;
    }
}
```

And here's the result:

You can see a demo I created in CodePen at
http://codepen.io/ricardozea/pen/f4ddc6443bc060004b58a7301aae83db.

The navigation patterns for RWD

One of the most mystifying features of RWD is the navigation. It can be as simple or as complex as we want it to be.

In this section, I'm going to show you how to build three commonly used navigation patterns:

- **Toggle navigation**: This is based on Brad Frost's *Toggle Menu* demo (`http://codepen.io/bradfrost/pen/sHvaz/`).

- **Off-Canvas or Off-Screen navigation**: This is based on Austin Wulf's SitePoint *Pure CSS Off-Screen Navigation Menu* demo (`http://codepen.io/SitePoint/pen/uIemr/`).

- **Flexbox-based navigation**: This is our custom solution.

Before we look at the details of each, let's clarify a few features about the mentioned patterns:

Design

On small screens, all navigation patterns use the hamburger icon as a trigger except the Flexbox-based navigation. On large screens, the navigation bar on all examples is a horizontal group of links with centered links.

To improve usability in both the Toggle and the Off-Canvas navigations, the hamburger icon gets the class `.active` added/removed to offer a visual cue showing that the item has been tapped. This is done with a bit of jQuery.

Including jQuery is part of these demos, so it's necessary to call it for them to work.

Scope

The markup shown is only for the menu itself, elements and directives such as the `<html>` tag and HTML5 Doctype have been purposely left out.

The examples work in all major browsers that have support for relatively advanced CSS3 properties. They don't use the FastClick script to remove the 300 ms delay that mobile devices have by default.

Vendor prefixes have been left out; after all, we should be using Autoprefixer to handle this for us.

Third-party demos

Since there's no need to reinvent the wheel, the following examples are based on other authors' demos, such as the ones by Brad Frost and Austin Wulf.

However, all original demos have been forked and *extensively* scaled, enhanced, cleaned up, optimized, restyled, and ported to Sass in order to fit the scope and style of this book. In other words, the markup and code you'll see has been heavily customized exclusively for you.

Let's begin.

The Off-Canvas or Off-Screen navigation

This is by far the most commonly used pattern for navigation both in RWD and mobile apps. It uses the hamburger icon as the trigger for the menu when tapped/clicked. When this happens, the main container slides to the right to reveal the menu on the left and slides back again to the left to hide it.

This example does not depend on JavaScript to work. However, it uses a few unsemantic elements to make it work: the `<input>` and `<label>` elements. In defense of this method, it uses the `:checked` pseudo-class, which has perfect support across the board.

Here's our HTML:

```
<!DOCTYPE html>
<html>
<head>
    <meta charset="UTF-8">
    <meta name="viewport" content="width=device-width,
        initial-scale=1">
    <script
src="https://ajax.googleapis.com/ajax/libs/
jquery/2.1.3/jquery.min.js"></script>
</head>
<body>
    <!-- Checkbox whose checked/unchecked states
                trigger the navigation -->
```

```html
<input type="checkbox" id="nav-trigger" class="nav-trigger">
<!-- Hamburger icon -->
<label for="nav-trigger"
       class="label-trigger"><span>Menu</span></label>
<!-- Navigation -->
<nav role="navigation">
    <ul class="menu">
        <li><a href="#">Link 1</a></li>
        <li><a href="#">Link 2</a></li>
        <li><a href="#">Link 3</a></li>
        <li><a href="#">Link 4</a></li>
        <li><a href="#">Link 5</a></li>
    </ul>
</nav>
<!-- Main container -->
<main class="main-container" role="main">
    <h1>The "Off-Canvas" or "Off-Screen" Navigation</h1>
    <p>On <strong>small screens</strong>, the menu
        is triggered with a hamburger icon.
        The menu slides left/right.</p>
    <p>On <strong>large screens</strong>
        starting at 40em (640px),
        the menu is a horizontal nav.</p>
</main>
</body>
</html>
```

And here's our SCSS:

```scss
*, *:before, *:after { box-sizing: border-box; }
//Globals
html, body {
    height: 100%;
    width: 100%;
    margin: 0;
}
//Mobile-first Media Query Mixin
@mixin forLargeScreens($media) {
    @media (min-width: $media/16+em) { @content; }
}
//Mixin for animating the hamburger icon
@mixin animation-nav-icon ( $direction: left, $duration: .2s) {
    transition: $direction $duration;
}
//Menu itself
```

```scss
.menu {
    width: 100%;
    height: 100%;
    margin: 0;
    padding: 0;
    position: fixed;
    top: 0;
    right: 0;
    bottom: 0;
    left: 0;
    z-index: 0;
    list-style: none;
    @include forLargeScreens(640) {
        max-width: 980px;
        min-height: 50%;
        margin: 10px auto 0;
        position: relative;
        text-align: center;
        border: #999 1px dotted;
    }
    //List items
    li {
        width: 100%;
        border-bottom: 1px dotted #999;
        @include forLargeScreens(640) {
            display: inline;
            border: none;
        }
        //Links themselves
        a {
            display: block;
            padding: 1em;
            color: #2963BD;
            text-decoration: none;
            @include forLargeScreens(640) {
                display: inline-block;
            }
        }
    }
}
//Main Container
.main-container {
    max-width: 980px;
    min-height: 100%;
```

```scss
        margin: auto;
        padding: 20px 0 20px 80px;
        position: relative;
        top: 0;
        bottom: 100%;
        left: 0;
        z-index: 1;
        background: #eee;
        @include forLargeScreens(640) {
            padding: 20px;
        }
    }
    //Navigation Trigger - Hide the checkbox
    .nav-trigger {
        position: absolute;
        clip: rect(0, 0, 0, 0);
    }
    //Label that triggers the checkbox
    .label-trigger {
        position: fixed;
        left: 10px;
        top: 10px;
        z-index: 2;
        height: 50px;
        width: 50px;
        cursor: pointer;
        background: #fff;
        border-radius: 2px;
        border: 1px solid #ccc;
        //Hamburger icon
        &:before {
            display: block;
            padding-top: 25px;
            text-align: center;
            content: '≡';
            font-size: 3em;
            line-height: 0;
        }
        //Active hamburger icon
        &.active {
            background: #333;
            color: #fff;
        }
        //Hide the term 'Menu' from displaying without sacrificing
            accessibility
        span {
            display: inline-block;
```

```scss
            text-indent: -100%;
            overflow: hidden;
            white-space: nowrap;
        }
    }
    //Animate the menu
    .nav-trigger {
        & + label {
            @include animation-nav-icon;
            //Hide the checkbox and label in large screens
            @include forLargeScreens(640) {
                display: none;
            }
        }
        //Animate the label when checkbox is checked
        &:checked + label {
            left: 215px;
        }
        //Animate the main container when checkbox is checked
        &:checked ~ .main-container {
            left: 200px;
            box-shadow: 0 0 5px 1px rgba(black, .15);
        }
    }
    //Animate the main container
    .main-container {
        @include animation-nav-icon;
    }
    //Avoid horizontal scrollbars due to repositioning of elements
    body, html { overflow-x: hidden; }
    //Styling stuff not needed for demo
    html, body { font-family: Arial, "Helvetica Neue", Helvetica,
                sans-serif; }
    h1, p { margin: 0 auto 1em; }
    p { line-height: 1.5; }
```

Here's the jQuery script:

```javascript
$(function() {
    //Set up the click behavior
    $(".label-trigger").click(function() {
        //Toggle the class .active on the hamburger icon
        $(this).toggleClass("active");
    });
});
```

Let's take a look at the screenshots.

Here is what it looks like on small screens in the *collapsed* state:

Here is what it looks like in the *expanded* state:

This is what it looks like on large screens:

You can see a demo I created in CodePen at `http://codepen.io/ricardozea/pen/fd504cbcf362069320d15a4ea8a88b27`.

The Toggle navigation

In the Toggle pattern, when the hamburger icon is tapped or clicked, the navigation bar slides down and the links are stacked. The navigation bar collapses when the hamburger icon is tapped again.

The HTML is as follows:

```
<!DOCTYPE html>
<html>
<head>
    <meta charset="UTF-8">
    <meta name="viewport" content="width=device-width,
        initial-scale=1">
    <script
src="https://ajax.googleapis.com/ajax/libs/
jquery/2.1.3/jquery.min.js"></script>
</head>
<body>
    <!-- Hamburger icon -->
    <button class="menu-link"><span>Menu</span></button>
    <!-- Navigation -->
    <nav id="menu" class="menu" role="navigation">
        <ul>
            <li><a href="#">Link 1</a></li>
            <li><a href="#">Link 2</a></li>
            <li><a href="#">Link 3</a></li>
            <li><a href="#">Link 4</a></li>
            <li><a href="#">Link 5</a></li>
        </ul>
    </nav>
```

```
    <!-- Main container -->
    <main class="main-container" role="main">
        <h1>The Toggle Navigation</h1>
        <p>On <strong>small screens</strong>, the menu
is triggered with a hamburger icon.
The menu slides down/up.</p>
        <p>On <strong>large screens</strong> starting
at 40em (640px), the menu is a horizontal nav.</p>
    </main>
</body>
</html>
```

The SCSS is as follows:

```
*, *:before, *:after { box-sizing: border-box; }
//Mobile-first Media Query Mixin
@mixin forLargeScreens($media) {
    @media (min-width: $media/16+em) { @content; }
}
//General Styling
.main-container, .menu {
    width: 98%;
    max-width: 980px;
    margin: auto;
    padding: 20px;
    background: #eee;
}
//Link that triggers the menu
.menu-link {
//Change to float: left; if you want the hamburger menu
        on the left side
    float: right;
    margin: 0 1% 5px 0;
    padding: 1.5em 1em 1em;
    background: #f6f6f6;
    line-height: 0;
    text-decoration: none;
    color: #333;
    border-radius: 2px;
    cursor: pointer;
    //Hamburger icon
    &:before {
        display: block;
        padding: 10px 0;
        content: '≡';
```

```scss
            font-size: 3em;
            line-height: 0;
        }
        //Active hamburger icon
        &.active {
            background: #333;
            color: #fff;
        }
        //Hide the term 'Menu' from displaying without
sacrificing accessibility
        span {
            display: inline-block;
            text-indent: -100%;
            overflow: hidden;
            white-space: nowrap;
        }
        //On large screens hide the menu trigger
        @include forLargeScreens(640) {
            display: none;
        }
    }
    //If JavaScript is available, hide the menu.
    .js .menu {
        overflow: hidden;
        max-height: 0;
        @include forLargeScreens(640) {
            max-height: inherit;
        }
    }
    //Menu itself
    .menu {
        padding: 0;
        clear: both;
        transition: all .3s ease-out;
        //Define height of the menu
        &.active {
            max-height: 17em;
        }
        //Normalize the unordered list and add a bit of styling
        ul {
            margin: 0;
            padding: 0;
            list-style-type: none;
            border: 1px #999 dotted;
```

```scss
          border-bottom: none;
          text-align: center;
          //In large screens remove the border
        @include forLargeScreens(640) {
            background: #fff;
        }
      }
    }
    //List items
    li {
      //Links themselves
      a {
        display: block;
        padding: 1em;
        border-bottom: 1px #999 dotted;
        text-decoration: none;
        color: #2963BD;
        background: #fff;
        @include forLargeScreens(640) {
            border: 0;
            background: none;
        }
      }
      //On large screens make links horizontal
      @include forLargeScreens(640) {
    display: inline-block;
    margin: 0 .20em;
        }
      }
}


//Styling stuff not needed for demo
body { font-family: Arial, "Helvetica Neue", Helvetica,
sans-serif; }
p { line-height: 1.5; }
h1 { margin: 0; }
```

The jQuery is as follows:

```
$(function() {
    //Add class .js to the body if JS is enabled
    $("body").addClass("js");
    //Set up the click behavior
    $(".menu-link").click(function() {
        //Toggle the class .active on the hamburger icon
        $(this).toggleClass("active");
        //Toggle the class .active on the menu
            to make it slide down/up
        $(".menu").toggleClass("active");
    });
});
```

Let's take a look at the screenshots.

Here is what it looks like on small screens in the *collapsed* state:

And here is the *expanded* state:

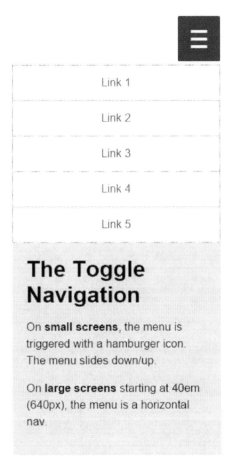

Here is what it looks like on large screens:

You can see a demo I created in CodePen at
http://codepen.io/ricardozea/pen/e91a5e6ea456d41f4128d9bd405ccaa0.

You can also visit `http://responsive-nav.com/` for a nice Toggle navigation functionality.

The Flexbox-based navigation

This custom solution using Flexbox is incredibly versatile and it doesn't necessarily require the use of media queries. The other two menu solutions (Toggle navigation and Off-Canvas navigation) do require media queries.

With this solution, the menu items adapt to the available space, making the target zones as large as possible, automatically enhancing the usability of the menu. Another major plus of this Flexbox-based solution is that it's not JavaScript dependent.

This is the HTML:

```html
<!DOCTYPE html>
<html>
<head>
    <meta charset="UTF-8">
    <meta name="viewport" content="width=device-width,
        initial-scale=1">
</head>
<body>
    <nav role="navigation">
        <ul class="menu">
            <li><a href="#">Link 1</a></li>
            <li><a href="#">Link 2</a></li>
            <li><a href="#">Link 3</a></li>
            <li><a href="#">Link 4</a></li>
            <li><a href="#">Link 5</a></li>
        </ul>
    </nav>
    <!-- Main container -->
    <main class="main-container" role="main">
        <h1>The Flexbox-based Navigation</h1>
        <p>On both <strong>small and large screens</strong>
            the menu and its items are always visible.</p>
        <p>However, on <strong>small screens</strong>
            the links are more clearly defined and occupy all
            the available space.</p>
    </main>
</body>
</html>
```

And now the SCSS:

```scss
*, *:before, *:after { box-sizing: border-box; }
//Mobile-first Media Query Mixin
@mixin forLargeScreens($media) {
    @media (min-width: $media/16+em) { @content; }
}
//Menu itself
.menu {
    display: flex;
    flex-wrap: wrap;
    justify-content: space-around;
    max-width: 980px;
    margin: auto;
    padding: 2px;
    list-style: none;
    border: #999 1px dotted;
    //List items
    li {
        //Expand to use any available space
        flex-grow: 1;
        margin: 3px;
        text-align: center;
        flex-basis: 100%;
        @include forLargeScreens(320) {
            flex-basis: 30%;
        }
        @include forLargeScreens(426) {
            flex-basis: 0;
        }
        //Links themselves
        a {
            display: block;
            padding: 1em;
            color: #2963bd;
            text-decoration: none;
            background: #eee;
            @include forLargeScreens(426) {
                background: none;
            }
        }
    }
```

```
        }
    }
    //Main Container
    .main-container {
        max-width: 980px;
        margin: auto;
        padding: 20px;
        background: #eee;
    }

    //Styling stuff not needed for demo
    body { margin: 8px; font-family: Arial, "Helvetica Neue",
            Helvetica, sans-serif; }
    p { line-height: 1.5; }
    h1 { margin: 0; }
```

Let's take a look at the screenshots.

Here is what it looks like on small screens (320px):

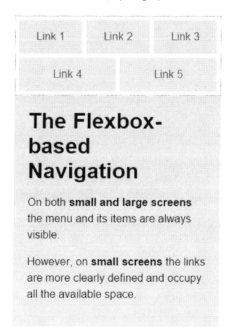

Here is what it looks like on small screens (426px):

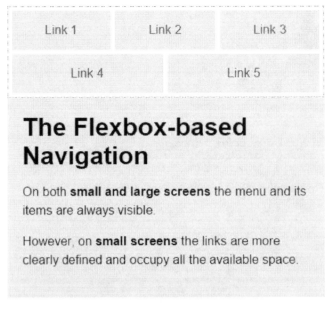

Here is what it looks like on a large screens (980px):

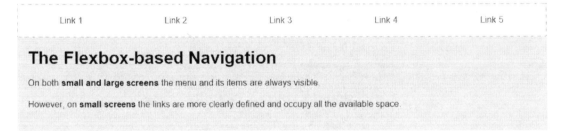

You can see a demo I created in CodePen at
http://codepen.io/ricardozea/pen/022b38c6c395368ec4befbf43737e398.

Summary

We are now halfway through mastering RWD with HTML5 and CSS3. What a milestone! A *huge* thanks for coming this far!

RWD is clearly more than media queries, Sass mixins, and CSS grids. It's also about understanding the different sizes of our target zones, the location of our controls (links, buttons, form fields, and so on), and the touch zones in different devices.

There will always be different approaches to creating a menu button, just make sure the functionalities never break on any screen size. Once we defined the style of our menu button, we defined which navigation pattern would work best for our content and our users.

There isn't really one single, best solution for menu button or navigation pattern; it all depends on each project's specific conditions. What I do recommend is that whatever you build, make sure you always maintain a high level of browser support, scalability, and performance, so that the users can have a great experience and the client/company can meet its goals.

Now that we are talking about performance, in the next chapter we're going to talk about the "ugly child" of RWD: images.

Let's dance!

6
Working with Images and Videos in Responsive Web Design

I've always called images the "ugly child" of **RWD**. Why? Until the last minute, I always tried to avoid having to deal with them. Do I use image sprites? If so, do I export my transparent PNG as an 8 bit or 24 bit, or 32 bit? Some legacy IEs don't support PNG with alpha channel, so I have to export a GIF sprite. I can use SVG instead, but IE8 and below don't support SVG. I can use icon fonts, but what happens if the icon font doesn't load? I'm going to have to look up some analytics then. There's a new *iDevice* with a new type of high-density screen? Now I have to export two (or more) images every single time. Great! But I can't serve a high-quality image that's more than double the size of the regular size image to small-screen devices! Yeah, it may look good but it'll take forever to download, they just might as well leave the site even before the first H1 loads.

You get the picture. That's barely scratching the surface of working with media in RWD.

Some of these thoughts are still very alive today, but I've learned through the years that with a bit of common sense and staying on top of the technologies that address all these issues, having a straightforward system to deal with images (and video) can go a long way.

As in the other chapters, we are going to keep things simple but meaningful. There is no silver bullet when it comes to images, specifically in RWD, we can stay here all day long and that's certainly something we don't want with this book. I want you to go build awesome responsive sites as soon as possible. But I do encourage you to spend some time researching a bit more about images for RWD; it is truly a memorable topic among the web design and developer communities.

In this chapter, we're going to address the following topics:

- Tips for exporting images and considerably reducing their final file size while maintaining the image quality.

- How and when to use the `srcset` and `sizes` attributes, and the `<picture>` element.

- Using `Retina.js`.

- Making videos responsive.

- Using `FitVids.js`.

- Using vector formats: Icon Fonts and SVGs.

- Using the right CSS image replacement technique.

Now, here's the image we're going to use in our examples:

These awesome individuals are two Kung Fu grandmasters from the Shaolin Temple in China. Their names are Shi DeRu and Shi DeYang.

Shi DeRu and Shi DeYang by Shi Deru (Shawn Xiangyang Liu), who is the sole owner and copyright-holder of the authenticity of the picture taken at the Shaolin Temple's front gate. It is licensed under CC BY-SA 3.0 via Wikipedia. It can be found at `http://en.wikipedia.org/wiki/Shaolin_Kung_Fu#/media/File:Shi_DeRu_and_Shi_DeYang.jpg`.

Since we are also *mastering* RWD with HTML5 and CSS3, I thought this photo fit right in with our mission.

The properties of the original image of the Kung Fu grandmasters I'm going to describe will help set a baseline to understand the before/after effect when optimizing images for RWD.

Here are the original image's properties:

- It is a 24-bit JPG image.

- The file size is 556KB, but it is compressed thanks to the magic of the JPG algorithm (about 12 MB decompressed).

- The dimensions are 2496 x 1664 pixels, which is about 4.15 megapixels. To put it in perspective, this image has more resolution than my 55" LED TV in my living room.

By the end of book, I assure you two things. One, you'll be absolutely ready to build responsive sites and apps. Two, when it's time to start a new project, you're going to get up from your seat and strike the same pose these grandmasters are doing.

Image editing is out of scope of this book and the following steps will require image manipulation of some sort. At this point, you can use your favorite image editor of choice. I personally use Adobe Fireworks (indeed I do), but the vast majority uses Photoshop.

If you don't use any of those, you can always use **GNU Image Manipulation Software (GIMP)** or Paint.NET—both are free. You can download them from here:

- GIMP: `http://www.gimp.org/`
- Paint.NET: `http://www.getpaint.net/`

You can also use an online image editing tool. However, I have to admit though that I've never used any of them, so I can't recommend one. At this point what I can say is try some of them out and choose the one that best fits your needs.

Let's get started.

Tips for reducing the file size in images for RWD

In design, the rule of thumb when creating copies of an image is to go from large to small—never the other way around. In other words, the larger the image, the better its subsequent copies will be.

Resizing

Just by resizing the image from 2496 x 1664 pixels to 1024 x 683 pixels, the file size is now 331 KB. This is nearly a 40 percent reduction in file size from 556 KB. A huge improvement, but we're not there yet.

Blurring the background

Blurring the background is actually quite effective in itself, but it also has another benefit from the *art direction* point of view: It helps draw attention to the important part(s) of the image.

After blurring the background, the file now weighs 185 KB. That's about a 67 percent reduction in file size from 556 KB. We're starting to get somewhere.

Here's the new image with the blurred background:

A huge win for optimization!

Darkening or lightening the less important areas

Darkening or lightening the less important areas is very subjective and many may not necessarily agree with it. Under special circumstances, this process — just like the background blurring technique — can help reduce the file size and bring the important parts of the image out.

What we're basically trying to accomplish by darkening or lightening an image is to reduce the amount of colors by creating *solid color* areas, or at least as solid as possible. In other words, we're reducing the contrast. Use this trick with discretion.

In the case of our Kung Fu grandmasters, after darkening the less important parts of the image in the background, the image now weighs 178 KB. Admittedly, that's not much different from the former process (only 7 KB difference), but any kilobyte we can extract from the image without affecting the quality is always a good thing, and 178 KB is about a 68 percent reduction in file size.

This is how the image looks after darkening the background a little:

Every kilobyte counts.

Optimizing an image

This is the last step in the process. This step can actually be divided in two smaller steps.

Using Adobe Fireworks (optional)

Save a JPG that balances quality versus file size well. There are no determined values that can always be applied to every single image. It all happens on the fly. When doing this step, you don't want to save the image with too much low quality since the image is going to go through another optimization step.

I'm actually going to use a software that Adobe stopped developing back in May 2013: Fireworks.

Fireworks has been known to have a superior image optimization engine than Photoshop, I've run tests myself and Fireworks compression versus. quality always showed the best results. Fireworks is as relevant to today's web design processes and workflows as any other image editing software out there today. So don't be afraid to use it.

After exporting the image from Fireworks at 80 percent quality, the image of the Kung Fu grandmasters weighs now only 71 KB. That's about an 87 percent reduction in file size from the original 556 KB.

Compressing the image

Run the image through another image optimization tool, either a standalone application such as ImageOptim for Mac or Radical Image Optimization Tool (RIOT) for Windows, or through an online service such as https://tinypng.com/ or http://www.jpegmini.com/.

We're going to use the https://tinypng.com/ online image compression service. After running the image exported from Fireworks through https://tinypng.com/, the file size is now about 52 KB, that's about a 91 percent reduction in file size from the original 556 KB. This is a massive win for image optimization.

 If you didn't run the image through Fireworks first, don't worry. Even though your image may be a bit larger, it will still be incredibly optimized and that's the objective here.

Here's the before (left) and after (right) comparison between the 556 KB image and the final 52 KB image:

1024 x 683 @ 52KB

2496 x 1664 @ 556KB

Third-party image resizing services

We have to acknowledge that if the manual process of optimizing images can be quite tedious and time consuming in the scenario where many images need to be resized and optimized, doing it manually may not be the best idea.

There are a few third-party and server-side services out there that automate this process for us. We're going to leave the tutorials of how to implement these services for another book. However, we're going to list some of the most popular services so you can have a reference in case you want to dive deeper.

Here are a few examples of third-party image resizing services:

- **Sencha.io Src** from Sencha.com (`http://www.sencha.com/learn/how-to-use-src-sencha-io/`)
- **ReSRC** by Dom Fee and Ed Thurgood (`http://www.resrc.it/`)
- **WURFL** Image Tailor (`http://web.wurfl.io/#wit`)

Here are a few examples of server-side (`.htaccess` and/or `.php`) image resizing services:

- Adaptive Images by Matt Wilcox (`http://adaptive-images.com/`)
- RESS.io (`http://ress.io/`)

The \<picture\> element and the srcset and sizes attributes

Let me start by saying that there is no 100 percent optimal solution to the image issues in RWD. This is because of the current lack of support for the recommended properties, or because there's a double download of assets. Granted, Dave Newton's article in `http://ww1.smashingmagzine.com/`, *How To Avoid Duplicate Downloads In Responsive Images*, tries to address this issue (`http://www.smashingmagazine.com/2013/05/10/how-to-avoid-duplicate-downloads-in-responsive-images/`).

However, that solution is very verbose. If you have to work with many images, this solution may not be the best option and allowing a double download starts making more sense. Every project is different, so trying to make the most informed decisions possible is incredibly important.

As soon as browser vendors decide to fully support any of the solutions mentioned here, there won't be a need to worry about double downloads or polyfills of any kind.

The `<picture>` element and the `srcset` and `sizes` attributes are maintained by the **Responsive Images Community Group (RICG)** and are now part of the HTML specification. In other words, we can use them without any type of polyfill and have the confidence that modern browsers will support them. Well, to some degree at least.

The only reason we would need to use a polyfill is to support those browsers (legacy and modern) that haven't yet implemented support for them.

Both the `<picture>` element and the `srcset` attribute have a fallback feature for those browsers that don't support them. You can opt to use a polyfill, but you are not required to do so. If you think using a polyfill enhances the user experience, by all means, go for it. Read this article about it from the creator of the Picturefill polyfill, Scott Jehl (`http://www.filamentgroup.com/lab/to-picturefill.html`).

There are many polyfills out there, here's a short list of the ones we can use today:

- Picturefill by Scott Jehl (recommended by the RICG: `http://scottjehl.github.io/picturefill/`)
- PicturePolyfill by Andrea Verlicchi (`http://verlok.github.io/picturePolyfill/`)
- respimage by Alexander Farkas (`https://github.com/aFarkas/respimage`)

Some people in the web design and web development communities feel strongly about considering that a new HTML element (`<picture>`) isn't the solution to the issues we are experiencing with images in RWD. They feel that the solution should come from within an already existing tag, the `<img>` tag.

> The `sizes` attribute can also be used with the `<picture>` element, but we're going to focus on using the `sizes` attribute with the `<img>` tag.

Good for us, that the solutions come in both flavors. It doesn't matter which method you use to serve your images in a responsible way, what matters is that you should be using one of these methods. If you already are, that's awesome. If not, don't sweat it. The following explanations will help clear up any questions you have about this matter.

When to use <picture> and when to use srcset

When to use `<picture>` and when to use `srcset`? This is a very legit question that I myself couldn't wrap my head around when first heard these terms. So I decided to ask Brad Frost at a workshop he conducted in Dayton, OH.

The recommended approach boils down to this concept: art direction. In responsive images, art direction basically means that you have different images that are cropped a certain way so that less important parts of the image are left out in order to focus on the important ones.

This is different from just resizing the same image. Granted, you can use whatever method you want, but to keep things simple, you can use the `<picture>` element when you want to serve art directed images and the `srcset` attribute when you just want to serve resized versions of the same image.

Before we dive into the markup, let's see a visual example of an art directed image versus a resized image using the photo of the Kung Fu grandmasters:

Let's see what happened here. The original image has a lot of space around the Kung Fu grandmasters: we can see the trees and the buildings in the back. The resized versions maintain all aspects and proportions 1:1 of the original image.

However, the art directed images have a lot of differences. The first art directed image is cropped to show both grandmasters in a close up; the second art directed image has been cropped even more to accentuate the focus on Shi DeRu only (the grandmaster on the left). We could've cropped the image to focus on Shi DeYang (the grandmaster on the right), but this was the "art direction" I wanted to give the image. This is a subjective decision but based on a solid intent.

Now, let's see the *Picturefill polyfill/script* in action.

Implementing the Picturefill polyfill

The first thing we need to do is download the JavaScript file, which can be downloaded from `https://github.com/scottjehl/picturefill/blob/2.3.0/dist/picturefill.min.js`

Then, all we need to do is include it in the `<head>` section of our document:

```
<!DOCTYPE html>
<!--[if IE 8]> <html class="no-js ie8" lang="en"> <![endif]-->
<!--[if IE 9]> <html class="no-js ie9" lang="en"> <![endif]-->
```

```
<!--[if gt IE 9]><!--><html class="no-js"
    lang="en"><!--<![endif]-->
<head>
    <meta charset="utf-8">
    <meta name="viewport" content="width=device-width,
initial-scale=1">
    <meta http-equiv="X-UA-Compatible" content="IE=edge">
    <script src="js/picturefill.min.js"></script>
    <title>Picturefill polyfill</title>
</head>
```

Using the <picture> element

When using the <picture> element, you (the author) tell the browser which image to use at which breakpoint. The good thing about this is that we can define exactly when a certain image should be displayed by using media queries. The media queries work exactly the same as the media queries used in CSS, and they even look exactly the same.

This is what a basic <picture> snippet looks like:

```
<picture>
    <source srcset="images/grandmasters-small.jpg"
     media="(max-width: 40em)">
    <source srcset="images/grandmasters-medium.jpg"
     media="(max-width: 64em)">
    <source srcset="images/grandmasters-default.jpg">
    <img src="images/grandmasters-default.jpg"
     alt="Fallback image">
</picture>
```

Now, even with a polyfill, IE9 has issues with the <picture> element. As weird as it sounds, we need to inject a <video> tag within conditional comments for IE9 to work correctly.

This is what the markup looks like after amending it for IE9:

```
<picture>
    <!--[if IE 9]><video style="display: none;"><![endif]-->
    <source srcset="images/grandmasters-small-ad.jpg"
     media="(max-width: 40em)">
    <source srcset="images/grandmasters-medium-ad.jpg"
     media="(max-width: 64em)">
    <source srcset="images/grandmasters-default.jpg">
    <!--[if IE 9]></video><![endif]-->
    <img src="images/grandmasters-default.jpg" alt="Fallback image">
</picture>
```

As you can see, I also highlighted the `<img src="grandmasters-default.jpg" alt="Fallback image">` tag. This is the fallback image for those browsers that do not support the `<picture>` element.

One thing to keep in mind is that not so long ago, this fallback image caused double download in some modern browsers. My last tests showed that this was not the case in Chrome and Firefox, which do support the `<picture>` element. So make sure you run all necessary tests to see where you stand and then think of a solution if you need to support those legacy browsers.

Here's a demo I created for this in CodePen: `http://codepen.io/ricardozea/pen/cf6c0965785d552bad5e200acb761ffe`

Using the srcset and sizes attributes

The `srcset` and `sizes` attributes actually come from the `<picture>` specification, but are implemented in the `<img>` element. When using the `srcset` and `sizes` attributes, the browser does all the work of deciding which image to use for each specific circumstance. You can also use media queries if you want, although, not required. The word `vw` means *viewport width* and it's used to let the browser know that it should display an image at a certain percentage in relation to the width of the viewport. If you see something like `80vw`, it means that the image should be 80 percent of the width of the current viewport.

The `w` descriptor means *the width of the image*. If you see something like `255w`, it means the browser will understand that specific image is 255px wide.

Let's take a look at an `<img>` tag with the `srcset` and `sizes` attributes:

```
<img src="images/grandmasters-default.jpg"
    srcset="images/grandmasters-small-rsz.jpg 255w,
            images/grandmasters-medium-rsz.jpg 511w"
    sizes="(min-width: 30em) 80vw, 100vw"
    alt="Mastering RWD with HTML5 and CSS3">
```

The letters *rsz* are an abbreviation of the word *resize*. That's because for images that are just going to be resized in RWD, the `srcset` attribute keeps things a bit simpler.

The following markup is truncated in order to focus on the specific explanations easily.

The first thing we see is the already known `src` attribute which acts as the fallback image:

```
<img src="images/grandmasters-default.jpg"…
```

Keep in mind that the image `grandmasters-default.jpg` *will not* be used by browsers that do understand `srcset`. In other words, the *default* image in browsers that support `srcset` is going to be first image in the list. In our case, it is `grandmasters-small-rsz.jpg`. Then, we see the `srcset` attribute.

This is where the magic starts happening:

```
srcset="images/grandmasters-small-rsz.jpg 255w,
        images/grandmasters-medium-rsz.jpg 511w"
```

In this example, our plan is to show two different image files in browsers that support `srcset`. This is accomplished by listing the images separated by commas. Also, the value defined after each image is the width of the image:

```
images/grandmasters-small-rsz.jpg 255w
```

> We can use height as well:
>
> ```
> grandmasters-small-rsz.jpg 170h
> ```
>
> However, the most common use case is that dealing with the width and allowing the height to adjust proportionally gives authors a bit more control over the image.

Giving the size of the image to the browser will allow it to make a more informed decision about what image to use based on the media query in the `sizes` snippet:

```
sizes="(min-width: 30em) 80vw, 100vw"
```

Remember, `30em` is the same as 480px. With the media query `min-width: 30em`, the browser goes through the following process:

- If my viewport is 30em (480px) or less, I should show the image that's 255px wide. There's no need to show the image that's 511px in a viewport that's only 480px. That's a waste of bandwidth!

- But if my viewport is *more* than 30em (480px), then I should show the image that's 511px wide.

The last part of the `sizes` attribute is the viewport widths: `80vw, 100vw`.

```
sizes="(min-width: 30em) 80vw, 100vw"
```

This means that if the viewport is 30em (480px) or less, the browser will show the image at 80 percent width. If it's more than 30em (480px), it will show the image at 100 percent width.

Finally, we have the `alt` attribute:

```
alt="Mastering RWD with HTML5 and CSS3">
```

Adding an `alt` attribute is always a good accessibility practice for users with assistive technology. Also, in case the images aren't loaded, browsers can display this text instead.

 The order of the attributes doesn't matter. In other words, you can have `srcset` first, then `alt`, then `sizes`, and then the `src` attribute (or vice versa).

Targeting high-density screens with srcset

High-density screens will always be something in the RWD world that we'll never get away from. So if you can't defeat them, join them.

Here's a snippet that addresses normal and high-density screens:

```
<img src="images/grandmasters-default.jpg"
     srcset="images/grandmasters-small-rsz.jpg 1x,
             images/grandmasters-medium-rsz.jpg 2x">
```

As you can see, this is a much shorter and concise markup. It's really self-explanatory: use a fallback image in case there's no `srcset` support. If there is support, then use the `1x` image if the device has a normal density display. You will have to use the `2x` image if the device has a high-density display up to two times the density. If we are supporting even higher than 2x density devices, a 3x suffix should be added.

The `sizes` attribute is not required. If your design or conditions merit the use of the `sizes` attribute, you're free to use it.

Here's a demo I created for this in CodePen:
http://codepen.io/ricardozea/pen/a13993f05a4cdc5f714a311a94f48a69

<picture> versus srcset

Some web designers and developers say that using media queries inside HTML like we saw with `<picture>` and `srcset` goes against the principle of separation of concerns: styling and markup should always remain as separated, independent assets.

Others, as I mentioned before, think that a new HTML element is unnecessary and that any solutions should be based on enhancing and extending already existing elements like the `<img>` tag.

All I can say is that at the end, none of that matters. What matters is that as web designers and developers, we should be using anything we have at our disposal to make users happy and create memorable experiences, while adhering to the best practices for long lasting implementations.

Replacing 1x images with 2x images on the fly with Retina.js

The `Retina.js` script is one of those scripts that makes things so much easier that sometimes you wonder why responsive images are so difficult.

If you don't feel ready to deal with the `<picture>` and/or `srcset` and `sizes` attributes, I don't blame you. It's scary but I recommend that you keep trying to understand these tools since that's the state of the art of responsive images.

The `Retina.js` script was developed by the folks at Imulus (`http://imulus.com/`). The `Retina.js` script isn't a JavaScript-only solution; they also have a Sass mixin that produces the same results without the dependency on JavaScript.

Let's take a look at the JavaScript solution first.

Retina.js – a JavaScript solution

Using the script couldn't be any simpler. We need to download the script from `https://github.com/imulus/retinajs/blob/master/dist/retina.min.js`

Then, we place the script at the bottom of the HTML, right before the closing `<body>` tag:

```
<!DOCTYPE html>
<!--[if IE 8]> <html class="no-js ie8" lang="en"> <![endif]-->
<!--[if IE 9]> <html class="no-js ie9" lang="en"> <![endif]-->
<!--[if gt IE 9]><!--><html class="no-js" lang="en">
<!--<![endif]-->
<head>
    <meta charset="utf-8">
    <meta name="viewport" content="width=device-width,
      initial-scale=1">
```

```
        <meta http-equiv="X-UA-Compatible" content="IE=edge">
        <title>Retina.js - JavaScript Solution</title>
</head>
<body>
    ...
    <script src="js/retina.min.js"></script>
</body>
</html>
```

 The Retina.js script is not framework dependent. In other words, it doesn't need jQuery or Mootools or Dojo or any framework to… well, work.

Then, we add an image to our markup:

```
<!DOCTYPE html>
<!--[if IE 8]> <html class="no-js ie8" lang="en"> <![endif]-->
<!--[if IE 9]> <html class="no-js ie9" lang="en"> <![endif]-->
<!--[if gt IE 9]><!--><html class="no-js" lang="en">
<!--<![endif]-->
<head>
    <meta charset="utf-8">
    <meta name="viewport" content="width=device-width,
     initial-scale=1">
    <meta http-equiv="X-UA-Compatible" content="IE=edge">
    <title>Retina.js - JavaScript Solution</title>
</head>
<body>
    <img src="images/grandmasters-default.jpg" alt="">
    <script src="js/retina.min.js"></script>
</body>
</html>
```

That's it! We don't have to do anything to the markup, unless we want to exclude an image from being replaced. I explain how to do this coming up next.

The basic function of the JavaScript solution of Retina.js is that it looks for images in the page and replaces them with high-resolution versions if they exist on the server.

You need to name your high-resolution images with the @2x modifier right at the end of the name.

In other words, if you have the following image:

```
<img src="images/grandmasters-default.jpg" alt="">
```

Retina.js replaces it with the following one:

```
<img src="images/grandmasters-default@2x.jpg" alt="">
```

As long as the @2x image exists on the server, Retina.js replaces it. If the image doesn't exist, then it won't replace it.

Excluding images

If you have excluded or want to exclude, images from being replaced by Retina.js, you can add the data-no-retina attribute to your images:

```
<img src="images/grandmasters-default.jpg" alt="" data-no-retina>
```

Retina.js – a Sass mixin solution

Well, this is weird—a JavaScript solution that somehow also happens to have a CSS solution? Sweet! Note that this Sass mixin is for applying background high-resolution images.

The Sass mixin looks like this:

```
@mixin at2x($path, $ext: "jpg", $w: auto, $h: auto) {
    $at1x_path: "#{$path}.#{$ext}";
    $at2x_path: "#{$path}@2x.#{$ext}";

  background-image: url("#{$at1x_path}");

    @media all and (-webkit-min-device-pixel-ratio : 1.5),
        all and (-o-min-device-pixel-ratio: 3/2),
        all and (min--moz-device-pixel-ratio: 1.5),
        all and (min-device-pixel-ratio: 1.5) {
          background-image: url("#{$at2x_path}");
          background-size: $w $h;
    }
}
```

The usage is quite simple:

```
.hero {
    width: 100%;
    height: 510px;
    @include at2x('../images/grandmasters-default',
        jpg, 100%, auto);
}
```

We need to declare the **file extension**, the **width**, and the **height** as comma-separated values. The preceding Sass snippet will compile to this:

```
.hero {
    width: 100%;
    height: 510px;
    background-image: url("../images/grandmasters-default.jpg");
}
@media all and (-webkit-min-device-pixel-ratio: 1.5),
all and (-o-min-device-pixel-ratio: 3 / 2), all
and (min--moz-device-pixel-ratio: 1.5), all and
(min-device-pixel-ratio: 1.5) {
    .hero {
        background-image:
url("../images/grandmasters-default@2x.jpg");
        background-size: 100% auto;
    }
}
```

Here's a demo I created for this in CodePen: `http://codepen.io/ricardozea/pen/c3af015b325da6ee56cf59e660f3cc03`

 With `background-size: 100% auto;`, the background image will stretch to the maximum width of its parent container. However, if the container is wider, the image will be repeated.

Making videos responsive

The videos we're going to talk about are the videos that come inside our good old friend, the `<iframe>` element, such as videos from YouTube, Vimeo, Dailymotion, and so on. There are several ways to make videos responsive, some more involving than others. Let's break it down.

Responsive videos with HTML and CSS

YouTube is an amazing video service that makes life easier for everyone—video authors, as well as web designers and developers. The fact that YouTube takes care of the hosting of the video, the streaming, and the technological conditions of browsers that don't support Flash (iOS), or browsers that don't support the `<video>` tag (legacy browsers), is just awesome.

The first thing we need to do is create a container that will hold the video. This container is the one we're going to manipulate to give the video the width we want while maintaining its aspect ratio:

```
<div class="video-container"></div>
```

Then, we create a container for the video we're going to embed:

```
<div class="video-container">
    <div class="embed-container"></div>
</div>
```

Then we embed the video, which is inside the `<iframe>` element:

```
<div class="video-container">
    <div class="embed-container">
        <iframe width="560" height="315"
src="https://www.youtube.com/embed/vpRsLPI400U" frameborder="0"
allowfullscreen></iframe>
    </div>
</div>
```

Ok, that's it for our markup. Now, let's tackle the CSS from inside out.

Let's give the `<iframe>` element a few properties:

```
.embed-container iframe {
    position: absolute;
    top: 0;
    left: 0;
    width: 100%;
    height: 100%;
}
```

Then, let's give the `.embed-container` wrapper some context:

```
.embed-container {
    position: relative;
    padding-bottom: 56.25%;
    padding-top: 35px;
/* This padding is only needed for YouTube videos */
    height: 0;
    overflow: hidden;
}
```

Now the `<iframe>` element will be positioned correctly and take up all the space of its parent container. The parent container will make sure the video is visible and anything sticking out of it will be hidden.

 For videos with 16:9 aspect ratio, use `padding-bottom: 56.25%;`.
For videos with 4:3 aspect ratio, use `padding-bottom: 75%;`.

All we need to do now is define the width of the whole thing. We do that by adding a width to the outer container, the `.video-container` wrapper:

```
.video-container {
    width: 80%; /* This can be any width you want */
}
```

Responsive videos with jQuery

If you're a jQuery fan, this plugin is for you. It may also come in handy when you have to retrofit already published videos on your site, or if there are too many of them to update manually.

The plugin is called FitVids.js. It was developed by Chris Coyer and the guys at Paravel. Using FitVids.js is pretty straightforward. First, we need to download the FitVids JavaScript file from the following URL: `https://github.com/davatron5000/FitVids.js/blob/master/jquery.fitvids.js`

Then, we call jQuery and the FitVids.js files in the `<head>` of our document. Finally, we add a script at the bottom of our markup to call the `fitVids` function. That's pretty much all there is to it.

The actual file name of `FitVids.js` is `jquery.fitvids.js`. This is the file name we're going to see in the example.

Here's an HTML snippet with two videos within `<iframe>`, one from YouTube and another one from Vimeo:

```
<!DOCTYPE html>
<!--[if IE 8]> <html class="no-js ie8" lang="en"> <![endif]-->
<!--[if IE 9]> <html class="no-js ie9" lang="en"> <![endif]-->
<!--[if gt IE 9]><!--><html class="no-js" lang="en">
<!--<![endif]-->
<head>
```

```html
    <meta charset="utf-8">
    <meta name="viewport" content="width=device-width,
     initial-scale=1">
    <meta http-equiv="X-UA-Compatible" content="IE=edge">
<script src="js/jquery.min.js"></script>
<script src="js/jquery.fitvids.js"></script>
    <title>Responsive Videos with: jQuery Using FitVids.js</title>
</head>
<body>
    <h1>Responsive Videos with: jQuery Using FitVids.js</h1>
    <main class="main-container" role="main">
        <h2>YouTube</h2>
        <iframe width="560" height="315"
src="https://www.youtube.com/embed/vpRsLPI400U" frameborder="0"
allowfullscreen></iframe>
        <h2>Vimeo</h2>
        <iframe width="560" height="315"
src="https://player.vimeo.com/video/101875373" frameborder="0"
webkitAllowFullScreen mozallowfullscreen allowFullScreen></iframe>
    </main>
    <script>
        $(function(){
        //Look for all the videos inside this element
          and make them responsive
         $(".main-container").fitVids();
        });
    </script>
</body>
</html>
```

If you're curious about how `FitVids.js` modifies the DOM to make the videos responsive, here's the markup:

```html
<div class="fluid-width-video-wrapper"
    style="padding-top: 56.25%;">
    <iframe src="https://www.youtube.com/embed/vpRsLPI400U"
frameborder="0" allowfullscreen="" id="fitvid0"></iframe>
</div>
```

Document Object Model (DOM): When you read, or hear, someone say *modify the DOM*, it basically means *modify the generated HTML*.

Here's a demo I created for this in CodePen:
http://codepen.io/ricardozea/pen/9e994c213c0eeb64ccd627e132778a42.

Responsive videos with plain JavaScript

If you are not using jQuery or don't want any framework dependencies, but still need a simple JavaScript solution, the best option is to use a script developed by Todd Motto: Fluidvids.js.

Using it is very simple as well. First, we need to download the Fluidvids JavaScript file: https://github.com/toddmotto/fluidvids/blob/master/dist/fluidvids.min.js

Then, we need to call the fluidvis.js file in the <head> element of our document. Once we have that in place, we add a small script snippet at the bottom of our markup. That's it. The script will read through the markup, modify the DOM, and make any videos it finds *responsive*.

> Make sure to always give a width and height value to the <iframe> element. Otherwise you'll see a blank space on the page.

Here's the HTML snippet you'll need for this to work:

```
<!DOCTYPE html>
<!--[if IE 8]> <html class="no-js ie8" lang="en"> <![endif]-->
<!--[if IE 9]> <html class="no-js ie9" lang="en"> <![endif]-->
<!--[if gt IE 9]><!--><html class="no-js" lang="en">
<!--<![endif]-->
<head>
    <meta charset="utf-8">
    <meta name="viewport" content="width=device-width,
initial-scale=1">
    <meta http-equiv="X-UA-Compatible" content="IE=edge">
    <script src="js/fluidvids.min.js"></script>
    <title>Responsive Videos with: Plain JavaScript
- FluidVids.js</title>
</head>
<body>
    <h1>Responsive Videos with: Plain JavaScript
- FluidVids.js</h1>
    <main class="main-container" role="main">
        <h2>YouTube</h2>
        <iframe width="560" height="315"
src="https://www.youtube.com/embed/vpRsLPI400U" frameborder="0"
allowfullscreen></iframe>
        <h2>Vimeo</h2>
```

```
        <iframe width="560" height="315"
src="https://player.vimeo.com/video/101875373" frameborder="0"
webkitAllowFullScreen mozallowfullscreen allowFullScreen></iframe>
    </main>
    <script>
        fluidvids.init({
            selector: ['iframe'],
            players: ['www.youtube.com', 'player.vimeo.com']
        });
    </script>
</body>
</html>
```

Here's the modified DOM:

```
<div class="fluidvids" style="padding-top: 56.2%;">
    <iframe src="https://www.youtube.com/embed/vpRsLPI400U"
width="560" height="315" frameborder="0" allowfullscreen
class="fluidvids-item" data-fluidvids="loaded"></iframe>
</div>
```

Here's a demo I created for this in CodePen: http://codepen.io/ricardozea/pen/fda7c2c459392c934130f28cc092dbbe

Third-party services to embed video

What can I say? All you need to do is point your browser to http://embedresponsively.com/ and select the tab of the video service you want to use. Let's choose Vimeo. Input the URL of the video you want to make responsive, press the **Embed** button, and voilà—the HTML and CSS that you need to use appears right below the example video.

Here are the HTML and CSS snippets produced by embedresponsively.com for a video with the well-known Dan Mall about RWD (it has been formatted for easier reading):

The HTML is as follows:

```
<div class='embed-container'>
    <iframe src='https://player.vimeo.com/video/101875373'
frameborder='0' webkitAllowFullScreen mozallowfullscreen
allowFullScreen></iframe>
</div>
```

The CSS is as follows:

```css
.embed-container {
    position: relative;
    padding-bottom: 56.25%;
    height: 0;
    overflow: hidden;
    max-width: 100%;
}
.embed-container iframe,
.embed-container object,
.embed-container embed {
    position: absolute;
    top: 0;
    left: 0;
    width: 100%;
    height: 100%;
}
```

However, with the following snippets, the container of the video looks much higher than it should be. In order to make the preceding snippets work properly, we need to wrap the embed-container inside an outer container. Here are the amended markup and CSS.

The HTML is as follows:

```html
<div class="video-container">
    <div class='embed-container'>
        <iframe src='https://player.vimeo.com/video/101875373'
frameborder='0' webkitAllowFullScreen mozallowfullscreen
allowFullScreen></iframe>
    </div>
</div>
```

The CSS is as follows:

```css
.video-container {
    width: 100%;
}
.embed-container {
    position: relative;
    padding-bottom: 56.25%;
    height: 0;
    overflow: hidden;
    background: red;
}
```

```
.embed-container iframe,
.embed-container object,
.embed-container embed {
    position: absolute;
    top: 0;
    left: 0;
    width: 100%;
     height: 100%;
}
```

The `.video-container` wrapper is what we manipulate in order to define any width we want while maintaining the aspect ratio of the video. Now, all we need to do is place the markup in our HTML document and the CSS snippet in our SCSS file.

Here's a demo I created for this in CodePen: `http://codepen.io/ricardozea/pen/10262216eeb01fc9d3b3bedb9f27c908`

The Vector Formats

We're going to see some HTML and CSS/SCSS snippets to get an idea of how to work with icon fonts and **SVGs**, but we're not going to go through the creation of such assets since that process is out of the scope of this section.

Vectors or bitmaps/raster images

When people ask what the difference between vectors and bitmaps/raster images is, the answers I often hear are usually around the idea, "If you enlarge it, it won't lose its quality. No worries for mobile devices." Although true, it doesn't fully answer the question. So here are the differences:

A **vector image** is a file made out of mathematical equations. The results of these equations are represented by a graphic (lines, shapes, colors). If the size of the image changes in any way, the values of those equations are recalculated and the resulting graphic is painted again.

A **bitmap or raster image** is a file made out of pixels. These pixels have a specific/defined width, height, and color. If an image is enlarged, the pixels are stretched and that's why the image looks blurry or pixelated.

With those definitions out of the way, let's talk about some of the vector formats used for RWD. Vector formats include:

- Web fonts
- Icon fonts
- SVGs

Let's see how to rapidly implement icon fonts and SVGs; web fonts will be addressed in the next chapter.

Icon fonts

Icon fonts are basically a font file but instead of having letters as glyphs it has, well, icons. Some people love icon fonts (I do), and some aren't really too fond of them, especially since SVG has gained so much popularity.

Let's see the pros and cons of icon fonts.

Some advantages are:

- Icon fonts are very likely smaller in file size than their SVGs counterparts. We can have many more icons in a single font file and it weighs a lot less than having an SVG sprite.

- The properties of icon fonts can be modified with any properties used to modify text, for example, color, font-family, font-weight, and so on. After all, it's a font. This means that we don't have to learn any new syntaxes or properties.

- They are relatively easy to implement. Once all the `@font-face` properties are set once, calling an icon font is a matter of adding a class to the HTML and calling a specific code called the Unicode Point in the CSS.

- Icon fonts are vectors so they retain their optimum quality on any screen density, screen size, and zoom level.

- They're very design-versatile. A single icon font can be wrapped in a colored container, have the icon reserved (knockout), and still be the same icon—no need for a separate file.

Some disadvantages are:

- Updating a custom-designed icon can take some work, since we'd have to work with a third-party app to generate our icon font files.

- Icon fonts can only use a single color. I honestly don't think this is a disadvantage.

- One of the main disadvantages of icon fonts is that implementing a fallback in case the font file doesn't load is a bit complex and if you ask me, verbose. The name of the pattern is "A Font Garde". If you want to read about it, check out Zach Leatherman's post *Bulletproof Accessible Icon Fonts* (`http://www.filamentgroup.com/lab/bulletproof_icon_fonts.html`). The GitHub repo can be found at `https://github.com/filamentgroup/a-font-garde`.

Here are a few recommendations I can give you when using icon fonts:

- If possible, avoid using them for critical content.
- Always provide a `title=""` attribute in the element you're using the icon font on. If the font file fails to load, at least the text in the title tag can be seen.
- If you're ok with it, use an extra HTML element to hold the icon. If the icon font file fails to load, users with and without assistive technologies can still use the feature the icon font represents.
- In my years of experience, I have yet to see icon font files failed to load, but that doesn't mean it can't happen. So I recommend staying on top of your server logs to determine if the icon font file is or isn't being downloaded. If it's not, then you need to remedy the issue as soon as possible.

Let's implement an icon font then.

Implementing icon fonts

The fastest way to get icon font files is by using a third party web app like IcoMoon. io or Fontello.com. You can also get a copy of Font Awesome.

Be careful when considering using Font Awesome. Using a full font file with tenths of icons only to use a fraction of them is wasted bandwidth. If you're only going to use a handful of icon fonts, using IcoMoon.io or Fontello.com for custom icon selection is a better option.

Once you are able to unzip the provided files, the only file you're going to need is the `.woff` file. The reason you only need this file is because browser support for `.woff` files goes all the way back to IE9. Unless you want/need to support legacy browsers (desktop and mobile), you can then use `.eot`, `.ttf`, and `.svg` files.

I recommend that you keep it simple and avoid unnecessary headaches when trying to support icon fonts in legacy browsers. All they get is the text instead of the icon, or display the text in the `title=""` attribute.

Let's name our icon font file `icon-font.woff`. Create a `/fonts` folder and save the `icon-font.woff` file in it. This is what we are going to try to accomplish: a soft-blue link with an icon on the left, no underline, and 40px Arial/Helvetica font:

Using a pseudo-element

The great thing about using a pseudo-element is that our source markup always stays clean. In this case, we're going to use the `:before` pseudo-element, but this technique also works with an `:after` pseudo-element.

Let's take a look at the build.

This is the HTML snippet:

```
<a href="#" class="icon icon-headphones"
title="Headphones">Headphones</a>
```

Here's the SCSS. The first thing we need is a mixin to handle any custom web fonts. In this case, it is an icon font:

```scss
//Web font mixin
@mixin fontFace($font-family, $file-path) {
    @font-face {
        font: {
            family: $font-family;
            weight: normal;
            style: normal;
        }
    src: url('#{$file-path}.woff') format('woff');
    }
}
```

> Notice the nested properties in the `font: {...}` block. By doing this, we keep things DRY and avoid repeating the term *font* for the following instances: `font-family`, `font-weight` and `font-style`.

Then, we create a rule using *attribute selectors* to handle the basic styling properties of the icon font:

```
//Icon Font specific rule
[class^="icon-"], [class*=" icon-"] {
    font: {
        family: icon-font, Arial,
            "Helvetica Neue", Helvetica, sans-serif;
        weight: normal;
        style: normal;
        variant: normal;
    }
    text-transform: none;
    line-height: 1;
    speak: none;
    // Improve Font Rendering
    -webkit-font-smoothing: antialiased;
    -moz-osx-font-smoothing: grayscale;
}
```

 Notice the ^ and * characters in the attribute selectors. The first one means *select elements starting with the term* icon- and the second *select elements containing the term* icon-.

Then, we need to call the fontFace mixin in order to bring the font into the compiled CSS file:

```
@include fontFace(icon-font, '/fonts/icon-font');
```

The great thing about the fontFace mixin is that all we need to do is declare the font name and then the file path. There is no need to declare the file extension; that's taken care of by the mixin.

This will compile to:

```
@font-face {
    font-family: icon-font;
    font-weight: normal;
  font-style: normal;
  src: url("/fonts/icon-font") format("woff");
}
```

Here is the rule that makes the magic happen using `:before`:

```
.icon-headphones:before {
    content: "\e601";
    margin-right: 10px;
}
```

For basic styling enhancement, we create these other two rules. However, they are not required. The code is as follows:

```
.icon { font-size: 40px; }

a {
    padding: 5px;
    text-decoration: none;
    color: #2963BD;
    transition: .3s;
    &:hover { color: lighten(#2963BD,20); }
    &:focus { outline: 2px solid orange; }
}
```

The final compiled CSS looks like this:

```
[class^="icon-"], [class*=" icon-"] {
    font-family: icon-font, Arial, "Helvetica Neue",
    Helvetica, sans-serif;
    font-weight: normal;
    font-style: normal;
    font-variant: normal;
    text-transform: none;
    line-height: 1;
    speak: none;
    -webkit-font-smoothing: antialiased;
    -moz-osx-font-smoothing: grayscale;
}
@font-face {
    font-family: icon-font;
    font-weight: normal;
    font-style: normal;
    src: url("https://s3-us-west-
2.amazonaws.com/s.cdpn.io/9988/icon-font.woff") format("woff");
}

.icon-headphones:before {
    content: "\e601";
```

```scss
        margin-right: 10px;
    }
    .icon {
        font-size: 40px;
    }
    a {
        padding: 5px;
        text-decoration: none;
        color: #2963BD;
        -webkit-transition: .3s;
            transition: .3s;
    }
    a:hover {
        color: #6d9adf;
    }
    a:focus {
        outline: 2px solid orange;
    }
```

Here's a demo I created for this in CodePen: `http://codepen.io/ricardozea/pen/e62b201350efe7f59f91c934f9fc30fa`

Here's another demo I created in CodePen with the icon fonts a bit more advanced: `http://codepen.io/ricardozea/pen/5a16adffb6565312506c47ca3df69358`

Using an extra HTML element

To be honest, using an extra HTML element goes a little against the principle of separating content from styling, since adding an extra HTML element for styling reasons is not something some developers recommend. However, we can also argue that the icon itself really is content, not styling. Either way, here's the run down.

Here's the HTML snippet:

```html
<a href="#" title="Headphones"><i class="icon-headphones"
aria-hidden="true"></i>Headphones</a>
```

 In order to hide irrelevant content from screen readers, we use the `aria-hidden="true"` directive.

The SCSS code from the previous example is practically the same, except we move the `font-size: 10px;` declaration from the `.icon` class to the `a` rule and then delete the `.icon` class altogether. You will also see some extra properties but only for styling reasons.

The final SCSS looks like this:

```scss
//Web font mixin
@mixin fontFace($font-family, $file-path) {
    @font-face {
        font: {
        family: $font-family;
        weight: normal;
        style: normal;
        }
        src: url('#{$file-path}.woff') format('woff');
    }
}
//Icon Font specific rule
[class^="icon-"], [class*=" icon-"] {
    font: {
        family: icon-font, Arial, "Helvetica Neue",
          Helvetica, sans-serif;
        weight: normal;
        style: normal;
        variant: normal;
    }
    text-transform: none;
    line-height: 1;
    speak: none;
    // Improve Font Rendering
    -webkit-font-smoothing: antialiased;
    -moz-osx-font-smoothing: grayscale;
}
@include iconFont(icon-font, '/fonts/icon-font');
.icon-headphones:before {
    content: "\e601";
    margin-right: 10px;
}
a {
    font-size: 40px;
    //Styling stuff
    padding: 5px;
    text-decoration: none;
    color: #2963BD;
    transition: .3s;
    &:hover { color: lighten(#2963BD,20); }
    &:focus { outline: 2px solid orange; }
}
```

The compiled CSS looks like this:

```css
[class^="icon-"], [class*=" icon-"] {
    font-family: icon-font, Arial, "Helvetica Neue",
      Helvetica, sans-serif;
    font-weight: normal;
    font-style: normal;
    font-variant: normal;
    text-transform: none;
    line-height: 1;
    speak: none;
    -webkit-font-smoothing: antialiased;
    -moz-osx-font-smoothing: grayscale;
}

@font-face {
    font-family: icon-font;
    font-weight: normal;
    font-style: normal;
    src: url("https://s3-us-west-
2.amazonaws.com/s.cdpn.io/9988/icon-font.woff") format("woff");
}
.icon-headphones:before {
    content: "\e601";
    margin-right: 10px;
}

a {
    font-size: 40px;
    padding: 5px;
    text-decoration: none;
    color: #2963BD;
    -webkit-transition: .3s;
            transition: .3s;
}
a:hover {
    color: #6d9adf;
}
a:focus {
    outline: 2px solid orange;
}
```

Here's a demo I created for this in CodePen:

http://codepen.io/ricardozea/pen/8ca49cb06aeb070f4643f0a8e064126c.

Scalable Vector Graphics

SVG graphics have gained incredible popularity very quickly. Browser support is 100 percent, even Opera Mini supports SVG images. Let's discuss some pros and cons of SVG images:

The pros of SVGs:

- They can be created and edited with a text editor.
- They are 100 percent accessible.
- They can have multiple colors.
- They are SEO-friendly since they can be indexed.
- Since they are vectors, they maintain their quality on any screen density, screen size, or zoom level.
- They can be animated, even the elements inside the `<svg>` tag.
- The SVG spec is an actual, open standard developed by the W3C.
- It's arguably more semantic than using a font for graphics.
- Third-party online icon tools can also export to SVG in addition to icon font.
- Browser support is 100 percent available in modern browsers.

The cons of SVGs:

- An SVG sprite file can weigh more than its icon font counterpart.
- If legacy browser support is required (IE8 and below), an image fallback is required.
- Software that can save as SVG usually adds extra unnecessary markup in the final file, so we either have to remove it manually or use a third-party optimization tool to do it for us for every file. This in turn adds another layer of complexity to development workflow.
- Although SVGs are made with XML structure, it requires a pretty advanced level of understanding to perform edits in a text editor.

An SVG file is basically an XML-formatted file. This is what the markup of the headphones graphic looks like:

```
<svg xmlns="http://www.w3.org/2000/svg" width="32"
height="32" viewBox="0 0 32 32">
        <path id="left-ear-pad"
d="M9 18h-2v14h2c0.55 0 1-0.45 1-1v-12c0-0.55-0.45-1-1-1z"/>
    <path id="right-ear-pad"
d="M23 18c-0.55 0-1 0.45-1 1v12c0 0.6 0.5 1 1 1h2v-14h-2z"/>
```

```
        <path id="headband"
d="M32 16c0-8.837-7.163-16-16-16s-16 7.163-16 16c0 1.9 0.3 3.8 1
5.464-0.609 1.038-0.958 2.246-0.958 3.5 0 3.5 2.6 6.4 6 6.929v-
13.857c-0.997 0.143-1.927 0.495-2.742 1.012-0.168-0.835-0.258-
1.699-0.258-2.584 0-7.18 5.82-13 13-13s13 5.8 13 13c0 0.885-0.088
1.749-0.257 2.584-0.816-0.517-1.745-0.87-2.743-1.013v13.858c3.392-
0.485 6-3.402 6-6.929 0-1.29-0.349-2.498-0.958-3.536 0.62-1.705
0.958-3.545 0.958-5.465z"/>
</svg>
```

There are many ways to use SVG images: inline via the `<img>`, `<object>`, `<use>`, or `<svg>` tags; as background images with CSS; using Modernizr in conditional classes to address fallbacks; or with jQuery or plain JavaScript, using third-party services such as grumpicon.com, you name it.

To keep things simple, we're going to focus on two methods:

- Inline via the `<svg>` tag.
- File-based with the `<img>` tag.

Inline via the `<svg>` tag

Inlining SVGs is the go-to method of many web designers and developers. The fact that we can control individual parts of the SVG with CSS and JavaScript makes it very appealing for animations.

One of the drawbacks of inlining SVG markup is that the image is not cacheable. In other words, every time the image appears, the browser has to read the XML of the SVG. If you have too many SVGs on your page, these can potentially be detrimental to the page speed and eventually the user experience. So be careful of the objective of the page and the types of visitors using your website/app.

Here's an HTML snippet of the SVG of the headphones inlined in a link tag:

```
<a href="#">
    <svg xmlns="http://www.w3.org/2000/svg" width="32"
height="32" viewBox="0 0 32 32">
        <path id="left-ear-pad"
d="M9 18h-2v14h2c0.55 0 1-0.45 1-1v-12c0-0.55-0.45-1-1-1z" />
    <path id="right-ear-pad"
d="M23 18c-0.55 0-1 0.45-1 1v12c0 0.6 0.5 1 1 1h2v-14h-2z" />
        <path id="headband"
d="M32 16c0-8.837-7.163-16-16-16s-16 7.163-16 16c0 1.9 0.3 3.8 1
5.464-0.609 1.038-0.958 2.246-0.958 3.5 0 3.5 2.6 6.4 6 6.929v-
13.857c-0.997 0.143-1.927 0.495-2.742 1.012-0.168-0.835-0.258-
1.699-0.258-2.584 0-7.18 5.82-13 13-13s13 5.8 13 13c0 0.885-0.088
1.749-0.257 2.584-0.816-0.517-1.745-0.87-2.743-1.013v13.858c3.392-
```

```
0.485 6-3.402 6-6.929 0-1.29-0.349-2.498-0.958-3.536 0.62-1.705
0.958-3.545 0.958-5.465z"/>
    </svg>Headphones
</a>
```

To control its size, distance from the text, and appearance, we add the following CSS:

```
svg {
    width: 40px;
    height: 40px;
    margin-right: 10px;
    fill: #2963BD;
}
a {
    font-size: 40px;
    text-decoration: none;
    color:#2963BD;
}
```

> SVGs files called via the `<img>` tag *are not* affected by CSS. If you
> want to make any style changes to it, you have to either make them
> in the actual SVG file or place the SVG markup inline.

However, this markup has a problem. It doesn't provide a fallback for legacy browsers, specifically IE8 and below. Let's try to fix this.

Providing fallback images to legacy browsers for inline SVGs

There are two ways to provide fallback images to legacy browsers for inline SVGs.

Using the <foreignObject> and <img> tags

Create a `<foreignObject>` element inside the `<svg>` tag and include an `<img>` tag that calls the fallback image:

```
<a href="#">
    <svg xmlns="http://www.w3.org/2000/svg"
xmlns:xlink="http://www.w3.org/1999/xlink" version="1.1"
width="32" height="32" viewBox="0 0 32 32">
        <path
d="M9 18h-2v14h2c0.55 0 1-0.45 1-1v-12c0-0.55-0.45-1-1-1z"/>
        <path
d="M23 18c-0.55 0-1 0.45-1 1v12c0 0.6 0.5 1 1 1h2v-14h-2z"/>
        <path
d="M32 16c0-8.837-7.163-16-16-16s-16 7.163-16 16c0 1.9 0.3 3.8 1
```

```
5.464-0.609 1.038-0.958 2.246-0.958 3.5 0 3.5 2.6 6.4 6 6.929v-
13.857c-0.997 0.143-1.927 0.495-2.742 1.012-0.168-0.835-0.258-
1.699-0.258-2.584 0-7.18 5.82-13 13-13s13 5.8 13 13c0 0.885-0.088
1.749-0.257 2.584-0.816-0.517-1.745-0.87-2.743-1.013v13.858c3.392-
0.485 6-3.402 6-6.929 0-1.29-0.349-2.498-0.958-3.536 0.62-1.705
0.958-3.545 0.958-5.465z"/>
        <foreignObject>
            <img src="https://s3-us-west-2.amazonaws.com/s.cdpn.
io/9988/headphones.png" alt="Headphones">
        </foreignObject>
    </svg>Headphones
</a>
```

Using an <image> tag

As we all know, there's isn't an `<image>` tag... or is there? In the SVG world, there is! This solution is very similar to the first method. The two differences are that we do not use a `<foreignObject>` element and we use an `<image>` tag. This is all *inside* the `<svg>` tag:

```
<a href="#">
    <svg xmlns="http://www.w3.org/2000/svg" width="32"
height="32" viewBox="0 0 32 32">
        <path id="left-ear-pad"
d="M9 18h-2v14h2c0.55 0 1-0.45 1-1v-12c0-0.55-0.45-1-1-1z" />
        <path id="right-ear-pad"
d="M23 18c-0.55 0-1 0.45-1 1v12c0 0.6 0.5 1 1 1h2v-14h-2z" />
        <path id="headband"
d="M32 16c0-8.837-7.163-16-16-16s-16 7.163-16 16c0 1.9 0.3 3.8 1
5.464-0.609 1.038-0.958 2.246-0.958 3.5 0 3.5 2.6 6.4 6 6.929v-
13.857c-0.997 0.143-1.927 0.495-2.742 1.012-0.168-0.835-0.258-
1.699-0.258-2.584 0-7.18 5.82-13 13-13s13 5.8 13 13c0 0.885-0.088
1.749-0.257 2.584-0.816-0.517-1.745-0.87-2.743-1.013v13.858c3.392-
0.485 6-3.402 6-6.929 0-1.29-0.349-2.498-0.958-3.536 0.62-1.705
0.958-3.545 0.958-5.465z"/>
        <image src="https://s3-us-west-2.amazonaws.com/s.cdpn.io/9988/
headphones.png" xlink:href="" alt="Headphones">
    </svg>Headphones
</a>
```

Now, the reason this works is because we are combining a feature of SVGs and HTML into one element.

The SVG feature is that the `<image>` tag is a valid element within the SVG world. Now, as weird it sounds, all browsers see the `<image>` tag as an out-of-standards tag that resembles the `<img>` tag from HTML.

The HTML feature is that normally we use the `src` attribute to point to the asset's location. In the SVG world, assets are called with the `xlink:href` attribute. If we add a `src` attribute pointing to the asset and leave the `xlink:href` attribute empty, then legacy browsers will see the fallback image while modern ones won't because the `xlink:href` attribute is empty.

I recommend sticking with the second method; it's just more succinct and less hassle. Just remember that instead of `<img>`, we use `<image>`. Also, for the purpose of the book, I left the `xlink:href` attribute in the markup but this is optional. If it's empty, you can remove it altogether if you want.

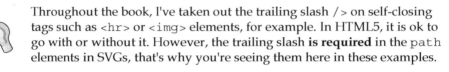

Throughout the book, I've taken out the trailing slash `/>` on self-closing tags such as `<hr>` or `<img>` elements, for example. In HTML5, it is ok to go with or without it. However, the trailing slash **is required** in the `path` elements in SVGs, that's why you're seeing them here in these examples.

None of these methods I just mentioned cause double download on browsers that support SVG. That's a win-win situation if you ask me.

File-based with the xlink:href and src attributes

SVG is a type of image file, so calling it within an `<img>` is perfectly valid:

```
<img src="images/headphones.svg" alt="Headphones">
```

We know that SVG has flawless support in modern browsers, but the prior image isn't displayed in legacy browsers (IE8 and below).

Remember the previous explanation about the `xlink:href` and `src` attributes in SVG and HTML? Well, we're going to do pretty much exactly the same we did there. However, instead of inlining the SVG markup, we're just going to link to an SVG file while providing a fallback image for old browsers.

This clever trick was created by Alexey Ten. Here's the markup:

```
<a href="#">
    <svg width="39" height="39">
        <image xlink:href="https://s3-us-west-
2.amazonaws.com/s.cdpn.io/9988/headphones.svg" src="https://s3-us-
west-2.amazonaws.com/s.cdpn.io/9988/headphones.png"
width="39" height="39">
    </svg>Headphones
</a>
```

There are issues here as well. Alexey's technique is not the offender, it is the browsers—specifically IE9, 10 and 11 as well as iOS 3 and 4. They download both the SVG and the fallback image.

If this double download is acceptable for you and you understand the consequences, go for it. Nonetheless, keep a mental note of where you can improve things like this for your next project.

Here's a demo I created for this in CodePen:

`http://codepen.io/ricardozea/pen/594e718f36976f8e77d4f9cf1640e29a`

Other sources to learn about SVG

We can't talk about SVGs without referencing three of the most noticeable names in the web design and development industry today: Amelia Bellamy-Royds, Sara Soueidan, and Chris Coyer. Amelia and Chris created one of the most complete guides about how to use SVG with fallbacks that I've read, *A Complete Guide to SVG Fallbacks* (`https://css-tricks.com/a-complete-guide-to-svg-fallbacks/`).

Sara Soueidan's blog is a must-read if you want to learn everything about SVG: `http://sarasoueidan.com/articles/`.

Summary

Here we are, looking at the horizon and thinking something along the lines of `srcset` or `<picture>`? Resize or art direction? `Retina.js` or Sass mixin? FitVids or FluidVids? Icon fonts or SVG? Inline SVG of file-based SVG? What's the best way to offer our visitors the best experience?

Yes, I know the feeling. And you know what? That's a good problem to have. Otherwise, we wouldn't be learning how to master RWD.

Since most of the time we're just resizing images, `srcset` is the way to go. Wrapping our videos in a container and a few lines of CSS make those videos responsive in no time. Boom! Too many videos to make responsive? No problem, `FitVids.js` makes it happen with a single jQuery function. Icon fonts weigh less than their big brother SVGs, but keep an eye on those server logs in case the icon font files aren't downloading. Using SVGs is always going to be a win, even if there are double downloads, but keep leveling up by using different techniques and sharing your findings and experiences with others.

Let's change gears and talk about a fascinating subject that can make or break your responsive design: typography.

Let's ride!

7
Meaningful Typography for Responsive Web Design

As I said in one of my talks at the Dayton Web Developers meeting:

> *"With a solid typographic scale you might even get away with not using a single image on your website."*

The power of typography has got to be one of the most underappreciated assets in web design. Admittedly, we are seeing more and more designs where typography has been strongly considered, playing a major role in creating the intended atmosphere of a website or app.

In this chapter, our focus is going to be on a few aspects, tips, and tricks about the things we need to consider for RWD from a typography stand point.

We're going to talk about:

- Pixels, ems or rems for typography?
- Calculating relative font sizes.
- Creating a Modular Scale for a harmonious typography.
- Using the Modular Scale for typography.
- Web fonts and how they affect RWD.
- Using `FitText.js` for fluid-size headings.
- Using `FlowType.js` to improve legibility.

Pixels, ems, or rems for typography?

It is difficult to decide whether to use pixels, ems, or rems for typography. It's a matter of style. Some web designers/developers still use pixels as their unit to declare font sizes. It's just a lot easier to wrap our heads around the sizes.

The issues with setting font sizes in pixels were basically on legacy IEs, where, if the user wanted to zoom in on the page for whatever reason, the text would stay fixed at the pixel size it was given.

Now, that's a thing of the past as far as modern browsers are concerned. When you zoom in any modern browser, if it's zoomed in enough, it will trigger the media queries, hence showing the mobile version of the site.

Another problem with pixel-based font sizing is that it's hard to scale and maintain. What this basically means is that we'd have to declare the font sizes of many more elements in every media query, over and over and over.

On the other hand, we have relative units, ems and rems, which are pretty much the recommended way of setting our font sizes.

However, the problem with ems is that we have to keep track (mentally, in CSS/ HTML comments, or in a text file somewhere) of the sizes of the parent containers, which can easily turn into a font management nightmare. A font size in ems depends on the font size of its parent container. So if we have different levels of nested containers, things could get ugly really fast because keeping track of the parent container's font sizes is not easy.

But then *rems* came along. Rem means *root em*. The *root* is the `<html>` element.

Rems bring pretty much the best of both worlds: we can declare font sizes in rems with the same mental model that we declare pixels, but with the benefit of using relative units like ems. The only problem with using rems is that legacy browsers don't support this unit, so a pixel-based, font size fallback value needs to be accounted for. This is where a short Sass mixin comes and saves the day.

But let's start with the core strategy of this chapter before trying any Sass tricks.

Calculating relative font sizes

Remember the RWD magic formula we mentioned in *Chapter 3, Mobile-first or Desktop-first?*:

(target ÷ context) x 100 = result %

There's also another similar magic formula to calculate relative font sizes (ems) when the font size has been set in pixels. The only difference is that we don't multiply by 100.

This is that formula:

target ÷ context = result

The *target* is the font size defined in pixels. The *context* is the font size defined in the parent container. The *result* is the value defined in ems.

Here's an example considering that the font size in the parent container, the body in this example, is 16px:

```
header {
    font: 30px Arial, "Helvetica Neue", Helvetica, sans-serif;
}
```

To calculate the relative font size, we use the following formula:

30px ÷ 16px = 1.875em.

So our CSS rule will look like this:

```
header {
    font: 1.875em Arial, "Helvetica Neue", Helvetica, sans-serif;
}
```

We would have to do this for every font size in our design.

This is fine in terms of understanding the math. However, the real value is in the thought process that goes into creating those pixel-based values in the first place. This is where the Modular Scale comes in.

Creating a Modular Scale for a harmonious typography

The Modular Scale was created by Tim Brown. There are different ways to create a Modular Scale for typography. In our example, we're going to create a Modular Scale using two base numbers and one ratio. The multiplication of these numbers creates a scale that's harmonious and proportional between all the values.

The most well-known ratio is the *golden ratio* also known as the *golden section*, *divine proportion*, and so on. Its value is *1.618*.

Now, to avoid unnecessary mathematics, the golden ratio is based on the Fibonacci sequence: 1, 1, 2, 3, 5, 8, 13, 21, and so on.

These numbers have the following pattern: the next number is the result of adding up the two numbers before it. For example:

$0 + \mathbf{1} = 1 + \mathbf{1} = 2 + \mathbf{1} = 3 + \mathbf{2} = 5 + \mathbf{3} = 8 + \mathbf{5} = 13 + \mathbf{8} = 21\ldots$

The idea here is to understand the intent of creating a set of numbers that are harmonious when used together. We are going to do the same to create a typographic scale to use in our projects with the Modular Scale web app and forget about *manually* calculating the relative font sizes for your project.

So let's check out the Modular Scale web app built by Tim Brown and Scott Kellum: `http://www.modularscale.com/`.

Once the web app opens, there are three steps we need to do in order to create our Modular Scale:

1. Define the first base number.
2. Define the second base number.
3. Choose a ratio.

The Modular Scale can be used in anything that uses a value of some sort, not only typography. It can be used for `padding`, `margin`, `line-height`, and so on. Our focus in this chapter is, however, on typography.

Defining the first base number

The recommended way to define this first number is to use the body text size, that is, the font size that is used in the paragraphs. But keep in mind that using the body text size as the first base number is not mandatory. We can use our typeface's x-height, or some other length within that typeface, that we think could be a good starting point.

Although we can choose any font size, let's start with the default one we all know all browsers use, 16px. So we type `16px` in the first base field.

Click on the plus icon and add a second base field.

Don't worry about the font size preview of the app yet, as you can see, as we type numbers for our base values, the font sizes on the right preview pane change. We'll get to that in the next step.

Defining the second base number

The second base field is what I call a *magic number* because this number is completely subjective and arbitrary, however, it's tightly related to the project we're working on.

When I say *tightly related* I mean something like using the width of the main container, for example, 960px, 980px, 1140px, and so on. Alternatively, it can also be the number of columns used in the grid, such as 12 or 16. It can also be the width of a column at the maximum width of the site, such as 60px, or even the gutter spacing, say 20px.

This *magic number* is anything we want it to be, but it's directly related to our project in one way or another. For this example, let's say we're going to target screens at a maximum width of 1280px, so our main container is going to have a maximum width of 1140px. So let's type `1140px` in the second base field.

Choosing a ratio

This is where the magic takes place. Choosing a ratio means that this ratio will be multiplied by the base numbers creating a scale of values that are proportionally related.

The ratios are based on musical scales, and in that list is the golden ratio (1.618) as well, if we decide to use it. From the **Ratios** dropdown, select **1:1.618 – golden section** ratio.

That's it! We have now created our first Modular Scale.

The font sizes provided by this Modular Scale are totally harmonious because they are proportionate to each other based on relevant values that are directly related to our project:

- The ideal body font size is 16px
- The maximum width of our main container is 1140px
- The Golden Ratio is 1.618

Our typography now has a solid modular foundation, let's use it.

Using the Modular Scale for typography

If you click on the **Table** view, all the text is now gone and we're left with a list of font sizes—ranging from ridiculously small values to just as ridiculously large values. But that's ok. That's the power of a modular scale.

This is what we see:

As you can see in the preceding image, there are three columns:

- The first column shows the font size in pixels.
- The second column shows the font size in ems.
- The third column shows the font size if the base was 16px.

What we need to do is focus on the first and second columns only. The highlighted row that says 16px, or 1em, is going to be the font size of our paragraphs. 16px is the default font size in most browsers.

Then, we define our header elements. Let's say we define only h1, h2 and h3. This means that we're going to select the rows above 16px that have larger font sizes:

- `<h1>`: **39.269px** that is 2.454em
- `<h2>`: **25.888px** that is 1.618em
- `<h3>`: **24.57px** that is 1.517em

For the `<small>` element, if we have any disclaimers on our site, we select the font size right below 16px:

`<small>`: **9.889px** that is 0.618em

That's it! All the numbers in this Modular Scale are harmonious and when used together will provide a clear visual hierarchy, and a relationship difficult to obtain through other methods.

Here's an example.

This is the HTML:

```
<h1>Meaningful Typography for RWD</h1>
<blockquote>
    <p>"With a solid typographic scale you might even get away
with not using a single image on your website."</p>
    <p>&mdash; Ricardo Zea</p>
</blockquote>
<h2>Creating a Modular Scale for a Harmonious Typography</h2>
<p>A Modular Scale is a combination of a ratio of two or more
numbers, and a base number.</p>
<h3>The Golden Ratio</h3>
<p>The most well-known ratio is the Golden Ratio also known as the
Golden Section, Divine Proportion, etc. It's value is 1.618.</p>
```

This is the SCSS:

```scss
//Mobile-first Media Query Mixin
@mixin forLargeScreens($media) {
    @media (min-width: $media/16+em) { @content; }
}
body {
    font:16px/1.4 Arial, "Helvetica Neue", Helvetica, sans-serif;
    @include forLargeScreens(640) {
        font-size: 20px;
    }
}
h1 { font-size: 2.454em; }
h2 { font-size: 1.618em; }
h3 { font-size: 1.517em; }
```

> Notice how I'm including the mobile-first Sass mixin as well.

Here's the compiled CSS:

```css
body {
    font: 16px/1.4 Arial, "Helvetica Neue", Helvetica, sans-serif;
}
@media (min-width: 40em) {
    body {
        font-size: 20px;
    }
}
h1 {
    font-size: 2.454em;
}
h2 {
    font-size: 1.618em;
}
h3 {
    font-size: 1.517em;
}
```

The Modular Scale looks like this on small screens (510px wide):

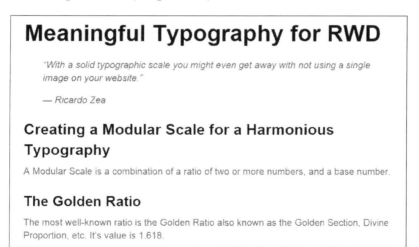

And like this on large screens (850px wide):

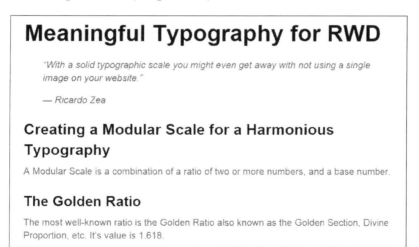

The only potential problem we have here is what I mentioned before about using ems: keeping track of the font size of the parent elements can turn into a font management nightmare.

Using pixels is a no-go because of its scalability issues in legacy browsers. Using rems, however, keeps things in the "relative font size" realm, while providing a pixel-based mentality but without the scalability problems. This allows us to support legacy browsers that do not support rems.

Here's a demo I created for this in CodePen:

http://codepen.io/ricardozea/pen/0b781bef63029bff6155c00ff3caed85

The rems-to-pixels Sass mixin

All we need is a Sass mixin that allows us to set the font values without a specific unit and the mixin takes care of adding the font sizes for both rem-based for modern browsers, and the pixel-based for legacy browsers.

This is the Sass mixin created by Chris Coyer:

```
//Pixels to Rems Mixin
@mixin fontSize($sizeValue: 1.6) {
    font-size: ($sizeValue * 10) + px;
    font-size: $sizeValue + rem;
}
```

 I made a small modification to the original name of the mixin from using dash-separated to camelCase. The reason I did this is because it's easier to spot the name of a mixin from a class name when scanning the document.

The usage is like this:

```
@include fontSize(2);
```

This example uses the same markup used in an earlier chapter, so I'm going to show you only the SCSS and some screenshots.

The SCSS is as follows:

```
//Mobile-first Media Query Mixin
@mixin forLargeScreens($media) {
    @media (min-width: $media/16+em) { @content; }
}
//Pixels to Rems Mixin
@mixin fontSize($sizeValue: 1.6) {
    font-size: ($sizeValue * 10) + px;
    font-size: $sizeValue + rem;
}
```

```
//Base-10 model
html { font-size: 62.5%;
    @include forLargeScreens(640) {
        font-size: 75%;
    }
}
h1 { @include fontSize(3.9269); }
h2 { @include fontSize(2.5888); }
h3 { @include fontSize(2.457); }
p { @include fontSize(1.6); }
```

Consider the following points:

- We're setting the root font size to 62.5 percent, which reduces the font size to 10px. This makes declaring the font values a lot easier. For example, a font size of 1.2rem is the same as 12px, .8rem is 8px, and so on.

- We need to move the decimal dot from the pixel-based values one spot to the left when declaring the font size in rems. For example, according to our Modular Scale the <h1> pixel size is 39.269px, so when declaring the font size in rems, we declare it as 3.9269, *without a unit*.

The compiled CSS is as follows:

```
html {
    font-size: 62.5%;
}
@media (min-width: 40em) {
    html {
        font-size: 75%;
    }
}
h1 {
    font-size: 39.269px;
    font-size: 3.9269rem;
}
h2 {
    font-size: 25.888px;
    font-size: 2.5888rem;
}
h3 {
    font-size: 24.57px;
    font-size: 2.457rem;
}
p {
    font-size: 16px;
    font-size: 1.6rem;
}
```

This is what the Modular Scale using the rems-to-pixels mixin looks like on small screens (510px wide):

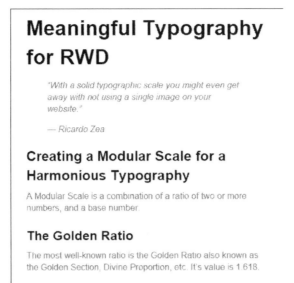

This is what it looks like on large screens (850px wide):

Meaningful Typography for RWD

"With a solid typographic scale you might even get away with not using a single image on your website."

—— Ricardo Zea

Creating a Modular Scale for a Harmonious Typography

A Modular Scale is a combination of a ratio of two or more numbers, and a base number.

The Golden Ratio

The most well-known ratio is the Golden Ratio also known as the Golden Section, Divine Proportion, etc. It's value is 1.618.

Here's a demo I created for this in CodePen:

`http://codepen.io/ricardozea/pen/8a95403db5b73c995443720475fdd900`

The examples we just saw are using the system font Arial. Let's go ahead and spruce these examples up with some web fonts to give them a bit more *character*.

Web fonts and how they affect RWD

Web fonts are almost mandatory to use nowadays, and I say *almost* because we need to be mindful of the implications they bring to our projects, and if necessary, we may actually not use them at all.

Before we get into the nitty gritty of how to work with web fonts, here are a few web font resources that may be helpful for many of you:

- **Font Squirrel** (`http://www.fontsquirrel.com/`): I've used this service extensively with great success. To use the fonts, you need to download the file(s) and then use with `@font-face` in your CSS. They have the best web font generator tool you'll ever find (`http://www.fontsquirrel.com/tools/webfont-generator`)

- **Google Fonts** (`https://www.google.com/fonts`): I can't talk about web font resources without mentioning Google Fonts. If I can't find it on Font Squirrel I come here, and vice versa. You can either download the font file(s) or use JavaScript. The fonts used in the following examples were downloaded from Google Fonts (`https://github.com/google/fonts/tree/master/ofl/oswald`).

- **Adobe Edge Web Fonts** (`https://edgewebfonts.adobe.com/`): This is also a great tool. This service is powered by TypeKit (the first web font service). I've used TypeKit extensively as well. You can't download the fonts though, you have to use JavaScript instead.

Now, let's see the pros and cons of using web fonts:

The advantages are:

- They help accentuate the brand and create consistency across different media.
- When used correctly, they make designs look more appealing.
- There is no need to use image replacement techniques anymore.
- This keeps the text as HTML making the content more accessible and *indexable*.

- Legacy browsers support web fonts.

- Great resources for free fonts.

- All these in turn help keep the markup cleaner.

The disadvantages are:

- They slow down the website/app due to HTTP requests or their dependency on third-party servers.

- Not all web fonts are legible at small and/or large sizes.

- If legacy browsers are required to support, there are more files to manage.

- Licensing the use of a font requires some sort of payment: monthly, per font family, per font style, and so on.

- Some free fonts are not well built.

- There are rendering side effects:

    ○ **Flash Of Unstyled Text (FOUT)**: On modern browsers, when the page loads, the text is first rendered on the screen with a system font, and then a second later it's swapped and styled with the web font.

    ○ **Flash Of Invisible Text (FOIT)**: On legacy browsers, when the page loads, the text is not visible but a second later it's rendered with the web font.

There are others not worth getting into, such as **Flash Of Fallback Text** and **Flash Of Faux Text (FOFT)**.

How to tackle all the "flash-of-whatever-texts" is not part of the scope of this section. However, I encourage you to read about Font Load Events in Zach Leatherman's article on the Opera blog called *Better @font-face with Font Load Events* (https://dev.opera.com/articles/better-font-face/).

Sass mixin for implementing web fonts

To implement web fonts, we need to use the @font-face directive in our CSS… well, SCSS.

The @font-face declaration block looks like this in its vanilla CSS form:

```
@font-face {
    font-family: fontName;
    src: url('path/to/font.eot'); /*IE9 Compat Modes*/
    src: url('path/to/font.eot?#iefix')
format('embedded-opentype'), /*IE6-IE8 */
```

```
        url('path/to/font.woff') format('woff'),
/*Modern Browsers*/
        url('path/to/font.ttf') format('truetype'),
/*Safari, Android, iOS*/
        url('path/to/font.svg#fontName') format('svg');
/*iOS devices*/
    font-weight: normal;
    font-style: normal;
}
```

Now, if you're using more than one style or font family, you need to repeat the whole @font-face declaration block for each font file. This is not very DRY (Don't Repeat Yourself).

 Web fonts are expensive in terms of file size and server requests, so please use web fonts moderately. The more you use, the slower your website/web app will become.

Yes that's a pretty hefty piece of CSS to handle web fonts, oh man.

To keep our sanity, let's turn the prior @font-face CSS declaration block to a Sass mixin:

```
@mixin fontFace($font-family, $file-path) {
    @font-face {
        font: {
            family: $font-family;
            weight: normal;
            style: normal;
        }
        //IE9 Compat Modes
        src: url('#{$file-path}.eot');
        //IE6-IE8
        src: url('#{$file-path}.eot?#iefix')
format('embedded-opentype'),
        //Modern Browsers
        url('#{$file-path}.woff') format('woff'),
        //Safari, Android, iOS
        url('#{$file-path}.ttf') format('truetype'),
        //Safari, Android, iOS
        url('#{$file-path}.svg') format('svg');
    }
}
```

The usage is a single line of code to call the font file. Let's use the typeface Oswald:

```
@include fontFace(oswald-light, '../fonts/oswald-light');
```

Using it on any element is a matter of adding the font name at the beginning of the font stack, as shown here:

```
p { font: 2.2rem oswald-bold, Arial, "Helvetica Neue",
Helvetica, sans-serif; }
```

If we need to include more than one font file, just add another line calling the mixin but specifying the other font name:

```
@include fontFace(oswald-light, '../fonts/oswald-light');
@include fontFace(oswald-regular, '../fonts/oswald-regular');
```

The preceding two lines of code will compile to the following CSS:

```
@font-face {
    font-family: oswald-light;
    font-weight: normal;
    font-style: normal;
    src: url("../fonts/oswald-light.eot");
    src: url("../fonts/oswald-light.eot?#iefix")
format("embedded-opentype"), url("../fonts/oswald-light.woff")
format("woff"), url("../fonts/oswald-light.ttf")
format("truetype"), url("../fonts/oswald-light.svg")
format("svg");
}
@font-face {
    font-family: oswald-regular;
    font-weight: normal;
    font-style: normal;
    src: url("../fonts/oswald-regular.eot");
    src: url("../fonts/oswald-regular.eot?#iefix")
format("embedded-opentype"), url("../fonts/oswald-regular.woff")
format("woff"), url("../fonts/oswald-regular.ttf")
format("truetype"), url("../fonts/oswald-regular.svg")
format("svg");
}
```

That's a pretty nifty way of creating all that CSS with a mere two lines of code, eh? However, if we want to make things right, let's analyze what we're doing here:

- We're supporting legacy browsers:
    - IE8 and below with a `.eot` font.
    - Old Safari on Android in iOS with a `.ttf` font.
    - Old iOS for the, practically forgotten, iPhone 3 and below with a `.svg` file.

- Modern browsers only need a .woff font. According to CanIUse.com, .woff font files are 99 percent supported, with the exception of Opera Mini at the time of writing this book (http://caniuse.com/#search=woff).

So the question is: Can we gracefully degrade the experience for legacy browsers and OS's and let them use a system font instead?

Sure we can!

After optimizing the mixin to use only .woff fonts, this is what it looks like:

```
@mixin fontFace($font-family, $file-path) {
    @font-face {
        font: {
            family: $font-family;
            weight: normal;
            style: normal;
        }
      //Modern Browsers
        src: url('#{$file-path}.woff') format('woff');
    }
}
```

The usage is exactly the same:

```
@include fontFace(oswald-light, '../fonts/oswald-light');
@include fontFace(oswald-regular, '../fonts/oswald-regular');
```

The compiled CSS is much shorter:

```
@font-face {
    font-family: oswald-light;
    font-weight: normal;
    font-style: normal;
    src: url("../fonts/oswald-light.woff") format("woff");
}
@font-face {
    font-family: oswald-regular;
    font-weight: normal;
    font-style: normal;
    src: url("../fonts/oswald-regular.woff") format("woff");
}
```

Using it on a couple of elements looks like this:

```
h1 { font: 4.1rem oswald-regular, Arial, "Helvetica Neue",
Helvetica, sans-serif; }
p { font: 2.4rem oswald-light, Arial, "Helvetica Neue", Helvetica,
sans-serif; }
```

Serving only the .woff font puts a lot less file management on our plate, which helps free our brains from unnecessary tasks and allow us to focus on what matters most: building a memorable experience. Not to mention, it makes our CSS code more streamlined and scalable.

But wait, we're letting legacy browsers gracefully degrade to system fonts, and we still need to define the font sizes in pixels for them!

Pixels-to-rems Sass mixin to the rescue!

Remember to see the base-10 model in the <html> tag for easier calculations:

```
//Base-10 model
html { font-size: 62.5%; }
```

Then let's declare the font sizes and font families:

```
h1 {
    @include fontSize(4.1);
    font-family: oswald-regular, Arial, "Helvetica Neue",
Helvetica, sans-serif;
}
p {
    @include fontSize(2.4);
    font-family: oswald-light, Arial, "Helvetica Neue",
Helvetica, sans-serif;
}
```

The compiled CSS looks to this:

```
h1 {
    font-size: 41px;
    font-size: 4.1rem;
    font-family: oswald-regular, Arial, "Helvetica Neue",
Helvetica, sans-serif;
}

p {
    font-size: 24px;
    font-size: 2.4rem;
    font-family: oswald-light, Arial, "Helvetica Neue",
Helvetica, sans-serif;
}
```

We're declaring two separate font sizes in the same rule, therefore we can't use the font shorthand in this case.

Thus, by harnessing the superpowers of two simple Sass mixins, we can easily embed web fonts and use rems for our font-sizes while providing pixel-based font sizes for legacy browsers.

This is a great example of robust scalability.

Here's a demo I created for this in CodePen:

`http://codepen.io/ricardozea/pen/9c93240a3404f12ffad83fa88f14d6ef`

Without losing any momentum, let's change gears and talk about how to improve the legibility of our pages by accomplishing a minimum line length with the awesome FlowType.js jQuery plugin by Simple Focus.

Using FlowType.js for increased legibility

One of the most compelling editorial principles states that the ideal line length for the most legible typography is between 45 and 75 characters.

That's a pretty decent range if you ask me. However, actually making your paragraphs long enough, or short enough for that matter, is like a "blind leading the blind" game. How can we tell whether the combination of the width of a container and its font size actually meet the 45 to 75 characters recommendation? Also, on small or medium screens, how can you tell this is the case?

Tricky one, eh?

Well, no need to worry because with FlowType.js, we can address these issues.

You can download the plugin from `http://simplefocus.com/flowtype/`.

The first thing we need is the HTML, so here's the markup we're going to use:

```
<!DOCTYPE html>
<!--[if IE 8]> <html class="no-js ie8" lang="en"> <![endif]-->
<!--[if IE 9]> <html class="no-js ie9" lang="en"> <![endif]-->
<!--[if gt IE 9]><!--><html class="no-js" lang="en">
<!--<![endif]-->
<head>
    <meta charset="utf-8">
```

```
    <meta name="viewport" content="width=device-width,
        initial-scale=1">
    <meta http-equiv="X-UA-Compatible" content="IE=edge">
    <title>Meaningful Typography for RWD</title>
    <script src="//code.jquery.com/jquery-latest.min.js"></script>
    <script src="js/flowtype.js"></script>
</head>
<body>
    <main class="main-ctnr" role="main">
        <h1>Meaningful Typography for RWD</h1>
        <blockquote>
            <p>"With a solid typographic scale you might even get
away with not using a single image on your website."</p>
            <p>&mdash; Ricardo Zea</p>
        </blockquote>
        <p>One of the most compelling editorial principles states
that the ideal line length for the most legible typography is between
45 and 75 characters.</p>
    </main>
</body>
</html>
```

Once you get comfortable with FlowType.js, you might actually start thinking, "If FlowType automatically modifies the font size at pretty much any viewport width, I don't think I need to declare any font sizes in my SCSS! After all, they are going to get overwritten by FlowType."

Well, we do need to set the font size regardless, because if FlowType.js doesn't load, we'd be left at the mercy of the browser's default styles, and we designers do not want that.

With that being said, here's the SCSS to declare the necessary font sizes:

```
//Pixels to Rems Mixin
@mixin font-size($sizeValue: 1.6) {
    font-size: ($sizeValue * 10) + px;
    font-size: $sizeValue + rem;
}
//Base-10 model
html { font-size: 62.5%; }
h1 { @include fontSize(3.9269); }
p { @include fontSize(1.6); }
```

This will compile to the following CSS:

```css
html {
    font-size: 62.5%;
}
h1 {
    font-size: 39.269px;
    font-size: 3.9269rem;
}
p {
    font-size: 16px;
    font-size: 1.6rem;
}
```

This is where the magic happens. We create a jQuery function where we can specify which element(s) to target. This function can be placed either inside a separate JavaScript file or within the markup.

In our example we're telling FlowType.js to apply the resizing of the font to the `<html>` element. Since we're using relative font size units, rems, all the text will automatically resize/adjust at any screen width, maintaining the ideal line length.

Here's the jQuery function:

```javascript
$(function() {
    $("html").flowtype();
});
```

Defining thresholds

There's a potential problem with the solution we just saw: FlowType.js will modify the font size of the paragraphs indefinitely. In other words, on small screens the text will be extremely small and on large screens it will be way too big.

We can solve this issue with two separate threshold approaches or a combination of both.

Now, one thing we need to make clear is that this part will require some tweaking and adjusting in order to get the best results, there aren't specific values that will work for all situations.

We are going to use the following approach:

- Define the minimum and maximum widths of the container or element.
- Define the minimum and maximum font sizes of the container or element.

Threshold widths

Defining the minimum and maximum widths will tell FlowType.js at which points it should stop resizing.

Let's define the width thresholds:

```
$(function() {
    $("html").flowtype({
      //Max width at which script stops enlarging
        maximum: 980,
      //Min width at which script stops decreasing
      minimum: 320
   });
});
```

> The thresholds I selected work specifically for this example and it may not necessarily work for other situations. Tweak and test until you get the ideal widths that work with the recommended 45-75 characters per line recommendation.

Threshold font sizes

Just like with the width thresholds, defining the minimum and maximum font sizes will tell FlowType.js what the smallest and largest font sizes it should scale the text to.

We're also going to declare our own font size using the `fontRatio` variable; the higher the number, the smaller the font, and the lower the number, the larger the font. If this feels counterintuitive, look at it this way: the higher the number, the higher the compression (thus making it small) and the lower the number, the lower the compression (thus making it large).

Adjusting the `fontRatio` value is an *eyeballing* exercise, so tweak and test like there's no tomorrow.

Let's take a look at the font sizes values:

```
$(function() {
  $("html").flowtype({
      //Max width at which script stops enlarging
      maximum: 980,
      //Min width at which script stops decreasing
      minimum: 320,
      //Max font size
      maxFont : 18,
      //Min font size
```

```
    minFont : 8,
    //Define own font-size
    fontRatio : 58
  });
});
```

> There's no need to include a comma after the last value in the list.

FlowType.js just plain rocks man!

Here's a demo I created for this in CodePen:

`http://codepen.io/ricardozea/pen/c2e6abf545dbaa82a16ae84718c79d34`

Summary

So here we are, levelled up in typography for RWD. Is there more about typography? You bet! This amazing subject is a whole industry in itself, without it we wouldn't be reading this book.

We can now say that we understand why using relative units for typography is a good approach: scalability. Also, using our little magic formula, we can calculate relative font sizes for each of our text elements in our design, but why go through all that trouble? Modular Scale for typography saves the day in that regard, and it injects our projects with awesome typographic harmony. Who knows, maybe we may not need to use images at all!

Brands can now be extended to the web via web fonts, but we need to be careful and consider the impact of using them on our sites/apps. Also, as far as modern browsers go, we only need to use a single file type (WOFF font files), which make things a lot easier to manage—for browsers to download and for users to enjoy.

FlowType.js enhances our headers and body text while maintaining a good level of legibility.

Now, an important part of RWD is (believe it or not) doing things like we did many, many years ago. In the next chapter, we're going to keep things simple and we're going to talk about RWD in e-mail.

Time to go back in time!

8
Responsive E-mails

Here we are, after traveling back in time. Think of the late 90s and designing with tables; oh yes, you read right, designing with tables.

Today, things are not any different when it comes to creating e-mails: we have to use tables for layout. Why? It's simple. There aren't any wars. E-mail client wars, that is.

Unlike the browser wars of 1995, where Netscape and Internet Explorer battled for market supremacy, e-mail clients have been living their own separate lives practically oblivious to each other since anyone can remember.

Thanks to the browser wars, we now have such awesome standard-compliant browsers that are full of features, customization capabilities, constant updates, and so on, making everyone's online life a bit easier.

E-mail clients, on the other hand, evolve at their own pace and that pace is slow because there really isn't any competition. Moreover, the vast majority of corporations are already locked in with Microsoft's Outlook. In the more recent versions of Office, Outlook has actually become worse than its earlier counterparts, thus not really helping the e-mail landscape improve in support of more modern technologies.

To top this off, there are e-mail clients that are relatively new and radically reject support for the `<style>` element or even media queries altogether.

But e-mail is an incredibly efficient and formidable marketing tool that—regardless of the level of technology—we need to be prepared to work with soon or later.

In other words, e-mail as a medium of communication is not going anywhere any time soon, and we as web designers/developers have to design e-mails with tables and inline styles.

But don't worry, I will show you that with the basic principles of RWD, a little bit of common sense using progressive enhancement, and by always trying to keep things simple, designing and implementing responsive e-mails is not difficult and can be fun.

In this chapter, we're going to talk about the following topics:

- Why do we need to worry about responsive e-mails?
- Don't overlook your analytics.
- Things to consider for responsive e-mails.
- Responsive e-mail build.
- Third-party services.

Why do we need to worry about responsive e-mails?

The main reason we need to worry about responsive e-mails is simple: about 65 percent of e-mails are opened on mobile devices (smartphones and tablets). The remaining 35 percent of e-mails are opened on desktop. Additionally, responsive e-mails have more engagement than nonresponsive ones.

In addition to this, e-mails opened in desktop have more engagement than e-mails opened on mobile devices.

Check out the following articles:

- *Nearly 65% of e-mails in the U.S. are opened on mobile devices*: https://www.internetretailer.com/2014/01/23/nearly-65-e-mails-us-are-opened-mobile-devices
- *65% of marketing e-mails were opened on a mobile device last quarter; Android tablet use doubles*: http://www.phonearena.com/news/65-of-marketing-emails-were-opened-on-a-mobile-device-last-quarter-Android-tablet-use-doubles_id51864

 The term *engagement* means that the user clicks/taps. So, *more engagement* simply means *more clicks/taps*.

Don't overlook your analytics

Before starting to push pixels, nest tables, and style elements, it's absolutely imperative that we look at the analytics and have a bird's eye view of the landscape we're going to create e-mails for.

Doing this will allow us to understand:

- When are our e-mails being opened.
- Which days have more opens.
- Which hours have more opens.
- Whether the season is causing more/less openings.
- Which devices are being used to open our e-mails.
- What e-mail clients are being most used/less used.

If, for example, the analytics have data stating that Outlook 2013 is rarely used (wouldn't that be awesome), then we may not need to worry about this e-mail client at all.

If the Yahoo Mail app in Android is the most commonly used application and platform, then we can safely use more advanced CSS properties and progressively enhance, knowing that our ideas will display correctly.

Doing market share research is important, but your own analytics are ultimately the ones that will dictate how you're going to approach your e-mail development strategy.

Recommendations for building better responsive e-mails

Although some e-mail clients are getting better at rendering e-mails, there are other e-mail clients that are not really as good as they should be. This means that we need to build something basic and progressively enhance it for better e-mail clients.

There are a few guidelines that are important to consider when building responsive e-mails:

- **Define the e-mail client with the least CSS and HTML support**: Knowing which e-mail client has the least HTML and CSS support will save us unnecessary headaches and time during testing. Again, this is where analytics are crucial.

- **Use progressive enhancement**: First, design and build for the e-mail client that has the least CSS and HTML support. Then, we enhance the design and experience using that core base.

- **Stay within a width of 550px to 600px**: This is very important because most e-mail clients have very narrow preview panes. Moreover, 600px or less will look good on desktop clients and web browsers, and the e-mail will remain readable when scaled down or turned responsive on small screens.

- **Use tables for layout**: Most e-mail clients have nowhere near the same support for HTML and CSS as web browsers, so building layouts with tables is still the way to create e-mails.

- **Inline CSS**: Many e-mail clients remove the `<head>` section of the e-mail, thus anything we put there will be stripped out. So, we need to inline the CSS in order to achieve the necessary styling.

- **Use system fonts**: Although using web fonts is technically possible, it's best to stick to system fonts so the e-mails look as similar as possible across different devices and different e-mail clients. However, if you do decide to use web fonts, go for it and always use them as part of the progressive enhancement process.

- **Provide a fallback color for background images**: Using background images isn't really that difficult. Outlook is the only client that requires special markup (Conditional Comments) to make it work. However, always provide a fallback background color in case the image doesn't load.

- **Always use the alt attribute on images**: If images do not load or load too slowly, the e-mail client will show the alternate text. Make sure you put something descriptive in the `alt` attribute as well. Instead of *Logo*, something like *Company Logo - Tagline* would be ideal.

- **No need to do mobile-first**: Because we're doing progressive enhancement, we are starting with the e-mail client with the least support for HTML and CSS. Hence, this e-mail client very likely doesn't support media queries or the `viewport` meta tag. So a mobile-first approach may not be necessarily the best option, at least yet.

- **Use the HTML5 DOCTYPE**: We could certainly use the old HTML4 DOCTYPE, but we can use the HTML5 DOCTYPE as well which is always a good measure.

- **Avoid using HTML5 elements**: Although we can use the HTML5 DOCTYPE, support for HTML5 elements is practically nonexistent. So avoid using HTML5 elements in e-mails.

- **Keep it simple**: Most e-mails have a very short lifespan, so making an intricate layout is not really necessary. Create a simple, one-column layout and this will save us a lot of headaches. Focus strongly on the design itself. This is where a solid typographic Modular Scale can work wonders.

Responsive e-mail build

Defining the features of the e-mail is also part of the *build*, so let's define those:

1. Create a Modular Scale for typography.
2. Create two designs to help visualize the e-mail beforehand: one for large screens and one for small screens.
3. The e-mail will have a maximum width of 600px and minimum width of 320px.
4. Use progressive enhancement.

Modular Scale for typography

To build our Modular Scale, we're going to use the following values:

- **Base one** (16px): Which is our base font size.
- **Base two** (600px): Which is the maximum width of our e-mail.
- **Ratio** (1.618): The Golden ratio.

This Modular Scale can be found at

`http://www.modularscale.com/?16,600&px&1.618&web&table.`

Design – large and small screen views

The following designs will help get a better picture of the e-mail on large and small screens. This is how it looks at 600px wide:

This is how the e-mail looks at its smallest size, 320px wide:

Let's get right down to business and build a responsive e-mail.

Setting up a basic HTML template

Let's start with the most basic template. Then, we're going to add to it the different things we need to have a sound template.

Here's the first take on the HTML with a few initial elements in the `<head>` section:

- Define the language of our document with the `lang` attribute, English in our case.

- Since our design has a colored background, we need to give the `<html>` and `<body>` elements a height of 100 percent. This makes both elements stretch to the full height of the viewport. Otherwise, the background will end where the bottom of the e-mail is and then the page will show a white background.

- Add a `<title>` tag.

- Add the following meta tags:
  - Character set UTF-8
  - Viewport
  - Make Internet Explorer use the latest rendering engine possible
  - Remove the autostyling of phone numbers in OSX/iOS

- Who says we can't use the web fonts? Only a handful of e-mail clients support them, those that don't will just fallback to a system font in our font stack, very likely Arial or Helvetica. Let's use Roboto.

Here's the HTML:

```
<!DOCTYPE html>
<html lang="en" style="height: 100%;">
<head>
    <title>Mastering RWD with HTML5 and CSS3</title>
    <meta charset="utf-8">
    <!-- Responsive: Tell browsers that this template is optimized
for small screens -->
    <meta name="viewport" content="width=device-width,
     initial-scale=1.0">
    <!-- IE: Make IE use its best rendering engine rather than
Compatibility View mode -->
    <meta http-equiv="X-UA-Compatible" content="IE=edge">
    <!-- OSX/iOS: Remove auto styling of phone numbers -->
    <meta name="format-detection" content="telephone=no">
    <!-- Webfont from Google Fonts -->
    <link
href='http://fonts.googleapis.com/css?family=Roboto:300,500'
rel='stylesheet'>
</head>
<body style="height: 100%;">

</body>
</html>
```

Using CSS reset to normalize display

Let's add the necessary CSS reset styles that will help keep a relatively uniform display across as many e-mail clients as possible.

The following list outlines what exactly we'll *reset* (also called *normalizing*) across several e-mail clients:

- **Outlook (all versions)**:
  - ° Force it to provide a View in browser link.
  - ° Make it maintain any custom line heights defined.
  - ° Remove spaces on left- and right-hand side of `<table>` elements.
  - ° Fix the padding issues.

- **OSX/iOS/Windows Mobile**:
  - ° Fix automatic increase of font size to 13px when fonts are small.

- **Yahoo**:
  - ° Fix the paragraph issues.

- **IE**:
  - ° Fix the resized images issue.

- **Hotmail/Outlook.com**:
  - ° Make it display e-mails at full width.
  - ° Force it to display normal line spacing.

- **All e-mail clients**:
  - ° Remove the border around linked images.

Here's the embedded CSS:

```
<!DOCTYPE html>
<html lang="en" style="height: 100%;">
<head>
    <title>Mastering RWD with HTML5 and CSS3</title>
    <meta charset="utf-8">
    <!-- Responsive: Tell browsers that this template is optimized
for small screens -->
    <meta name="viewport" content="width=device-width,
      initial-scale=1.0">
    <!-- IE: Make IE use its best rendering engine rather than
Compatibility View mode -->
```

```html
<meta http-equiv="X-UA-Compatible" content="IE=edge">
<!-- OSX/iOS: Remove auto styling of phone numbers -->
<meta name="format-detection" content="telephone=no">
<!-- Webfont from Google Fonts -->
<link
href='http://fonts.googleapis.com/css?family=Roboto:300,500'
rel='stylesheet'>
<style>
    /*Force Outlook to provide a "View in Browser" link.*/
    #outlook a { padding: 0; }
    body {
        width: 100% !important;
        margin: 0;
        padding: 0;
        /*Outlook: Make Outlook maintain any custom line heights
defined.*/
        mso-line-height-rule: exactly;
        /*OSX/iOS/Windows Mobile: Fix automatic increasing of font
size to 13px when fonts are small.*/
        -webkit-text-size-adjust: 100%;
        -ms-text-size-adjust: 100%;
    }
    /*Yahoo: Fix paragraph issue*/
    p { margin: 1em 0; }
    /*Outlook: Remove spaces on left and right side of a table
elements.*/
    table {
        mso-table-lspace:0pt;
        mso-table-rspace:0pt;
    }
    /*Outlook 07, 10: Fix padding issue.*/
    table td { border-collapse: collapse; }
    img {
        outline: none;
        text-decoration: none;
        /*IE: Make resized images look fine.*/
        -ms-interpolation-mode: bicubic;
    }
    /*Remove border around linked images.*/
    a img { border: none; }
    /*Prevent Webkit and Windows Mobile platforms from changing
default font sizes, while not breaking desktop design.*/
    /*Force Hotmail to display e-mails at full width.*/
    .ExternalClass{ width:100%; }
    /*Force Hotmail to display normal line spacing.*/
```

```
            .ExternalClass,
            .ExternalClass p,
            .ExternalClass span,
            .ExternalClass font,
            .ExternalClass td,
            .ExternalClass div {
                line-height: 100%;
            }
        </style>
    </head>
    <body style="height: 100%;">

    </body>
</html>
```

With this basic template in place, let's start adding the content.

Adding the e-mail content

Building e-mails is pretty much a *you gotta do what you gotta do!* mentality. In other words, we do whatever we have to do to make things display as we want them to. Sometimes, we have to use nonbreaking spaces ( ) to separate things out, use the <br> tags to make things go to the next line, even use several <br> tags to create spaces between elements.

However, this does not mean that we're just going to throw all the good things we've learned out the window, no way.

Let's keep things as clean and lean as possible, nesting where necessary, and adding the necessary styles where required.

> To optimize space and help focus on the important parts, we're going to work with the markup inside the <body> tag only.

Creating a 100 percent wide wrapping table

This is our outermost table container and it's always a good practice to have one. This table will allow us to handle any padding we want or need in our design, because adding padding on the <body> tag may not be a reliable approach.

We can also use this outer table to add a background color if our design has one. We're going to give this outer table a width and height of 100 percent.

We're also adding 20px padding in the cells; this will give the whole e-mail a bit of room to *breathe*, because it won't be touching the top and bottom edges of the viewport/panel it's going to be seen in. The code is as follows:

```
<body style="height: 100%;">
    <table width="100%" height="100%" cellpadding="20"
cellspacing="0" border="0" bgcolor="#efefef"
class="outer-container-table">
        <tr>
            <td align="center"> </td>
        </tr>
    </table>
</body>
```

 I'm adding classes to some elements in the e-mail that I may not necessarily use right away. I'm adding them anyway in case in the future something changes, I already have those classes in place and can edit faster.

Creating the 600px inner table

We're declaring the width of this inner table with the HTML attribute `width`, rather than a width within an inline style. We're also adding a white background to this table so that our content sits over it and blocks the light gray background from the wide container.

The 1px border can be added using the border shorthand. Some say don't use CSS shorthands in e-mails! However, after testing several e-mail clients, the shorthand works just fine.

Adding a 10px margin at the top will help give the e-mail a bit more room. The code is as follows:

```
<body style="height: 100%;">
    <table width="100%" height="100%" cellpadding="20"
cellspacing="0" border="0" bgcolor="#efefef"
class="outer-container-table">
        <tr>
            <td align="center">
                <table width="600" cellpadding="0" cellspacing="0"
border="0" bgcolor="white" align="center"
class="inner-container-table" style="margin-top: 10px; border:
#999999 1px solid;">
                    <tr>
                        <td></td>
                    </tr>
```

```
                        </table>
                    </td>
                </tr>
            </table>
        </body>
```

Notice how I used the term *white* for the background color on the `.inner-container-table`? That's because I want to show you that you can also use HTML color names instead of hexadecimal values. All e-mail clients support this feature. It's also more descriptive.

There are plenty of resources out in the open Web listing all the HTML color names, but I like this one in particular because it groups the color names by categories. So, it is easier to use in a design: `http://html-color-codes.info/color-names/`.

Adding the header image

Inside the empty `<td>` element all we need to do is add the `<img>` tag that calls the header image.

Images are `inline-block` elements by default. In order to avoid unwanted behavior, make sure the image has `display: block;` and `width: 100%;` elements as shown here:

```
<body style="height: 100%;">
    <table width="100%" cellpadding="0" cellspacing="20" border="0"
bgcolor="#efefef" style="height: 100%;" class="outer-container-table">
        <tr>
            <td align="center">
                <table width="580" cellpadding="0" cellspacing="0"
border="0" bgcolor="white" align="center"
class="inner-container-table" style="margin-top: 10px; border:
#999999 1px solid;">
                    <tr>
                        <td>
                            <img
src="https://s3-us-west-2.amazonaws.com/s.cdpn.io/9988/header-email-
devices.png" alt="Mastering RWD with HTML and CSS3" style="display:
block; width: 100%;">
                        </td>
                    </tr>
                </table>
            </td>
        </tr>
    </table>
</body>
```

Creating the content wrapping table and all its content

This is where most of the magic happens because we are now creating the body of the e-mail, including the footer. A few things to note:

- The width of the first table is 88 percent. I did this to show you that you can be arbitrary if you want to. Moreover, you don't have to use pixels every time and you can also use other values different than 100 percent when using percentages.

- In some parts, I'm liberally using the `<br>` tags. This is because the spacing between some elements is where I wanted them to be. Under other circumstances, this would be a pretty bad practice; in e-mail, doing this is quite useful and very common.

- We're going to use three rows: one for the main header, one for the body, and one for the **Call to Action** (CTA) button. Doing this will allow us to handle each section independently, without having to worry about affecting the other two when debugging or styling.

- The footer will be separated from the main content structure, so we can handle the background image easily.

The markup is as follows:

```
<body style="height: 100%;">
    <table width="100%" height="100%" cellpadding="20"
cellspacing="0" border="0" bgcolor="#efefef"
class="outer-container-table">
        <tr>
            <td align="center">
                <table width="600" cellpadding="0" cellspacing="0"
border="0" bgcolor="  white" align="center"
class="inner-container-table" style="margin-top: 10px; border:
#999999 1px solid;">
                    <tr>
                        <td>
                            <img
src="https://s3-us-west-2.amazonaws.com/s.cdpn.io/9988/header-
email-devices.png" alt="Mastering RWD with HTML and CSS3"
style="display: block; width: 100%;">
                        </td>
                    </tr>
                    <tr>
                        <td align="center">
                            <table width="88%" cellpadding="0"
cellspacing="0" border="0" align="center" class="content-table">
                                <tr>
```

```
                                        <td align="center">
                                            <table width="100%"
cellpadding="10" cellspacing="0" border="0" align="center">
                                                <tr>
                                                    <td
style="font-family: Roboto, Arial, Helvetica, san-serif; font-weight:
500; font-size: 33.441px; text-align: center;"><br>Mastering
RWD<br>with HTML5 and CSS3</td>
                                                </tr>
                                                <tr>
                                                    <td>
                                                        <h2 style="font-
family: Roboto, Arial, Helvetica, san-serif; font-weight: 500; font-
size: 25.888px;">Responsive Emails</h2>
                                                        <p style="font-
family: Roboto, Arial, Helvetica, san-serif; font-weight: 300; font-
size: 16px; line-height: 26px">And here we sare after traveling back
in time: think of late 90's and designing with tables, oh yes you
read right, designing with tables.</p>
                                                        <p style="font-
family: Roboto, Arial, Helvetica, san-serif; font-weight: 300; font-
size: 16px; line-height: 26px"> And today things are not any
different when it comes to creating e-mails: we have to use tables
for layout.</p>
                                                        <p style="font-
family: Roboto, Arial, Helvetica, san-serif; font-weight: 300; font-
size: 16px; line-height: 26px">Why? Simple. There aren't any wars.
Email client wars that is&hellip; (continued).</p>
                                                    </td>
                                                </tr>
                                                <tr>
                                                    <td style="font-
family: Roboto, Arial, Helvetica, san-serif; font-weight:300; font-
size: 25.888px; text-align:center;">
                                                        <br>
                                                        <a href="#"
target="_blank" style="padding: 20px 30px; border: #663300 2px solid;
border-radius: 5px; text-decoration: none; color: white; background:
#ff8000;" class="main-cta">Get the Book! &raquo;</a>

                                                        <br><br><br>
                                                    </td>
                                                </tr>
                                            </table>
                                        </td>
                                    </tr>
                                </table>
```

```
                                        </td>
                                    </tr>
                                    <tr>
                                        <td>
                                            <table width="100%" cellpadding="0"
cellspacing="0" border="0" class="footer-table-ctnr"
style="background: #666666; background: linear-gradient(#333,
#666);">

                                                <tr>
                                                    <td background="https://s3-us-
west-2.amazonaws.com/s.cdpn.io/9988/trianglify-black.png">
                                                        <table width="95%"
align="center" cellpadding="30" cellspacing="0" border="0">
                                                            <tr>
                                                                <td style="font-
family: Roboto, Arial, Helvetica, san-serif; font-weight: 300; font-
size: 12px; line-height: 20px; color: white;">
                                                                    <p style="margin:
0;"><span style="font-weight: 500;">Book:</span> Mastering RWD with
HTML5 and CSS3</p>
                                                                    <p style="margin:
0;"><span style="font-weight: 500;">Author:</span> Ricardo Zea</p>
                                                                    <p style="margin:
0;"><span style="font-weight: 500;">Publisher:</span> Packt
Publishing</p>

                                                                    <br>
                                                                    <p>&copy; All
Rights Reserved - <a href="#" style="color:
white;">Unsubscribe</a></p>
                                                                </td>
                                                            </tr>
                                                        </table>
                                                    </td>
                                                </tr>
                                            </table>
                                        </td>
                                    </tr>
                                </table>
                            </td>
                        </tr>
                </table>
</body>
```

At this point, this is what the e-mail looks like:

And we're done! Are we? Not yet, we still have a few things to do:

- Add the Outlook 2007/2010/2013 Conditional Comments hacks for the background in the footer and the CTA button.
- Add the media queries.
- Add the Outlook web font fallback style.

Adding the Outlook 2007/2010/2013 Conditional Comments hacks

Just like IE in the times of table-based layouts, Outlook rules the landscape of e-mail clients in the desktop. So we can't ignore this client when creating e-mails.

That's all fine and dandy; the problem is that most Outlook versions have very poor HTML rendering capabilities, so HTML hacks via Conditional Comments are (unfortunately) necessary. They are not difficult to implement; you just have to know when to implement them.

Conditional Comments are most useful for background images and large CTA buttons. In our example, we have both: the black/gray triangles background pattern in the footer and the orange **Get the Book** » CTA that is Call To Action.

In the following markup, you'll be able to note the following points:

- The Conditional Comments wrap only the element in case. In other words, ensure that you don't wrap more elements than required, otherwise, we'll be creating more problems than solutions.

- Both the footer and the CTA buttons require us to edit things in two places: the element itself and inside the Conditional Comments.

- E-mail Conditional Comments look quite obscure; they don't adhere to any standards, since they are proprietary technology. Consider them more like a patch than part of progressive enhancement. They are a flat-out hack.

- Editing Conditional Comments isn't too difficult. The parts that are customizable are either inline CSS properties/values, or a `src` attribute for images—nothing we haven't seen before.

 For the purpose of clarity and to cover the scope of this book, I'm going to show you only the two sections that are wrapped in Conditional Comments.

Conditional Comments for the background image in the footer

This is how the HTML looks:

```
<td background="https://s3-us-west-
2.amazonaws.com/s.cdpn.io/9988/trianglify-black.png">
    <!--[if gte mso 9]>
    <v:rect xmlns:v="urn:schemas-microsoft-com:vml" strokecolor="none"
style="width: 600px; height: 184px;">
```

```
    <v:fill type="frame" src="https://s3-us-west-
2.amazonaws.com/s.cdpn.io/9988/trianglify-black.png"></v:fill>
    </v:rect>
    <v:shape style="position: absolute; width: 600px; height: 184px;">
<![endif]-->
    <table width="95%" align="center" cellpadding="30"
cellspacing="0" border="0">
        <tr>
            <td style="font-family: Roboto, Arial, Helvetica,
san-serif; font-weight: 300; font-size: 12px; line-height: 20px;
color: white;">
                <p style="margin: 0;"><span style="font-weight:
500;">Book:</span> Mastering RWD with HTML5 and CSS3</p>
                <p style="margin: 0;"><span style="font-weight:
500;">Author:</span> Ricardo Zea</p>
                <p style="margin: 0;"><span style="font-weight:
500;">Publisher:</span> Packt Publishing</p>
                <br>
                <p>&copy; All Rights Reserved - <a href="#"
style="color: white;">Unsubscribe</a></p>
            </td>
        </tr>
    </table>
    <!--[if gte mso 9]>
    </v:shape>
    <![endif]-->
</td>
```

Conditional Comments for the CTA buttons

The following snippet was adapted from Eli Dickinson's post *How to make HTML
e-mail buttons that rock* from IndustryDive.com (http://www.industrydive.com/
blog/how-to-make-html-email-buttons-that-rock/).

Here's what the markup looks like:

```
<td style="font-family: Roboto, Arial, Helvetica, san-serif;
font-weight:300; font-size: 25.888px; text-align: center;">
    <br>
  <!--[if mso]>
  <v:roundrect xmlns:v="urn:schemas-microsoft-com:vml"
xmlns:w="urn:schemas-microsoft-com:office:word" href="http:#"
style="height: 60px; width: 300px; v-text-anchor: middle;"
arcsize="10%" stroke="f" fillcolor="#ff8000">
    <center style="color: #ffffff; font-family: Roboto, Arial,
Helvetica, san-serif; font-weight:300; font-size: 25.888px;">
      Get the Book! &raquo;
    </center>
  </v:roundrect>
```

```
<![endif]-->
<![if !mso]>
    <a href="#" target="_blank" style="padding: 20px 30px;
border: #663300 2px solid; border-radius: 5px; text-decoration:
none; color: white; background: #ff8000;" class="main-cta">Get the
Book! &raquo;</a>
  <![endif]-->
  <br><br><br>
</td>
```

Adding media queries

The amount of code used in the media queries for this e-mail is minimal. This is the result of having a solid foundation of features before any HTML or CSS was created.

The things that made this e-mail a solid build are listed as follows:

- Setting a typographic Modular Scale.
- Keeping the layout to a single column.
- Building for the most problematic e-mail client first.
- Using progressive enhancement.
- Knowing where to apply Conditional Comments.

The media queries are simply as shown here:

```
/*Responsive Styles*/
@media (max-width: 380px) {
    .main-cta { padding:10px 30px !important;
white-space: nowrap !important; }
}
@media (max-width: 600px) {
    .inner-container-table { width: 95% !important; }
    .footer-table-ctnr td { padding: 10px 0 10px 5px !important; }
}
```

> Since inline styles have higher specificity than the ones in the
> `<style>` tag, we need to add the `!important` declaration to
> the end of the values in order to override those inline styles.

Here's what we see in the media queries:

- Since we are using the desktop-first approach, we use the `max-width` property.
- We see a media query at 380px, because the orange CTA looks a bit thick in small screens at this width. So, we reduce the top and bottom padding from 20px to 10px.

- We also add a `white-space: nowrap !important;` element for good measure and avoid having the button wrap to a second line.

- Once the viewport hits 600px, we're going to make the `inner-container-table` 95 percent wide. This will give the e-mail a bit of padding on the sides, allowing it to *breathe* and not feel *boxed* in such a small space.

- Then, we're going to reduce the padding on the table in the footer. This helps use a bit more of the available space while keeping the credits in a single line each.

Outlook web font fallback style

Outlook won't use any of the fallback fonts in the font stack. It will just use Times New Roman and sometimes this is not what we intend.

So using a specific style within Conditional Comments to target Outlook is the way to solve this problem. This style should go after the closing the `</style>` tag of the main embedded style sheet.

Here's what it looks like:

```
<!--[if mso]>
    <style>
    /* Make Outlook fallback to Arial rather than Times New Roman */
    h1, h2, p { font-family: Arial, sans-serif; }
    </style>
<![endif]-->
```

And that's it! Really, it is. Here's a demo I created in CodePen:
http://codepen.io/ricardozea/pen/d11a14e6f5eace07d93beb559b771263

Screenshot of various e-mail clients

This e-mail was tested on the following e-mail clients and platforms:

- Desktop:
    - Outlook 2010
    - Gmail
    - Yahoo! Mail
    - Outlook.com

- Mobile (iPhone):
    - Mail App
    - Gmail App (*mobile-friendly* view)

- ° Gmail App (original view)
- ° Yahoo Mail App

- Mobile (Android):

  - ° Gmail App

Here's an image of the e-mail on various desktop and mobile clients:

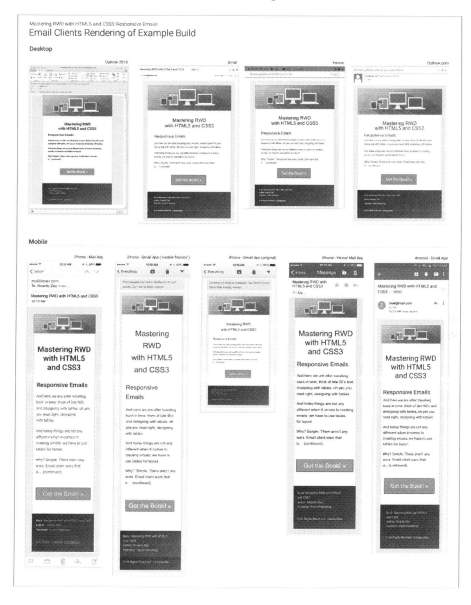

Here, a few of the e-mail clients, both desktop and mobile, were actually able to pick up Roboto, the web font we used. The rest of them used Arial from the font stack, which was our plan anyway.

On desktop, surprisingly, Outlook 2010 was the only one able to render Roboto—albeit the font looks bolder than it really is—yet it still was the only one.

On mobile, iPhone's mail app and Gmail on Android were the ones that were capable of using Roboto.

Third-party services

When building responsive e-mails, we have to complement our bag of tricks, hacks, and broad understanding of e-mail clients' quirks and mishaps, with tools that can allow us to test faster, optimize our workflow, improve our efficiency with more modern technologies, and learn from others.

There are as many tools out there as there are web designers; the ones we're going to mention are strongly related to what this book is about. Also, all these tools are free. Let's take a look.

Litmus's PutsMail

I have to admit that the name of this tool isn't very descriptive and doesn't make any reference to how useful this tool is. With Litmus's PutsMail, we can send an e-mail to any account we want for testing and debugging. With the click of a single button, PutsMail sends an e-mail to virtually any number of e-mail accounts we want.

PutsMail allows us to do the following things:

- Add any e-mail(s) to send the tests to
- Add a subject line
- Paste our HTML

Once we have that in place, we just click on the button to send the e-mail and off we go to test on all devices. No need for logins and cumbersome interfaces in e-mail management platforms.

I used this tool to send the e-mails you saw in the image with all the e-mail clients' screenshots a few paragraphs back.

The advantages are:

- It's very easy to use, and has a very low learning curve.
- Unlike some e-mail management services, PutsMail sends the test e-mails right away.
- Adding and removing e-mails from the list is very easy.
- In addition to testing regular HTML e-mails, it also allows you to test plain text and Apple Watch versions.
- It has the option to inline the CSS if needed.
- The markup is neatly highlighted in the HTML field.
- It's free.

The disadvantages are:

- Sometimes you need to delete an e-mail and add it again to be able to receive the test.
- Each e-mail marketing service has different rules about what gets stripped out or what is left in the markup upon sending the e-mail. So PutsMail's rules may be different from other e-mail marketing provider's rules.

Litmus's PutsMail can be found at the following URL: `https://putsmail.com/`.

CSS inliners

Writing inline CSS is quite a tedious task: if our paragraphs have `font-family: Arial, Helvetica, san-serif; font-style: italic; font-weight: bold; font-size: 18px;`, then we have to copy and paste all these attributes into each paragraph. Alternatively, we have to copy and paste the same paragraph and change the text inside of them.

Don't even think about using the font shorthand. What about a change in one of the properties? Well, we now have to make the change in every paragraph. Doing a find-and-replace can be risky, which means more time testing. Enter CSS inliners!

With CSS inliners, we can write our CSS inside a `<style>` tag in the `<head>` section of the e-mail template, just like we would do when creating a normal web page. Once we're done, we upload the e-mail template into the CSS inliner tool. The tool will *inline* the CSS automatically in each corresponding HTML tag.

So if we have the following paragraph:

```html
<p class="note__important">CSS inliners are an awesome tool!</p>
```

Then, we write this in the `<style>` tag in the `<head>` section:

```html
<style>
    p.note__important {
        font-family: Arial, Helvetica, san-serif;
        font-style: italic;
        font-weight: bold;
        font-size: 18px;
    }
</style>
```

The CSS inliner will do this:

```html
<p class="note__important" style="font-family: Arial, Helvetica,
san-serif;font-style: italic;font-weight: bold;font-size: 18px;" >CSS
inliners are an awesome tool!</p>
```

The advantages are as follows:

- We can include all our styles in a `<style>` tag in the `<head>` section of the e-mail template, just like in a regular web page build.
- It's simple to use CSS inliners: paste your markup, press the inline button, and you're done.
- It leads to considerable reduction in repetitive tasks, since placing a class in the `<style>` tag is all we need to do—the tool does the rest.
- Most CSS inliners are free.

The disadvantages are as follows:

- Testing e-mails is very time consuming, so using a CSS inliner to create test e-mails adds an extra step to the process.

  An exception to this is Litmus's PutsMail, since it has the option to inline the CSS upon sending the test e-mail.

- CSS inliners have different ways of writing the styles: some add spaces after the semicolon while others don't. This may or may not concur with one's style.

Some of the most popular CSS inliners are as follows:

- MailChimp (`http://templates.mailchimp.com/resources/inline-css/`)
- Campaign Monitor (`http://inliner.cm/`)
- Dialect's Premailer (`http://premailer.dialect.ca/`)
- Zurb's Inliner (`http://zurb.com/ink/inliner.php`)

Advanced e-mail frameworks

Who says we can't build e-mails with modern and more advanced technologies, such as Sass, Grunt, and Node.js?

For those who are a bit more technical and love frontend development, these e-mail frameworks can speed things up tremendously.

The advantages are as follows:

- These technologies boost the speed of the development and testing phases.
- These technologies run locally on one's machine; this means that everything executes much faster than using a third-party, web-based service.
- If you're a frontend developer who is familiar with such technologies, learning to use any e-mail framework can be much easier.
- Some e-mail frameworks allow us to reuse components, similar to using includes, like the header and footer, and so on.
- Creating plain text e-mails is an option in some e-mail frameworks.
- Any time any of us uses an open source project, we are helping a fellow web professional in their career, and any community around such projects, making a better web.
- There is support from the developer(s) and the ecosystem of contributors of the project.
- These technologies are free.

The disadvantages are as follows:

- The learning curve can be steep if one is not familiar with such frontend technologies.
- It requires knowing and understanding more than one frontend technology beforehand.

Some of the e-mail frameworks are as follows:

- Nathan Rambeck's Email Lab (`https://github.com/sparkbox/email-lab`) It uses the following:
    - Node.js
    - Grunt
    - Bundler
    - Sass
    - Ruby
    - Premailer
    - Nodemailer
    - Handlebars/Assemble

- Alex Ilhan's Zenith (`https://github.com/Omgitsonlyalex/ZenithFramework`)

    You can find a tutorial in Litmus at `https://litmus.com/community/learning/23-getting-started-with-sass-in-email`) It uses the following:
    - Sass
    - Compass
    - Premailer

- Lee Munroe's Grunt Email Workflow (`https://github.com/leemunroe/grunt-email-workflow`)

    It uses the following:
    - Grunt
    - Ruby
    - Node.js
    - Sass
    - Premailer
    - Mailgun (optional)
    - Litmus (optional)
    - Rackspace Cloud (optional)

Responsive e-mail template services

I've always believed that being hands-on is the best way to learn. However, in the world of e-mail, being hands-on means spending a lot of time working with HTML and CSS in ways that are no longer a good practice. Using tables for layout (not that using floats is any better), inlining CSS, dealing with quirky e-mail clients, and so on, takes a lot longer than necessary for testing and debugging, and all that other good stuff.

A way to speed things up is to use third-party e-mail templates because the authors have already, at least for the most part, done the dirty work for us. Let's take a look at the pros and cons of using third-party responsive e-mail templates.

The advantages are:

- It's likely that thorough testing has already been done; this reduces our own testing time tremendously.
- If we are happy with the layout, all we need to do is replace the content with our own.
- Some e-mail template services even allow you to send the e-mail itself after editing it.
- Some services don't require the author to know any HTML or CSS in order to create a responsive e-mail.
- Downloading the e-mail template is an option provided by some e-mail template services.
- Most responsive e-mail templates for download are free.
- Some paid drag-and-drop e-mail building services offer a free account with a lot of functionalities available with their free plan.

The disadvantages are:

- Although minimal, some testing of our own is still necessary.
- If we want to make changes to the layout, sometimes it's not possible. This depends on the e-mail template service.
- Although some e-mail template services allow us to send the e-mail, they don't provide any analytics or backend where we can see how the e-mail performed.
- Image optimization may or may not be ideal. There's no way to know.
- Reusing an old e-mail template is not possible with some services, so we have to edit everything again from scratch if we plan to use the same layout.

Some of the most common responsive e-mail templates for download are as follows:

- MailChimp's Email Blueprints
  (`https://github.com/mailchimp/Email-Blueprints`)
- Zurb Ink (`http://zurb.com/ink/templates.php`)
- Litmus's Slate
  (`https://litmus.com/resources/free-responsive-email-templates`)
- Brian Graves's Responsive Email Patterns
  (`http://responsiveemailpatterns.com/`)

The following are drag-and-drop e-mail building services:

- Stamplia Builder (`https://builder.stamplia.com/`)
- MailUp's BEE Free (`https://beefree.io/`)

  BEE is an acronym for Best E-mail Editor

See how an e-mail was built

This tool has got to be one of the most amazing and useful tools for e-mail development and learning. Litmus's **Scope** bookmarklet allows us to see, from within any webmail client, how an e-mail template was built.

 A *bookmarklet* is a JavaScript component that you store in your bookmarks, usually your bookmarks bar. When you click on the bookmarklet, a special functionality displays. A bookmarklet is not a bookmark per se; it happens to be stored with the bookmarks, but offers a very different functionality than a regular bookmark.

The way Scope works is quite simple:

1. Go to the Scope site: `https://litmus.com/scope/`.
2. Drag the bookmarklet to your bookmarks bar in your browser.
3. Open your webmail and view any e-mail.
4. Click on the **Scope It** bookmarklet in your bookmarks bar.
5. The Scope site opens with the e-mail in *design* mode.
6. Click on **code** and the design panel will slide away and allow us to see all the markup of the e-mail in question.

This is incredibly useful for learning how others are pulling off such amazing things like video on e-mails, gradients, responsiveness, and so on. Here's a screenshot showing us what the responsive e-mail template we just built looks like after sending it to my Gmail account and *scoping it* with the bookmarklet.

On the left we see the Scope side on Litmus's website, and on the right it's the file opened in Sublime Text. They are exactly the same… even the formatting is identical. Amazing tool!

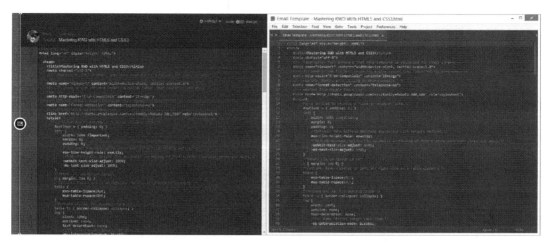

E-mail template using Litmus's Scope

Summary

Wow, we made it!

In this final chapter about responsive e-mails, we discussed some important things in addition to building an actual e-mail.

We now understand why e-mail is so important in any marketing campaign, since more and more e-mails are being opened on mobile devices. However, people like to interact with e-mails a lot more on their desktops—very solid reasons to make our e-mails responsive.

Analytics are a key factor in deciding which e-mail clients to support. We want to spend our time wisely. Then, setting up a basic HTML template can go a long way because we can reuse such template over and over.

Things like a CSS reset, wrapping our content in a 100 percent wide table, and creating the inner table is pretty much the go-to process for any e-mail design. We know now that the maximum width of an e-mail should be 600px.

Microsoft's Outlook 2007/2010/2013 versions are the IE6 of e-mail clients: they have very poor support for modern HTML and CSS, but they are the most popular e-mail client on desktop. So using Conditional Comments for nice CTAs and backgrounds is the way to go.

Also, in order to be as efficient as possible, using third-party e-mail templates and drag-and-drop e-mail building services are always an option.

With these final words about responsive e-mails, we have concluded our journey of mastering Responsive Web Design. If you have any questions, don't hesitate to look me up. I will be more than glad to help a fellow web professional wherever, whenever.

We can now strike that same pose the Kung Fu grandmasters from the Shaolin Temple, Shi DeRu and Shi DeYang did in *Chapter 6, Working with Images and Videos in Responsive Web Design*.

Hi Ya!

Huge thanks for reading, I hope you enjoyed it!

Index

used, for increasing accessibility 65
WAI-ARIA roles
URL 70
web font resources
Adobe Edge Web Fonts 259
Font Squirrel 259
Google Fonts 259
web fonts
advantages 259
defining 259, 260
disadvantages 260
working, with RWD 259, 260

wireframe page
URL 81
WURFL Image Tailor
URL 213

Z

Zenith framework
URL 298
Zurb Ink
URL 300
Zurb's Inliner
URL 297

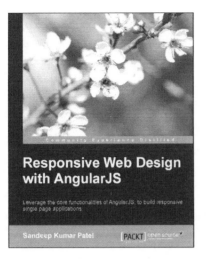
Responsive Web Design with AngularJS

ISBN: 978-1-78439-842-2 Paperback: 128 pages

Leverage the core functionalities of AngularJS, to build responsive single page applications

1. Get introduced to the key features of AngularJS and understand its role in responsive design.

2. Learn various approaches for responsive web application development.

3. Discover practical examples to incorporate responsive web design techniques to build a single page application.

Responsive Design High Performance

ISBN: 978-1-78439-083-9 Paperback: 162 pages

Leverage the power of responsive design to fine-tune your website's performance and increase its speed

1. Learn useful quick fixes to improve your website's performance.

2. Efficiently reduce the clutter in your code.

3. Become familiar with artefacts that could slow down your website.

Please check **www.PacktPub.com** for information on our titles

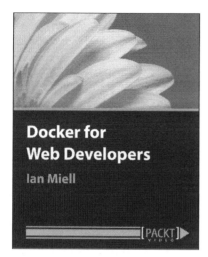

Docker for
Web Developers

Ian Miell

[PACKT]▶

Docker for Web Developers [Video]

ISBN: 978-1-78439-067-9   Duration: 01:31 hours

Accelerate your web development skills on real web projects in record time with Docker

1. Supercharge your web development process while ensuring that everything works smoothly.

2. Win at 2048 using Docker's commit and restore functionality.

3. Use the Docker Hub workflow to automate the rebuilding of your web projects.

4. Full of realistic examples, this is a step-by-step journey to becoming a Docker expert!

Web Development
with AngularJS
and Bootstrap

Simeon Cheeseman

[PACKT]▶

Web Development with AngularJS and Bootstrap [Video]

ISBN: 978-1-78439-150-8   Duration: 01:48 hours

Use dynamic AngularJS code and Bootstrap styling to create effective web applications

1. Leverage the power of AngularJS and Bootstrap to develop a functioning web application.

2. Explore the world of open source AngularJS libraries.

3. Understand how to create your own custom components.

Please check **www.PacktPub.com** for information on our titles